Roy R. Grinker, Sr., is Director of the Institute for Psychosomatic and Psychiatric Research and Training, Michael Reese Hospital and Medical Center, Chicago. Beatrice Werble is a research associate with the Institute. Robert C. Drye is Director of Education, Illinois State Psychiatric Institute.

The Borderline Syndrome

ROY R. GRINKER, SR.

BEATRICE WERBLE

ROBERT C. DRYE

BASIC BOOKS, INC., PUBLISHERS

THE
BORDERLINE
SYNDROME

A Behavioral Study of Ego-Functions

NEW YORK   LONDON

PREFACE

This book contains the first reported results of a lengthy research program on hospitalized borderline patients whose ego-functions were studied through multiple observations on their daily behaviors. In general the informal diagnostic term of borderline as well as several synonyms in our nosological classification have long been used without standard definition as a convenient term with which to label cases of clinical unclarity. In this first systematic investigation of the phenomena clinically observed for at least several decades as borderline, we have attempted to understand what the term really denotes, define its characteristics, and determine whether it encompasses subgroups or categories.

In a sense we have been working upstream against the forces opposing concepts of syndromes and accurate diagnostic criteria. The unpopularity of diagnosis and knowledge of the life history of describable entities is a reaction against the "disease" concept in psychiatry and the over emphasis on individual dynamic processes. Yet the pendulum has swung too far away in the direction of concern only with "the problem" of a specific patient. In truth there can be no science of psychiatry without classification and no sound classification without modifying the repetitive old observations and descriptions. Psychiatry needs a fresh look derived from modern theories of process and new methods of description, rating, and statistical analyses.

It is our hope that the clinician will now be able to diagnose with some degree of accuracy the borderline syndrome in general and each of the subgroups in detail, that future investigators can use the hypothesized subgroups for correlations with causes, course, natural history of the disturbance, and the effectiveness of various therapies, and finally, that our methods may prove useful for other clinical investigations of unclear syndromes and others whose clarity is more myth than substance. For some readers our method of observing, describing and then rating traits extracted from an ego-psychology theoretical framework and newly developed methods of clustering analyses may be as important as the results.

In this book, we have reported on a behavioral research study of hospital patients that included a post-hospital follow-up and an investigation of patients' families. We have in brief attempted to state *what* the borderline syndrome is and speculate on the *how* and the *why*.

Roy R. Grinker, Sr.

Chicago, Illinois   Beatrice Werble

February 1968   Robert C. Drye

ACKNOWLEDGMENTS

The pilot study and the major research were conducted at the Michael Reese Unit of the Illinois State Psychiatric Institute. Generous support was allotted by the State of Illinois Psychiatric Research and Training Authority (Grant No. 1769).

Individual cases were studied in depth at the clinical research center supported by the National Institute of Mental Health (Grant No. MH-5519) at the Institute for Psychosomatic and Psychiatric Research and Training of the Michael Reese Hospital and Medical Center.

The statistical research was performed at the New York Scientific Center of the International Business Machine Corporation.

We wish to express our gratitude to the many staff members of 8 East of the Illinois State Psychiatric Institute who were involved in this lengthy research program and to the associates who were employed on it.

We are grateful for the effective leadership of the Chief of the Reese Unit, Theodore Reid, Jr., M.D. He chose the research subjects, facilitated our work at every turn and maintained staff interest and morale continuously in spite of the required absence of feedback necessary to keep the participants from contaminating the data.

We express our appreciation to the following psychiatric residents and state hospital physicians: François Alouf, M.D., Hormoz Amjadi, M.D., Stuart Burstein, M.D., Oscar Canamar, M.D., Piero J. Cerruti, M.D., Thomas Chiu, M.D., Carlos Cuesta, M.D., Marvin DeHaan, M.D., Arnold Dinner, M.D., Walter Feldman, M.D., James Fisch, M.D., Dewey Gilbert, M.D., Zorislav Greblo, M.D., Andrew Gushwan, M.D., Leo Jacobs, M.D., Geoffrey Levy, M.D., Norman Litowitz, M.D., Chris Mahon, M.D., Richard Meyer, M.D., Pedro Mendez, M.D., Sheldon Meyers, M.D., Iran Pavkovic, M.D., Elly Roenau, M.D., David Rothstein, M.D., Fernando Sanetaella, M.D., C. Herbert Schiro, M.D., Stanley Stanmar, M.D., Thomas Stone, M.D., David Terman, M.D., Betty Wimberg, M.D., Ralph Yaney, M.D.

To the Nursing Staff: Madeline Gissell Bartsch, Diane Bartz, Robert Behrman, Jessie Blair, Fay Bridges, Darrell Chassin, Mary Hunt Dahlberg, Catherine Dainty Davidson, Mary Anne Horan Decker, Roy Edmonsen, Patricia Ehrsam, Anne Gleason, Carolyn Godfrey, Grace Hunter, Willie Mae Jackson, Oscar Jones, Essie Journigan, Elizabeth Moore, Robert Nicks, Benjamin Odie,

Regina Hughes Powell, Shirley West Randall, Antoinette Rottolo, Louis Shears, Edward Shores, Howard Skyles, Harold Synder, Patricia Stinson, Jack Tanton, Wayne Tipler, JoAnn Vicelli, Gertrude Watson, Inez Weinberg, Hazel Kennedy Wells, Frances Peckney Zebig.

To the Social Workers: Marian Waclawek Booth, Cornelia Cannon, Beryl Carter, Joyce Forsman, Zona Galle, Annette Maxey, Marcelene Reich Melendy, Ann Mitchell, Lou O'Donnell.

To the Activities Therapists and Vocational Rehabilitation Workers: Lolita Bevenue, Catherine Boyle, Gerald Bozarth, Mary Catherine Engel, Marian Kirby, Thaddeus LaBranch, Catherine Nance, Jean Rehmar, David Sandness, Nancy Wagers.

We are grateful for the excellent research assistants who interviewed the observers, rated the protocols, obtained family data and followed up the ex-patients: Gertrude Dworkin, Joan Massoquoi, Sandra Arbit, Michiko Fukazawa, Reva Heymann, Pearl German, Joan Traub, Laura Wingate, and the professional librarian, Mrs. Elizabeth Fredericks.

For facilitating our efforts whenever needed we are indebted to Lester H. Rudy, M.D., Director of the Illinois State Psychiatric Institute, George Magner, Ph.D., Chief of Social Service Department, Ana Marquinez-Castellanos, M.D., Assistant Chief of the Reese Unit and Kiyo Kobayashi, Medical Records Librarian, Illinois State Psychiatric Institute. Finally, we wish to thank Mary Russell, Head Nurse, 8 West and Ollie Knight, Research Assistant, 8 East, Illinois State Psychiatric Institute for their help in maintaining telephone contact with the subjects during our follow-up study.

Ora Benton, Kathleen Bell and Gayle Morales carried responsibility for trancription of protocols, various aspects of data tabulation, manuscript typing, and the many chores involved in a research program such as this.

CONTENTS

LIST OF APPENDIXES

LIST OF TABLES

The Borderline Syndrome

1 Introduction

THE PROBLEM

This monograph reports the theory, operations, data and conclusions of an extensive systematic research on a syndrome designated as *borderline* about which there has been little agreement and only vague definition. The impetus for our investigations arose from the increased frequency with which this diagnosis is being used by clinicians who are dissatisfied with the standard nomenclature for many patients they are seeing in practice. Does the increased use of the term represent a modern tendency toward diagnostic vagueness, a real increase in the incidence of the syndrome or the spreading recognition of a new clinical entity?

The borderline diagnosis has not yet appeared in the official American or International Classification of Psychiatric Disorders, or in Stengel's (1959) extensive survey of existing classifications prepared for the World Health Organization (W.H.O.). It did not appear in the design of the fact-finding program of the American Psychoanalytic Association. There are no statistics on prevalence, the term has no legal meaning and the label does not evoke a stereotype for most psychiatrists. There has been no published *systematic* study of these patients, and the term is now only part of the jargon of psychiatric practice.

From the literature discussed in Chapter 2 we are convinced that there is scarcely a general understanding of the term and no consensus on differentiating criteria that would lead to accurate, consistent and reliable diagnoses. There are few clinical descriptive or psychoanalytic reports based on supportive data, and there are only vague dynamic formulations. Several central ideas do run through the concepts and images that clinicians hold of these patients. They generally agree that borderline patients look clinically unclear and that they occupy an area in psychopathology where accurate diagnosis is difficult. Beyond this small island of common ground, varying assumptions are made.

To summarize the clinical positions: some say there is no such thing as borderline; others say that borderline may be a transitional state from neurosis to psychosis; and finally others believe that borderline is a relatively stable clinical entity with psychotic, neurotic and healthy ego-functions present simultaneously, and that the range of symptoms includes those characteristic of an extensive spectrum from neurotic to psychotic. Whichever of the last two positions is taken, there is agreement that among these patients certain ego-functions are rather severely impaired (Knight, 1953).

This then is the problem as derived from experiences in practice with patients who were unclearly defined and usually unsuccessfully treated. Is the term borderline a wastebasket into which all puzzling cases are dumped? Are there clinical, dynamic or other characteristics which could define them as members of a single nosological category, and are there multiple subcategories?

WHY DIAGNOSIS?

Is classification within the nosological systems in psychiatry important or is it essential? This is a debate that has generated considerable heat in the past. For those who consider psychiatry a part of medicine, the traditional formula of history-taking and examination, diagnosis, and then treatment is still unquestioned. When psychoanalytic psychiatry became dominant in the United States and the methods of observation and description were demoted, diagnosis was considered to be unimportant medical orthodoxy and only possible if at all necessary during treatment. The credo then became: "It is not the diagnosis but *this* patient's problems in living that are my concern." Indeed some went so far as to call mental illness a myth. All this denied the adage that "naming is knowing" (Bentley, 1950).

Kraepelin was the great classifier just as Freud was the dynamic innovator. Yet descriptive and dynamic concepts long preceded both Kraepelin and Freud. Even in modern times Kahlbaum, Hecker and Morel formed the foundations of Kraepelinian classification which too was not the last of its kind (Alexander and Selesnick, 1966). From the chaotic accumulation of hundreds of clinical observations, Kraepelin consolidated a few entities or syndromes—twelve in his first attempt in 1883. The American Psychiatric Association utilized the Kraepelin classification without change until 1934. Only by pressure from psychiatrists who had been in the military service was the classification radically revised in 1949; it is still slowly but constantly undergoing improvement. Stengel (1959) as a prelude to his survey of psychiatric classification states:

> Psychiatry has made considerable strides during the past three decades. There has been great therapeutic activity and an enormous intensification of research work. Medical men, public authorities and the community at large have become alive to the magnitude of the problems of mental disorders. Conditions for a concerted attack on mental ill health ought, therefore, to be highly propitious at the present time. Yet, in many respects, psychiatrists find themselves ill-prepared to meet the challenge. This is partly due to the incomplete integration of the various approaches to the study of mental illness, though there are signs that this process has been gaining momentum of late. A more serious obstacle to progress in psychiatry is difficulty of communication. Everybody who has followed the literature and listened to discussions concerning mental illness soon discovers that psychiatrists, even those apparently sharing the same basic orientation, often do not speak the same language. They either use different terms for the same concepts, or the same term for different concepts, usually without being aware of it. It is sometimes argued that this is inevitable in the present state of psychiatric knowledge, but it is doubtful whether this is a valid excuse.
>
> The lack of a common classification of mental disorders has defeated attempts at comparing psychiatric observations and the results of treatments undertaken in various countries or even in various centers of the same country. Possibly, if greater attention had been paid to these difficulties, there might be a greater measure of agreement about the value of specific treatments than exists today. Another field in which the lack of a common language threatens to defeat the purpose of much valuable

effort is that of experimental psychiatry where research has been very active of late. In recent years the epidemiological approach has been used in the study of mental disorders to an increasing degree. To be fruitfully employed on a broad front it requires a common basic terminology and classification. There is a real danger that the lack of such vehicle of communication will lead to confusion and to a waste of previous resources.

Recently Grinker (1964) wrote:

> Psychiatry in its role as a branch of medicine or as an applied science is concerned with diagnosis and various forms of therapy. This field is and has been extremely confused ever since man began to function as a medicine-man healer. It is only lately that scientific methods have been applied in an attempt to understand the rationale, methods and results of psychotherapy. If we dodge the issue that there are categories of mental disturbances with specific course, and prognosis, we have no science. There can be no scientific therapy without clinical categories as guidelines to facilitate the study of the life-history of specific disturbances, their spontaneous course and the interrelationships among causative factors. Studies of the various treatments for mentally ill patients require the establishing of diagnostic categories, defining the methods applicable to each and developing criteria for results.

Glover (1932) from the psychoanalytic point of view approaches the problem of classification as a "matted complexity," especially in complicated transitional forms which certainly includes the borderline. He states that psychiatric classifications based on clinical descriptions are unsatisfactory because as end products they do not include unconscious processes and genetic (developmental) elements. He believes that there is room for new syndromes achieved by "openness" for which a combination of descriptive words with genetic understanding is necessary to aid differential diagnosis and refine prognosis. Glover adds that there should be an intelligible relation between the phenomena of psychiatry and the psychological phenomena (behavior) of everyday life. The function of psychological adaptation is thus a boundary process between perceptual organization and drive processes as subserved by an ego which defines a sense of reality. For Glover the term borderline is unsatisfactory, as is prepsychotic, because in the phases of development there is a normal madness and everyone is a larval psychotic.

Is classification and the current nosology the true bible of modern psychiatry or does it hinder deeper understanding as a rigid and strict codifier? A pseudoquestion such as this has no answer except "both" (Menninger, 1963). No science can exist without a foundation of description and classification of its subject matter as the "what" of study.

Nor can the science develop beyond a primitive state without transcending the purely descriptive, to answer the dynamic question "how" which deals with process and the question "why" which considers purpose and meaning.

Therefore, what the borderline is and what kinds of patients may be classified under this rubric should be defined as clearly as possible. This is our problem. Once answered we may then attempt to determine the "how" in researches regarding its genesis, course, treatability and outcome. Then only may we place the borderline patient, or the syndrome into which he fits, into the larger economic, social and cultural systems of our civilization and speculate on the "why."

THE RESEARCH QUESTIONS

Our research program attempted to throw light on the uncertainty and vagueness that pervade the borderline. We set forth our questions as follows:

1. Is there a single borderline state that can be described? What are its boundaries?
2. Are there several types of borderline states that can be described?
3. If there are several, in what ways are they alike and in what ways do they differ from each other?

In embarking on our research program we took the position that the problem of the so-called borderline syndrome was worthy of empirical investigation in terms of an ego-functions framework. We also took the position that we would approach our problem through the study of patients' behavior because we held the conviction that behavior is a fruitful path for developing useful clinical knowledge about patients' ego-functioning.

OUTLINE OF RESEARCH STRATEGY

Our theoretical position is discussed extensively in Chapter 3, and the methodology which we developed is discussed in Chapter 4. Briefly stated in this introduction for the reader's general orientation, we set forth our strategy:

1. Patients with uncertain diagnoses or those diagnosed as borderline who were hospitalized in a psychiatric nursing unit within a research institute were carefully observed. All behaviors were observed and described repeatedly by all the professional and subprofessional personnel who had contact with the patients.

2. Transcribed descriptions of these behaviors were rated for specific variables by several experienced and trained raters within an ego-psychology framework, utilizing scales each of which was defined in detail. The ratings, therefore, were not made with reference to symptoms but in process terms according to allocated ego-functions.

3. Over and above these ratings, global ratings and more abstract "inferences" were developed on the basis of known behavioral referrents.

4. The ratings were analyzed statistically by new methods of cluster analysis; the subsequent groupings were factor-analyzed, resulting in the definition of the borderline syndrome and its subcategories.

5. Finally, from our ancillary studies and from a wide range of literature derived from a number of scientific disciplines, hypotheses were discussed regarding the "how" and "why" of the borderline.

CHAPTER **2** An Overview of
the Literature

It should not be surprising that a survey of what has been written on the subject of the borderline has proven extraordinarily difficult. This can be said about any vague clinical entity but especially when one diagnostic term has been applied to a variety of symptoms and syndromes. Whatever the term "borderline" means specifically, it implies a combination of neurotic and psychotic symptoms. Still, this is true of every psychiatric syndrome and of phases of development succeeded by states of relative health. Thus Glover (1966) writes of infantile psychoses ("We have all been larval psychotics since the age of two . . ."), and Anna Freud (1966a) of psychotic-like turbulence in the normal adolescent.

The utility of a survey of the literature on the borderline syndrome serves to point up the need for investigations into the problem of the increasing use of a clinical diagnosis that has no generally accepted meaning. We, therefore, have oriented ourselves to determining how the clinical syndrome or gestalt has been viewed, not to specific symptoms. Certainly this focus should precede attempts to define the developmental factors, dynamic patterns, clinical courses and end results, as well as the differential diagnosis. We shall attempt to cite briefly descriptions and dynamic formulations of the borderline when the term is used or implied, avoiding repetitive quotations from author to author of which there are many.

THE EARLY USE OF BORDERLINE IN PSYCHIATRY

An overview of the literature could extend to antiquity and we would probably find that our predecessors were at least somewhat aware of the problems that still puzzle us today. We could, moreover, interpret their generalized statements to apply to our current concepts. This difficulty is compounded when nontechnical terms such as "borderline" or "border-land" are employed to denote similarity to schizophrenia, an entity about which volumes of scientific literature have been written. It is, therefore, not worth the time or effort to pursue a review of the literature in detail prior to the era of modern psychiatry.

We have uncovered such statements as "the borderland of insanity is occupied by many persons who pass their whole life near that line, sometimes on one side, sometimes on the other" by Hughes (1884), or a description of patients as "in the twilight of right reason and despair" by Rosse (1890). Among the conditions considered in this borderland were severe obsessions, compulsions, phobias, hysteria and neurasthenia. After Kraepelin (1912) developed his first psychiatric classification, the borderline was drawn between the neuroses and the schizophrenias. Bleuler (1955), however, did not use the term borderline but accentuated the concept of latent schizophrenia to include character anomalies occurring before the onset of a schizophrenic psychosis.

Jones (1918) stated that dementia praecox has nothing to do with neuroses: "The borderland has already been crossed." Others thought that a variety of hysterical or obsessive symptoms could be considered as incipient dementia praecox. Clark (1919) described periodic depression and mild dementia praecox as borderland cases. A number of other papers indicated the opinion that borderline meant cases of mental illness which could not be considered as insanity, yet were not normal or neurotic.

In general the borderline or borderland appellation indicated diagnostic difficulties at a time when insanity meant commitability and loss of legal responsibility. Many seriously troubled patients for whom the current nosology was not applicable could manage to live outside of an institution. Were they latent or incipient schizophrenics, borderline or what? Was it possible that a combination of psychotic and psychoneurotic components could exist in the same case, or that a psychoneurosis could mask a psychosis? These and other similar questions troubled psychiatrists who were seriously and often entirely concerned with diagnosis and classification.

MODERN CLINICAL DESCRIPTIONS

Perhaps we can say that this era began when Glover (1932) wrote: "I find the term 'borderline' or 'prepsychotic' as generally used unsatisfactory. If a psychotic mechanism is present at all, it should be given a definite label." Glover believes that the terms "transitional" or "potential" clinical psychosis justify retention because they, unlike borderline, dovetail with the psychoanalytic concept of regression.

The increasing number of patients who did not fit into either the psychoneurotic or psychotic groups and who were not amenable to psychoanalytic therapy led Stern (1938) to define the borderline as a group of neuroses, thereby making them diagnostically respectable. His patients, as a result of deficient maternal affection, suffered from severe narcissistic damage leading to hypersensitivity, defects in self-esteem, rigidity of personality as defense against anxiety and "psychic bleeding" or paralysis, rather than active reactions. These patients' insecurities led to intense anxiety at disapproval which also interfered with psychotherapy because all interpretations were considered to be criticisms.

Stern wrote:

> A certain vagueness is at present unavoidable because the material which this group offers for study runs so clearly in two directions namely, toward the psychotic and the psychoneurotic. Much more time and investigation are necessary to evaluate the rather obscure phenomena these patients present. That they form a group by themselves, which one can designate as borderline, is a justifiable assumption.

Knight (1954) presented a definitive statement of the term borderline. In summary, he wrote that the term borderline has achieved almost no official status in psychiatric nomenclature, and conveys no diagnostic illumination of a case other than the implication that the patient is quite sick but not frankly psychotic. In those textbooks where the term appears it is used to apply to cases in which the decision is difficult as to whether the patients in question are neurotic or psychotic, since both phenomena are observed to be present.

Often these patients have been diagnosed as having psychoneuroses of severe degrees. Most often, they have been called severe obsessive-compulsive cases; sometimes an intractable phobia has been the outstanding symptom; occasionally an apparent major hysterical symptom or an anorexia nervosa dominates the clinical picture; and at times it is a question of the degree of depression, or the extent and malignancy of paranoid trends or the severity of a character disorder.

Knight noted that structured interviews are deceptive because during conventional circumstances these patients behave adequately. Fenichel (1945) also noted that the borderline appears normal as long as security prevails. Careful attention to details, however, enables the psychiatrist to detect peculiarities and contamination in thinking, suspiciousness and lack of concern about realities. There are few clues to possible precipitating factors.

Wolberg (1952) distinguishes the borderline from the psychotic even though the former may have temporary psychotic-like episodes. She enumerates a repetitive cycle of behavior and feelings as follows: (1) the patient is either controlling or controlled, exploiting or being exploited, child or parent; (2) the desire to be a good child is accompanied by a negativistic feeling of not wanting to obey; (3) constant needs for special consideration and rewards are never satisfied; (4) hypersensitivity to remarks and behavior of others; (5) grandiosity satisfied only by fantasies and search for attack which is feared; (6) feelings of failure, loneliness and emptiness; (7) hostile reactions with deep feelings of guilt—some aggressions expressed somatically or by overeating or use of drugs and alcohol; (8) self-punishment; (9) increasing anxiety and depression.

Schmideberg (1959) describes the borderline as a syndrome blending normality, neuroses, psychoses and psychopathy in a relatively stable lifelong pattern. Differentiation is made not from the specific symptoms but by severe disturbances of the personality which involve every aspect of living. Borderline patients have difficulty in feeling genuine emotions in work and study. They are nonsocial, often paranoid and aggressive. These patients are unhappy but not depressed, inconsistent with contrasting attitudes and often reveal poor observations of reality resulting in faulty judgments. They have difficulty in assuming responsibility and frequently utilize the defensive mechanism of denial. According to Schmideberg, the weak object-relations are associated with hostile acting-out behavior, in an attempt to break through insensitivity, and low tolerance for frustration. They acquire little real knowledge, tend to sponge on their families and drift through life.

Schmideberg states that one reason why the borderline should be regarded as a clinical entity is that the patient, as a rule, remains substantially the same throughout his life. He is stable in his instability and often even keeps his pattern of peculiarity constant. Parkin (1966) also states that the borderline is a stable state of transition in which the neurosis is a defense against psychosis. As the borderline condition rarely ushers in schizophrenia, it should not be regarded as a prepsychotic condition (a diagnosis usually made only ex post facto!), as latent schizophrenia or as pseudoneurotic schizophrenia. While some schizophrenics in remission may resemble borderlines, the latter are different because they have not been and are not likely to become schizophrenics. The borderline concept should also be distinguished from psychotic episodes, temporary or partial schizophrenic reactions to stress. The characteristic features of the borderline patient are not his symptoms. He certainly lacks the more obvious psychotic ones: delusions, far-reaching disorganizations or regressions, manic elation or melancholic depression. Though he is often suspicious and collects grievances, he has no true paranoid symptoms, nor has he the dramatic symptoms of the hysteric or the obsessional. Depression, anxiety and other painful feelings may accompany any disorder and are even experienced by normal people under stress; borderlines often suffer from them also. More interesting is their frequent lack of normal feelings.

According to Eisenstein (1952) borderline patients are made anxious by aloofness of manner in others, yet they are suspicious of warmth. They are plagued by negative feelings. Knight pointed out that despite severe damage patients' ego-functions in adaptation to the demands of the environment for conventional behavior are adequate, superficial object-relations are intact and habitual performances are unimpaired. Others have also pointed out that in a well-structured situation borderlines conform, although in a somewhat eccentric, whimsical or queer fashion. In an unstructured situation they may develop a wide variety of confusion indicating the essential pathology of the ego-functions.

In the literature there are many individual case reports from which are drawn extensive conclusions which seem to influence subsequent reports. Fortunately under the auspices of the Postgraduate Psychoanalytic Seminar at the Chicago Psychoanalytic Institute, first the late Albrecht Meyer and then Stanford Gamm held monthly meetings with sixteen psychoanalysts to discuss their pooled borderline cases in various forms of treatment. They state (unpublished):

> From the clinical diagnostic point of view the borderline spectrum includes cases variously described in the literature as character disorder, narcissistic character neurosis, narcissistic personality disorder, ego-defect

or distortion, schizoid personality, paranoid personality, pseudoneurotic or ambulatory schizophrenia, certain depressed characters, some patients with periodic depressions or manic depressive episodes, some alcoholics, gamblers, patients with sexual disturbances, perverse or promiscuous, severe obsessive compulsive characters, and many of patients with more serious psychosomatic illnesses.

The clinical characteristics of the borderline patient includes low self-esteem, extreme sensitivity to criticism and rejection, suspiciousness and distrust, and extreme fearfulness. They are very afraid of aggression, in themselves and others, of loving and being close, of responsibility and of change in general. Their interpersonal relationships tend to be tenuous and tentative, and their reality orientation is often deficient. They use denial and projection to a much greater extent than the neurotic person. Their intense longing for approval and closeness, and their simultaneous fear of it leads to marked feelings of loneliness and emptiness, in the extreme to utter void and despair.

These cases distribute themselves along a spectrum of increasing disturbance from the more severe psychoneurotic to the most disturbed "borderline" case that closely resembles the overt psychotic. At the healthier end of the spectrum are the narcissistic character neuroses that have strong narcissistic defenses, giving them an appearance of more or less normality. They come to analysis only after serious crises in their lives have cracked their armor. This group also includes those successful narcissistics whose defenses succumb only to old age or retirement. In the center of the spectrum are the bulk of the cases, that are less stable, less successful, more erratic, more actively disturbed. They tend to act out more, trying to fill up their emptiness with alcohol, excessive sexual indulgence, or in any other kind of excitement. But they do manage to preserve considerable successful adaptation. Closest to the psychotics are the most disturbed patients who show considerable paranoid ideation, marked feelings of void, very tenuous object relations, and the most marginal adjustment. In spite of their serious pathology, what seems to characterize the bulk of the borderline patients is their resistance to psychotic illness.

PSYCHODYNAMIC FORMULATIONS

It is under this heading that most of the literature on the borderline can be found. Unfortunately the reports are repetitive, discursive and not well documented by empirical references.

Knight's discussion of the borderline was the beginning of a steady interest in this syndrome by psychoanalysts who for many years had neglected to follow Helene Deutsch's work (1942) on the "as if" personality, which will be discussed separately. Knight believes that the superficial neurotic symptoms represent a forward "holding position" while the major portion of the ego regresses. He accepts the concept of the borderline state and the fact that neurosis and psychosis are not mutually exclusive.

Knight (1953) writes:

> We conceptualize the borderline case as one in which normal ego functions of secondary-process thinking, integration, realistic planning, adaptation to the environment, maintenance of object relationships, and defenses against primitive unconscious impulses are severely weakened. As a result of various combinations of the factors of constitutional tendencies, predisposition based on traumatic events and disturbed human relationships, and more recent precipitating stress, the ego of the borderline patient is laboring badly. Some ego functions have been severely impaired—especially, in most cases, integration, concept formation, judgment, realistic planning, and defending against eruption into conscious thinking of id impulses and their fantasy elaborations. Other ego functions, such as conventional (but superficial) adaptation to the environment and superficial maintenance of object relationships may exhibit varying degrees of intactness. And still others, such as memory, calculation, and certain habitual performances, may seem unimpaired. Also, the clinical picture may be dominated by hysterical, phobic, obsessive-compulsive, or psychosomatic symptoms, to which neurotic disabilities and distress the patient attributes his inability to carry on the usual ego functions.

It is generally accepted that the ego- or integrating functions of the borderline are severely damaged as a result of deep narcissistic injuries early in life. Eisenstein points out that borderline patients tend to "act out" by running away, becoming promiscuous or using drugs to excess. There is anxiety of coldness or aloofness in others and suspiciousness of their warmth or attempts at closeness. In moving toward closeness they seem to fear loss of differentiation or being "swallowed up" by another and, according to Fried (1956), react with hostility and detachment.

Two panel discussions on the borderline were held at meetings of the American Psychoanalytic Association and were reported by Rangell (1955) and Robbins (1956). The first discussant, Greenson, indicated the diagnostic problems involved and thought them due to the following:

> (1) We are trying to classify something which as yet we understand only imperfectly; (2) we use borderline to denote transition, usually in reference to neurosis and psychosis; (3) we also use it to denote a relatively stable clinical picture in which there are simultaneously indications of psychosis, neurosis, and even healthy ego functions.

Greenson also considers that in the borderline there is a defect in the development of basic ego-functions arising from poor early object-relations and identifications. The internalized good and bad introjects are not fused, resulting in confused identifications and faulty reality-testing. At the same symposium Zetzel differentiated between the borderline personality and the overt clinical syndrome of borderline states.

Suslick (1963) emphasizes that the predominating symptom and presenting mode of illness involve pathology in the process leading to identity. With increased frequency because of the weakening of our long-standing institutions and organizations, more people are asking, "Am I unique and isolated or one of the multitude and ordinary but not alone?"

Waelder (1960) ascribes the feeling of emptiness in the borderline as the basis of his attempt to appropriate from others, or of his feeling of danger of being engulfed by others. Some try to borrow from others, become satellitic to another, merge with a host or lay skin to skin. Others attempt to fill up with knowledge or experience.

According to Gamm and his group:

> The dynamic basis of the clinical picture is a developmental arrest resulting in excessive narcissism beyond that found in the normal or neurotic, deficiencies in crucial ego functions, such as the perceptual and executive, and the pregenital fixation. The ego defects deprive the patients of techniques for mastery that they need to deal with their internal and external world. The narcissistic, magical omnipotent fantasies erected by these patients to contend with these defects and to protect themselves from the painful memory-traces of a traumatic infancy and childhood are little help in coping with realities of the adult world. In spite of their unadaptive value, these fantasies are cherished by the patients who even live their lives around them, perhaps in an effort at belated mastery.

Contrary to Schmideberg, who considers that repression is weak in the borderline, Bernstein (1964) believes that there is a massive repression resulting in a decreased sense of reality and sense of identity. Although the borderline knows himself as an object, he feels like a phony, always acting. He needs to experience excitation but fears being overwhelmed by it. As Modell (1963) states: "It is the porcupine's dilemma; to sleep as close to his fellows to get the needed warmth from their bodies, yet to maintain sufficient distance to avoid being stuck by their quills." The cause of the borderline's early repression of large segments of his affective resources is not easily determined. These patients often come from intelligent, educated and involved parents of relatively high socioeconomic levels. Bernstein believes that these parents are overly intrusive and the child is forced to abandon his own motivations and remain dependent on his mother's clues. His adaptation thus depends upon guarding his own drives from expression. Conformation to the social image and restriction of one's own expressions, according to Bernstein, is the cost of modern cultural development.

Modell points out that schizophrenia is a final common pathway of a variety of pathological conditions. The borderline, however, is not an incipient or early schizophrenic although among the wide variety of its symptom-complexes are included withdrawal, depression and schizoid personalities. Although their object-relations are primitive, they still are able to maintain some ties with other people. As do others, Modell thinks that borderline indicates a structural diagnosis rather than a syndrome with specific symptoms. Among the qualities of the borderline he includes: (1) subtle disorder in sense of reality; (2) strained quality of identifications and sense of identity; (3) relations based on primary identification instead of love, with identity borrowed from the partner; (4) primitive destructive fantasies; (5) temporary and limited regressions; (6) wish for omnipotent protectors and enormous dependence on external objects, but at the same time intense fear of closeness. On the positive side the borderline is relatively stable and does not develop overt schizophrenic breakdowns. According to Modell the borderline is an example of developmental arrest because of deficient mothering.

Kernberg (1967) has presented the results of his therapeutic encounters with a large number of borderline cases. His general conclusions are: (1) the borderline represents a specific and stable form of pathological ego-structure; (2) the presenting symptoms do not differentiate the syndrome; (3) transient psychotic episodes occur as a reaction to severe stress, alcohol and drugs, or in therapy as a transference psychosis; (4) these patients otherwise maintain reality-testing and have intact formal organization of thought processes; (5) borderline cases are easily differentiated from psychoses but not so easily differentiated from neuroses.

Kernberg's patients presented neurotic symptoms, including anxiety, polymorphic perverse sexuality, schizoid or hypomanic prepsychotic personalities, impulse neuroses and addiction, infantile, narcissistic and antisocial character disorders and many polysymptomatic problems such as phobias, obsessions, conversions, dissociation, hypochondriasis and paranoia. All of these were occasionally present in varying combinations and did not differentiate the syndrome.

Kernberg considers that the borderline has an infantile personality or what he calls a "low level character neurosis." This is differentiated by generalized lability, childlike demanding overinvolvement, exhibitionistic dependency, pseudohypersexuality with perversions and inappropriate social behavior, oppositional rather than competitive strivings and extreme narcissism and a depressive-masochistic character structure.

Kernberg interprets the ego weakness in the borderline as structural, suggesting that there is a lack of anxiety tolerance and a lack of impulse control. The absence of sublimatory channels and the inability to reenact specific identificatory systems result in dispersion of tension through sudden outbreaks. Correspondingly, although the borderline has no formal thought disorder, there are shifts to primary-process thinking in the form of primitive fantasies on projective tests. Finally, the specific defenses consist of ego-splitting by which conflictual identifications based on aggression and affection are kept apart or alternatively activated. Hence there is no stable ego-identity.

BORDERLINE IN CHILDREN

Eckstein and Wallerstein (1954) write:

> Children whose adjustment is marginally located in their use of both neurotic and psychotic mechanisms are a clinical group described variously as borderline, schizophrenic-like, or severely neurotic. They and psychotic children are subject to marked and frequent fluctuation in ego states, visible in the treatment process.

Again they write:

> Time and again the child begins the therapy hour with conversation or play wholly suited to his chronological age, so the clinical observer may reasonably be ready to conjecture the presence of a relatively intact ego, well able to use and sustain the demands and vicissitudes of classical child therapy and analysis. Yet suddenly and without clearly perceptible stimulus, a dramatic shift may occur, the neurotic defenses crumble precipitously and the archaic mechanisms of the primary process and the psychotic defenses erupt into view. Then they recede just as rapidly and the neurotic defenses or perhaps more accurately the pseudo-neurotic defenses reappear.

Rosenfeld and Sprince (1963) report pooled cases of a group working with borderline children to demonstrate that the interpreted dynamics even in the early years of life are no different than for adults. These children have a precarious maintenance of object-cathexis, easily retreating into primary identifications (mimicry). Their disturbance is principally in the perceptive and integrative functions of the ego to select and inhibit stimuli. Considerable anxiety is aroused by primitive fears of disintegration. Most of the children are uncertain about their sexual identity and reveal a discrepancy in their sexual and aggressive drives. Among the clinical derivatives of the lack of pleasurable early experiences and hence lack of ego stability are: (1) hypersensitivity to the environment; (2) disintegration under stress; (3) inability to accept frustration; (4) aggression toward people to whom they are attached; and (5) difficulty in sorting out the importance of several possible choices of behavior.

IS THERE A BORDERLINE AT ALL?

Zilboorg (1957) discussed less advanced cases of schizophrenia under the rubric of ambulatory schizophrenic. He rejected terms such as borderline, incipient schizophrenia, schizoid personalities and mixed psychoses. He believed that schizophrenia should be used as a generic name, covering types of psychopathological processes which can present themselves in varying degrees of intensity, development and overtness of clinical manifestations. Rangell (1955) reported:

> In conclusion, Zilboorg stated that he did not believe there was such a thing as a borderline case, and that, if we wished to be static and classificatory, all cases were borderline. Each case is in a state of flux, having just left one point and being on the way to another. The so-called borderline case should be looked upon like any other case and treated in accordance with clinical necessity. As in general medicine, dosage depends on the degree of illness and on the individual reaction of the patient both to the remedy and to the illness.

Bychowski (1957) uses the term "latent schizophrenia" instead of borderline as did Federn (1952), following Bleuler (1950) who spoke of latent schizophrenia as a group of all sorts of deviant personalities in which are concealed all the symptoms and their combinations observable in the manifest types of the disease. Bychowski's clinical descriptions of the borderline, in comparison with those outlined by others, do not fit into this category but are indeed characteristic of the schizophrenias.

The term "pseudoneurotic schizophrenia" was coined by Hoch and Polatin (1949). In a letter dated February 7, 1963,* Hoch stated:

> In the paper, The Diagnosis of Pseudoneurotic Schizophrenia, you will find a discussion which would indicate why I do not feel that pseudoneurotic schizophrenia is synonomous with the borderline concept. To put it very plainly an ambulatory schizophrenic is a schizophrenic in any category who is not sufficiently ill or whose socio-economic condition is such that he does not have to be hospitalized. Pseudoneurotic schizophrenia is

---

* Personal communication to Roy R. Grinker, Sr.

a sub-entity of schizophrenia similar to the catatonic or paranoid states, and finally I believe borderline should be dropped completely because I do not know what borders on what. Furthermore, I do not believe that a neurotic becomes schizophrenic and vice versa. I think there are two different processes involved if one considers it purely from the point of view of ego function or ego control.

Hoch's patients did not deteriorate, nor did they have delusions or hallucinations. Nevertheless their clinical symptomatology could be termed schizophrenic, and in follow-up studies a considerable number had short psychotic episodes or became frankly schizophrenic. In another paper Hoch and Cattell (1959) vigorously opposed the borderline or latent schizophrenic terms as logically untenable. Here, however, the more specific details of their pseudoneurotic schizophrenias indicate that they are schizophrenic and not what other clinicians have called borderline.

Frosch (1964) has suggested that the concept of psychotic character be substituted for that of borderline as well as ambulatory schizophrenia, pseudoneurotic schizophrenia, pseudopathic schizophrenia, schizophrenia without psychoses, latent psychoses, larval psychoses, "as if" character and neurotic ego-distortion. This presupposes that symptoms or clusters of symptoms are not suitable for classification. Instead he has reference to a syndrome characterized by ego-functions in their relationships to reality, other objects and other psychic structures. The psychotic character differs from psychoses as follows: (1) relative preservation of capacity to test reality; (2) relatively higher level of object-relations but still on an infantile level; (3) capacity for reversibility of regression, giving transience to the appearance of psychotic symptoms; and (4) reality adaptation. The psychotic character reveals a wide range of clinical manifestations, all of which are subsumed under one syndrome characterized in essence by transient perceptual distortions, identification, depersonalization and regressions.

Helene Deutsch (1942) described a syndrome which she called the "as if" personality disorder composed of rare individuals whose relationships were based on mimicry or imitation of others. Thirty years later two of her treated patients who were successful in their careers were still utilizing the same method in relationships. Subsequent to Deutsch's presentation the "as if" syndrome was broadened to include the syndrome that now is called the borderline.

Deutsch's patients apparently had not regressed but were fixed at an early infantile level of development at which there was still a primitive stage of object-relations, with little consistency, poor superego development, primary processes of identification, lack of sense of identity, poverty of affect and lack of insight. These patients were sufficiently able to test reality to prevent the development of psychosis (Weiss, 1966).

The authors attempted to sample the opinions of contemporary psychiatric practitioners on their staff who had experience in diagnosing and treating what they termed borderline patients. Only ten per cent of over one hundred psychiatrists responded because opinions were so uncrystallized. Among the responders there was no single stereotype. In fact the divergencies of opinions confirmed the findings of our overview of the literature. Metapsychological pronouncements, observations, interpretations and inferences were presented with great semantic confusion. At best we concluded that the diagnosis of borderline represented a label for uncertainty and the search for a niche in which to place many varieties of human distress.

SUMMARY

We have presented an overview of the literature on the borderline in general. In subsequent chapters we refer to specific concepts of other writers when they apply to our own subject headings. Although we have not covered the entire literature as would historians, our overview does indicate what has been known and inferred, and encompasses the current speculations on the subject.

The reader is probably astonished at the paucity of clinical observations and descriptions and perhaps somewhat curious that the main body of writing stems from psychoanalysts rather than from general psychiatrists. That this clinical syndrome increasingly diagnosed in office practice and in psychiatric clinics has not been the subject of systematic empirical research is indeed surprising.

The dynamic formulations are somewhat repetitive, and the arguments regarding nuances of meaning are characteristic of modern psychoanalytic discussions in which definitions and semantic clarity are missing. For example, one contributor to a panel thought that there existed a "pseudo–as-if" character. Furthermore, for the most part the dynamic speculators rarely revealed the clinical data about which they were talking or writing, the number of patients they had observed or the techniques employed. Apparently the growing attention paid to the borderline by psychoanalysts is indicative of the increasing numbers of these patients seen in their private practices.

Despite these limitations the clinical descriptions and formulations do attain a general consensus, and the reader surely can grasp the currently accepted gestalt of the borderline. True, there are some who deny that the concept has heuristic value or empirical validity. They prefer to include the borderline among the latent, incipient, ambulatory or transitional schizophrenics. Yet they fail to identify their patients or discuss the absence of disturbances of associations or other cognitive functions characteristic of schizophrenia. It is striking, furthermore, that the data concerning the borderline syndrome are markedly similar in children and adults and in a wide socioeconomic range of the population.

The general consensus, without repeating the details, is that the borderline is not a regressive process but a developmental defect on which a wide variety of adaptive and defensive neurotic behavior is overlaid. The defect is fundamentally a deformity or distortion of ego-functions. The etiological factors for this arrest of development are not known, and the age or phase represented by the fixation has not been delineated.

The so-called structural defect of the ego due to some sort of narcissistic trauma produces a deficiency in the processes of identifications which are maintained at the infantile level of mimicry and do not reach the secondary level characterized by confidence, independence and the development of regulatory structures. Affectionate relations are sought but feared; loneliness is sometimes defended against by participating with others on an "as if" level; structured situations are more comfortable than the uncertainty of change; the sense of identity is woefully weak.

It is generally agreed that specific symptoms, most of which are neurotic, do not characterize the borderline nor do minor, transient psychotic withdrawals. The essential quality of the borderline is the defect or distortion of ego-functions. Indeed, the literature search presented as an overview points clearly to the need of systematic research into the ego-functions of the borderline. This is exactly what was planned and designed in our own investigations herein reported.

CHAPTER 3 The Conceptual and
Operational Theory
of the Research

HITCHES IN PREVIOUS CLINICAL RESEARCH

Before undertaking the current investigation the senior author and other colleagues had completed a similar study of depressions (Grinker et al., 1961). The intent was to subject depressed patients to a detailed analysis of their *feelings and concerns* as well as their *current behavior*. In recognition that both elements were necessary to develop data from which to uncover subcategories of the depressive syndrome we utilized both depth interviews and observations of overt behavior on a nursing unit.

In our pilot study there was considerable unreliability in the descriptions of behavioral aspects made by psychiatrists in contrast with the reliability of their interpretative judgments about the patients' internal feelings and concerns. Statistical studies revealed that psychiatrists are not so adept at observing behavior as they are at eliciting feelings and concerns. Apparently, even when specifically looking for behavioral traits, psychiatrists' interest in and familiarity with the content of thoughts and feelings interfere with their observations of what goes on in front of them. Paradoxically they can communicate better about what they have to infer and interpret. Therefore, in the main study of depressions we utilized the nursing staff on the ward for observational data and happily found their reliability to be excellent.

The study report (Grinker et al., 1961) commented on the current one-sided approach to clinical psychiatry as follows:

> An unfortunate by-product of focusing on the dynamics of depression has been the underemphasis on sound clinical observations and adequate descriptions of these and other mental patients. As a matter of fact, most of American psychiatry is dynamic psychiatry, and the word descriptive has become an appellation of derogation. Descriptive psychiatry is considered to be old-fashioned and obsolete. Clinical psychiatry is incompletely taught in most of our training centers; the teachers themselves are less interested in it since they for the most part have been trained to infer and formulate rather than to describe. As a result, the details of clinical syndromes are little known, and the natural history of psychiatric diseases has been neglected.

As stated in Chapter 1, the underemphasis and derogation of clinical observations of behavior is associated with a studied neglect of diagnosis and classification without which psychiatry cannot aspire to be scientific. Such negative approaches will always obstruct sound clinical research and inevitably studies of causal relations.

Paul Meehl (1959), a distinguished psychologist, critically states: "Rather than decrying nosology, we should become masters of it, recognizing that some of our psychiatric colleagues have in recent times become careless and even unskilled in the art of formal diagnosis." The philosopher Kaplan (1964) indicates how every classification serves some purpose to disclose relationships that must be taken into account no matter what.

SOURCES OF EVIDENCE FOR CATEGORIES OF DEVIANCE

The sources of evidence concerning problems of deviance in human beings fall into several categories. Deviance, or, in medical language, disease, indicates a comparison with what is supposedly healthy and normal. Offer and Sabshin (1961) have considered normality from four perspectives: normality as health, normality as utopia, normality as average and normality as process. The concept of normality as an ontogenic process necessitates its analysis as a system maturing and developing in a specific social and cultural setting. We are faced with the problem of the frames of reference from which the processes of health or illness are to be observed.

This problem is currently seen as a conflict of approaches to all nosological classifications. In Chapter 2 the literature overview discloses that the borderline case is described or defined from behavioral observations and from inferences derived from depth or psychoanalytic interviews which probe "intrapsychic" processes. Are these approaches complementary or in opposition? To put this very crudely, can a person be sick inside and behave well, or be internally healthy and outwardly deviant? In discussing the new or revived functions of psychiatrists in resocializing patients by means of short-term hospitalization, Ruesch (1966) indicates that adequate social behavior may exist in persons with severe pathology, and temporary deviant behavior may be associated with little psychopathology. There is something radically wrong with the above question. It presupposes that inside and outside are separable, that they follow different invariants and that they require radically different methods of observation. Actually they are inseparable both in structure and function. For example, the sociologist Goffman (1966), who defines mental illness as inappropriate behavior and states that we protect our gatherings and occasions by putting those who act unsuitably into asylums, writes. "The symptomatology of the 'mentally ill' may sometimes have more to do with the structure of the public order than with the nature of disordered minds." Concentrating on behavior unsuitable for specific occasions, Goffman neglects the internal lack or adequacy of the subjects' capacities to assume these various role behaviors.

Nevertheless whenever we reach a compromise indicating unity and use such terms as holistic, process or global, we become satisfied, sense closure and flee from the operational. Empirical research requires the observation of symptoms, behaviors or functions, but these are far from fundamental causes. The sociologist looks outward to the social world of experience with his special techniques. The psychologist looks inward at processes that he terms intervening variables, and the biologist, all too frequently reductionistic, searches for genic, biochemical or physiological deficits. Yet each focus constitutes a transacting part of the larger field for which hypothetical constructs or theory may be developed and tested. Actually a nosological and classificatory focus of the interdisciplinary components of psychiatry may facilitate their articulation.

The sources of evidences pertinent for research on types of health or illness may be outlined as follows: (1) the past developmental history; (2) anecdotal episodes derived from an anamnesis concerning reactions to various life situations and stresses, for example, critical periods of growth or responses to environmental changes; (3) behavior in the family group, at school, at work or in community activities; (4) behavior on the nursing unit of a mental hospital; (5) behavior in the two-person situation of patient and interviewer or therapist, or from the transference regression in the psychoanalytic situation; (6) appropriate psychological tests; (7) artificial (experimental) stress situations such as small periods of isolation or periods of forced group activity.

The clinician uses any one or all of these sources that are available to him. His diagnostic acumen is based on his capacity to utilize the essence from all sources with which to build a gestalt, characteristic of a symptom complex currently generally recognized and labeled. Such a technique does not suffice, however, as a method for scientific studies, for example, to delineate a new category or to develop subcategories or typologies.

In general, scientific information is obtained by collecting observations and measurements under specified conditions, encoding the data in terms characteristic of the statistical model to be used, processing the data, and checking the results again against the original events. Royce (1965) exemplifies this in terms applicable to clinical research: (1) standardized conditions of observations as on a nursing unit, (2) under specified conditions even though the variables are not controlled, (3) by many persons, (4) observing specified variables, (5) repetitive observations, (6) statistical analyses leading to the determination of the contribution of each variable. To this we must add the checking of results for their logical relationship with clinical experience.

THE PSYCHIATRIC-PSYCHOANALYTIC CONFLICT

We shall touch only lightly on this repetitive and futile conflict which has achieved no resolution over the last several decades because real conflict does not exist. However, there has been a consistent clash of ideologies which by definition are not amenable to reason. Its significance for us lies in the fact that we have attempted to utilize both positions theoretically as appropriate to the study of an organized system of clinical events, even though our operations were purely observational.

The conflict between psychoanalysis and psychiatry as "sciences" has been clearly described by Home (1966). He states that Freud took psychoanalysis out of the world of science into that of the humanities by his basic postulate that symptoms have meanings. In science including psychiatry we make observations from which we postulate explanations. In psychoanalysis we approach humans existing uniquely in time and interpret meanings inferentially. Mind is the meaning of behavior in a living subject; reification makes of mind a thing. Unfortunately, Home does not mention the proposition that even inferences and hence interpretations require the basic data of behaviors.

Among psychoanalysts there are differences in opinion which range from the complete negation of anything but "meaning" derived from introspection and imaginative empathy as, for example, Meissner (1966). He denies the significance of verbal reports and states that psychoanalytic concepts cannot be reduced to a behavioral or operational basis, thereby denying the operations of science as at the same time he speaks of scientific theory. This is what another psychoanalyst Glover (1966) calls the sophistry of modern psychoanalytic theory. On the other hand Anna Freud (1966b) advocates the use of methods other than psychoanalytic, indicating that relationships between surface behaviors as derivatives of the unconscious can signify id contents. As a matter of fact, child analysis is almost entirely dependent upon observations of *play behavior* in children.

Derivatives of the unconscious in behavior are observable diagnostic clues. From these the psychiatrist can assess genetic or dynamic processes but not as "confidently" as the psychoanalyst; however, he can adequately delineate ego-functions. In the psychoanalytic situation the transference neurosis presumably enables the analyst to observe in the regression so-called genetic processes, previous conflicts and the range of solutions. Although more indirectly, the behaviors of a subject expose not only present deficits but also past scars, ego-distortions and on-going conflicts.

Psychoanalytic techniques have been used to describe current ego-functions in terms of verbal and nonverbal behavior within the psychoanalytic situation which in itself is conducive to a weakening of ego-functioning and to regression to an earlier level of organization. Under these conditions the adequacy of ego-functioning in real-life situations cannot be determined except by the often distorted reports of the subject in retrospect. The special psychoanalytic techniques utilizing verbal behavior may reveal ego-functions in the living transference recapitulation but not always their relationship to current liabilities or assets.

In the light of this we can state the difficulties in utilizing the psychoanalytic method in clinical research: (1) transference behaviors are private; (2) they are limited in universality by differences in subjects and analytic investigators; (3) they are limited in numbers of subjects available; (4) behaviors are not replicable, because the situations are not replicable; (5) there is a single observer; (6) within the analytic transference, the individual inferences and interpretations do not always have external referrents, they often relate only to internal processes relatively independent of external events; (7) interpretations are selective.

Intrapsychic processes can be communicated to the self and others only through behaviors—verbal or nonverbal. Psychoanalysis as a process of introspection or as behavior verbally communicated exists in a setting conducive to transference regression. Since this setting, in which verbal, sometimes visceral and sometimes bodily behaviors are expressed, occurs in a constant dyadic relationship, the observations are private, nonreplicable and subject to biases and distortions of interpretations.

Despite these difficulties and the unreliability of inferences, observations of a large enough sample of subjects by a variety of observers may disclose patterns that cannot be discerned by observations in an open field with a multitude of transactions calling for many social roles. The scientific dilemma is the contamination by an initial reporter influencing all subsequent observers who can easily "confirm" in the "material" what they expect. There are few controls, no tests for reliability and great semantic vagueness.

Finally we should like to allay the conflict of dynamic vs. descriptive or more bluntly psychoanalytic vs. observational techniques. There should be no controversy because both are necessary and each method furnishes similar and different data. This is clearly indicated in the literature on the borderline, and as Glover (1933) states there is room for new syndromes achieved by "openness" for which a combination of descriptive words with genetic understanding is necessary to aid differential diagnosis and refine prognosis. In a more positive sense we should view the observable physical behaviors and the verbal introspective products as parts of one system. Mentation and behavior constitute a psychosomatic unity. It is a system composed of parts with allocated functions but integrated and organized.

PSYCHOANALYTIC EGO-PSYCHOLOGY

The theoretical framework utilized in this study is called in technical terms "ego-psychology." Without utilizing this name academic psychologists are constantly dealing with ego-functions in their experiments on cognition, learning and perception. Psychoanalytic theory from the very beginning utilized the concept of an ego as antithetical and in conflict with an id. Hartmann systematized and stimulated the development of what is called psychoanalytical ego-psychology when he postulated a conflict-free sphere of the ego or an autonomous ego. His contributions specified the many functions allocated to the ego which now enable us to link them to visible and measurable behaviors. Hartmann (1958, 1964) states, "Ego is the centralized functional control which integrates different parts of the personality with each other and with outer reality." However, he also calls ego a "sub-structure of the personality which is defined by its function." Forces acting on the ego include the impact of reality, the impact of the drives and autonomous factors (the hereditary core). This latter or the conflict-free structure of the ego furnishes the ground plan for maturation which is constantly sensitive to the environment.

The ego in psychological language is that allocated function of the psychic apparatus which lies at the border between internal psychological processes and the external environment. As a border process it filters perceptions of stimuli from the environment and screens action derived from internal motivation. Ego-functions have been described as strong or weak, brittle or flexible, rather than with reference to particular aspects of its several functions. Thus, for example, the latent or overt psychotic is supposedly characterized by a weak ego which succumbs to stress and then freely exposes internal archaic forms of thinking such as delusions, hallucinations or bizarre associations. On the other hand, the neurotic is characterized by a break or weakening of ego-functions in a limited sector.

The various functions attributed to the concept of ego may be arbitrarily considered under seven headings (Beres, 1965):

1. *Relation to Reality*

   a. Adaptation to reality depends upon the external demands or obstacles to need-satisfactions. The individual in action requires a repertoire of internalized social roles that he can play spontaneously and actions which on necessity he can devise (creativity) toward people, things and tasks. This means the capacity to grow, differentiate and integrate.

   b. Reality-testing requires an accuracy of perception, capacity to orient self in time and place, tolerance for ambiguity and judgment as to the differentiation of figure and ground (focusing).

   c. Sense of reality is manifested by unobtrusive ordinary functions which differentiate self from others based on effective automatic recognition of the boundaries of self (identity). According to Federn (1952) this involves an "ego feeling" which constitutes an effective awareness of self maintained over time (stability) which also resists diffusion or depletion.

2. *Regulation and Control of Drives*
This function concerns effective control of inner pressures which demands tolerance of frustration, anxiety and ambiguity. It depends on such tactics as detour-behavior, delay and sublimation.

3. *Object-Relations*
The ability to form such relations and to maintain their consistency not withstanding ambivalences, rejections or frustrations.

4. *Cognitive Functions*
These include concentration, selective scanning, memory, abstraction and ability to avoid contamination by drive expressions.

5. *Defensive Functions*
Included are the various types of defenses appropriate to both inner and outer pressures, such as repression, reaction-formation, denial, withdrawal, and adaptive or coping mechanisms.

6. *Autonomous Functions*
These cognitive functions are considered to be the "givens" of the conflict-free ego and include perception, intention (energy or will), intelligence, and language capacity.

7. *Synthetic Functions*
An important capacity includes the ability to organize, to form gestalts and to compromise.

THE EGO IN BEHAVIOR

Lately there has been increasing awareness that clinical psychiatry as one of the behavioral sciences requires new and more refined techniques of observation, description and analysis to become progressive. For this reason it is necessary to be explicit about our concepts of behavior.

We agree with Kantor (1963) that "behaviorism" means many things. It describes an objective nonintrospective approach to psychological processes; as Skinner (1957) states, psychology is the science of behavior and mental life. But for him meaning is a property of conditions under which behavior occurs and includes inferred variables of which response or behavior is usually a function. Behaviorism is a theory and a philosophy or according to Kantor all of science itself. It excludes the invisible and intangible, including introspection or self-observation, and maintains the physical as the object of its interest, rejecting the psychological.

Nagel (1961) explains in a discussion of the methodological problems in the social sciences that the term "behaviorism" does not today have a precise doctrinal connotation, as it did in the 1920's and 1930's, and students of human conduct who today designate themselves as behaviorists do so chiefly because of their adherence to a method that places a premium on objective data; behaviorism is a methodological orientation.

Elkes (1963) states that basic to a study of the pharmacology of behavior is its description. Behavior is not an epiphenomenon but the major phenomenon of life and also a method of study from which one can demand more precision. But the varieties and subtleties of behavior challenge established techniques. In the two-person or dyadic relationship the moment-to-moment behaviors are enormous. In larger groups transactions seem too varied for recording and miss the subjective component. According to Elkes rating scales of any precision are effective only when clinical judgments are possible.

A more controversial stance was adopted by Helen Sargent (1961) who criticizes the "behavior-observation-inference" model which can only be developed by our perceptive senses. Although direct observation of the inner state of another is impossible, common sense permits us to attribute sense to what goes on in a person's mind and know what it means. She implies that including reportable affects, dreams, conflicts and memories as behaviors are escape hatches, but since they are reportable only verbally with more or less indices of affect we believe that they must be included under behaviors. Sargent states that to predict behavior we must know attitudes, intents or motives rather than acts. We contend that knowing the acts and their circumstances we can in reverse identify attitudes or motives. Unfortunately Sargent has set up a dichotomy between content and method.

There are others who take a broader view of behavioral analysis. Kanfer and Saslow (1966) utilize five approaches which include self-descriptions obtained through interviews, transactions with significant others, informants from among family and friends, work behavior and psychological tests. Kantor again includes both physical acts and psychological sets of "interbehaviorism" (transactionalism), a symmetrical field composed of acts and sets, as component parts of a behavioral system and investigated by techniques which vary with the focus on parts of the field.

We cannot conceive of a fracture of behavior into acts and mentation;

they both comprise a system characterized by internal and external boundaries. They only seem to be separated in the face of disintegrations or regressions. Strauss (1967) from the sociological point of view writes about deviance as such or deviant acts. They can only be so defined if compared with standards or values held by the group or challenged by another group. Some abnormal or eccentric behavior in the larger group may not become deviant as long as the persons remain within a special and consistent line of culture and conflict is avoided. Usually, however, people belong to many groups in which they adapt successfully because they have acquired an internalized role repertoire sufficiently extensive (Grinker, 1957). In fact there are no total deviants. The question is in what way and to what extent is behavior deviant and in what setting. Thus in planning for mental health facilities the *demands* for help from the public are sometimes based on internal discomfort but more often on behavioral deviance from accepted standards of others. On the other hand *needs* are what the authoritative mental health disciplines decide and they "case-find" just those problems.

In their study of "milieu therapy" the Cummings (1962) view the fundamental principles as the practical management and control of the executive functions of the ego leading to an increase in the number of differentiated sets. An ego is a coherent system of ideas, events and values of which the greater the variety, the more flexible, adaptive and healthy the personality. Growth occurs through the resolution of crises which the milieu controls. Professional staffs are "for the deviant but against his deviance." Finally social improvement is *followed by* ego growth.

BEHAVIOR AS EGO IN ACTION

Our study is oriented toward the observation, description and ratings of behaviors of a subclass of psychiatric patients in a particular setting. In this sense we are attempting to improve on the deficiency exposed in our research on depression. The study of depressions, however, was an attempt to deal with a wide range of symptoms in an effort to place them in subcategories or syndromes. Here we are not dealing with symptoms but functions of a specified psychic structure, the ego, as evidenced in behaviors.

Obviously we could include observations of everything the subjects did or said as grist for our qualitative and quantitative scientific rating methods. This would be a waste of time, however, in that all that is known about psychopathology would have been discarded and mountains of detail would have been accumulated only to be discarded on the basis of a post-hoc theory. We, therefore, started with both conceptual and operational theories (Grinker, 1964).

Because a study of the whole range of ego-functions is important for the proper diagnosis and prediction of outcome in spontaneous growth, development and the prediction of psychosis and/or recovery under appropriate methods of treatment, we believe that it is important to describe, classify and quantify the various ego-functions as they are expressed in behavior.

Our position utilizes the psychoanalytic theory of ego-psychology in that the several allocated functions of the ego are employed in our design for the purpose of placing observations in appropriate frames. We are enabled to obtain a sufficient quantity of raw data from a large number of observations made by many observers over time. Tests of reliability and validity as well as replication are thus possible. We can be comfortable in seeing assets as well as liabilities and directly observe problems in social living. Based on the raw data we may develop hypotheses and make excursions into speculation specifically labelled as such and attached to external referrents. Whatever we lose from lack of depth interviews or psychoanalytic techniques can be overcome by bringing the results of both methods into juxtaposition. Indeed in Chapter 7 we report some patients studied carefully over time by depth interviews. Our hypotheses may enrich psychoanalysis and in turn be modified by it.

We affirm again that behavior—verbal and nonverbal—is the basic data of scientific psychiatry. Behavior represents in actuality functions allocated to a hypothetical ego which filters perceptions, on the one hand, and actions, on the other, expresses reportable motivations, affects, defenses and compromises, employs symptoms and sublimations and demonstrates integrative capacities and disintegrative trends. We espouse a form of behavioral study that acknowledges the existence of unconscious mental processes and accepts introspection reported by verbal responses that subjects make under given conditions.

In sum, we can state that the conceptual theory under which we operate involves ego-psychology in the sense that ego-functions are the final common pathway for the expression of mentation at any level no matter what technical means are adopted for their observation or in what situation—psychoanalytic (Rapaport, 1959) or in a mental hospital nursing unit—they occur. Ego-functions are expressed in behaviors which are observable and describable. The research task in defining a clinical syndrome is to observe well-defined aspects of behavior, the raw data of which can be rated and analyzed according to sound statistical methods. Furthermore the basic data may then be used for inferences and interpretations as to their meanings.

Operationally we may observe behaviors under various headings and subheadings and then utilize well-defined scales with which to rate them numerically. These headings correspond to the allocated functions of the ego translated into operational terms. These are discussed in Chapter 4 where our design is demonstrated. For now it is sufficient to indicate the close connection between ego-functions and behaviors by referring to such large categories as *outward behavior* (to people, environment, and tasks), *perception* (awareness, differentiation, assessment), *messages* (verbal, nonverbal, reception), *affects and defenses* (relations with people, control of affect and behavior, defense mechanisms and situational mastery) and *synthesis* (integration, capacity to resist disintegration and to carry on usual life processes).

CHAPTER 4 Research Design

This chapter describes the essential aspects of the research design of our study of ego-functions in the borderline. Following a brief outline of the pilot study we present a detailed description of the full-scale study which covers the selection of patients, the procedures for obtaining the behavioral observations and the techniques for ratings.

PILOT STUDY

The pilot study of the ego-functions research was initiated early in 1959 by a team composed of Drs. Roy R. Grinker, Sr., and Robert C. Drye, and Miss Joanne Holden who concentrated on the selection of a broad framework and the intensive study of a single patient whose treatment was being supervised by one member of the team.

The beginning framework was derived from the outline of seven allocated ego-functions presented by Beres (page 29). This served as an initial description to be modified, enlarged and made operational as the research developed. Although all sources of evidence for ego-functions were thought to be important, the decision was made during the pilot experience to rely most heavily on observable current behavior on the psychiatric nursing unit as an index of patterning which should reveal capacities to overcome difficulties and to change toward better adaptation (assets), as well as revealing defects (liabilities) in ego-functioning.

To aid in developing an appropriate research design an intensive study of a single patient was undertaken. Week by week for two months the patient's behaviors on the nursing unit and in therapeutic interviews were studied. In addition, observations of the behaviors made by other personnel such as occupational therapists and social workers were recorded. All descriptions of the patient's behaviors were elicited by means of interviews, which the team discussed in detail.

The seven allocated ego-functions were established as representatives of the highest levels of abstraction. Each category was then broken down into a number of behavioral variables serving to make the abstractions concrete and operational. From statements of behavior, sentences were developed which indicated what kind of interpretation could be made from the data. The categories and sentences were then tested for applicability to the pilot case and then further refined on two additional pilot cases.

The pilot experience taught us several important indications for the next step and validated again the importance of a preexperimental pilot study. Our original ideas for the design were too grandiose in an effort to be all-inclusive, and we realized that the focus of the research required sharpening. What we did in the study of one patient and the time spent in discussion obviously could not be carried over to an adequately sized sample of cases. On the other hand, stricter adherence to objectivity is a by-product of an increased number of cases since what we had to sacrifice were the least objective items. We also learned that direct questioning of the observers confused the discrimination between observations and inferences. Finally, the pilot experience successfully enabled us to improve our translation of the abstract definitions of ego-functions into operational terms.

Both the intensive pilot study and the full-scale study of the ego-functions of borderlines were conducted at the Illinois State Psychiatric Institute (ISPI). This modern well-equipped state institution was opened in 1959 as a research, training and service center. Soon after the doors of the hospital opened the pilot study was initiated, immediately implementing the research purpose of the hospital. At the same time the total program of the hospital was taking shape and was fairly well established when two years later, in July, 1961, the full-scale study got under way.

The hospital has seven patient floors each with 48 beds. On each floor 30 beds are allocated to an open and 18 to a closed unit. Each of six of the floors is affiliated with one of the six psychiatric training institutions in the city of Chicago, and the seventh with the state of Illinois. The specific setting for the full-scale study was the open nursing unit (Eight East, 8E) of the Michael Reese floor with nursing staff ratio of two to every three patients. Social services, occupational therapy, psychological services are available on each unit.

Beyond the commonality of the hospital-wide services, the programs and treatment models vary from floor to floor in accordance with the aspirations and goals of the staff and its sponsoring institutions. Since it opened, the treatment on the Michael Reese floor has been extensively developed as a milieu-therapy program. A concomitant of this environment is the staff's expectation that patients not only adhere to the rules and regulations of the unit, but that they actively involve themselves in some, if not all, of the group enterprises. The environment has structure.

FULL-SCALE STUDY

Selection of Patients for Study

The chief of the Reese psychiatric unit, Dr. Theodore Reid, Jr., was asked to admit as many borderline patients as possible which meant the definitely-not-schizophrenic patients. In retrospect he interpreted our general criteria into the following traits:

1. Young adult with repeated short-term hospitalizations but with good psychological functioning in the intervals.
2. Florid attention-provoking histrionic episodes preceding hospitalization.
3. Quite accessible during the diagnostic interview or rapidly becoming so.
4. Intellectual contact can be made and cognitive functions are intact.
5. Associations appropriate.
6. No systematized delusions or paranoid systems.
7. An ego-alien quality to any transient psychotic-like behavior.

Excluded from the study were patients (even though considered borderline) who:

1. Gave evidence of damage from alcohol or drugs.

2. Suffered from degenerative diseases.

3. Were beyond middle years.

4. Had experienced a discernible loss of memory from shock therapy.

Thus patients whose ego-functioning might be impaired for physical or organic reasons were excluded.

Although these definitions appear to be rather loose, from the point of view of the research they were a very satisfactory basis for referral. The purpose of the study which was the development of diagnostic typologies within an ego-functions framework required that we identify a range of behavior with considerable variety. Had we attempted a tighter definition of borderline we would have invalidated our purpose.

The syndrome may be manifested at times by behavior that seems sufficiently psychotic to warrant admission to a psychiatric receiving hospital. Many of our patients were procured for transfer to our unit from the Psychopathic Hospital. Yet on admission this behavior ceased almost at once in our structured milieu which furnished fewer tests of ability to cope with the world so that psychotic behavior hardly ever appeared or reappeared. That the patients understood the stresses for them on the outside world is evidenced by the fact that they were reluctant to leave the security of our hospital.

TABLE 1. *Precipitants to Hospitalization*

Predominant Precipitant	TOTAL	*51*
Depression without specific suicide attempt or ideation		5
Suicidal ideation		5
Attempted suicide		4
Impulse eruption; inability to regulate aggression		2
Anxiety—(acute and/or diffuse)		5
Phobias		4
Alcohol and/or drugs		4
Ritualistic compulsive behavior		2
Somatization		3
Disorders of thinking and association		3
Combination of above		11
Other		3

Table 1 shows the precipating causes for hospitalization of our patients when these could be determined. They fall into four groups: (1) depression, suicidal ideas and suicidal attempts; (2) anger, impulse eruption and anxiety; (3) defenses such as phobias, compulsions, alcohol and somatization; (4) disorders of thinking in temporary confusional states.

Social Characteristics of Sample

We had decided to select 50 patients for study. Referrals to the study were discontinued with the 51st patient who met our criteria, and the extra subject was kept in the sample. The selection of patients by clinical criteria and the list of exclusions resulted in a sample of patients who were relatively homogeneous in their social characteristics (cf. Appendix I).

TABLE 2. *Social Characteristics*

	Number	Per cent
Sex	*51*	*100*
Male	28	55
Female	23	45
Age	*51*	*100*
Less than 30 years	39	76
30 years or older	12	24
Race	*51*	*100*
White	46	90
Negro	5	10
Religion	*51*	*100*
Protestant	17	33
Catholic	27	53
Jewish	6	12
Other	1	02
Marital Status	*51*	*100*
Single (never married)	29	57
Married (living with spouse)	13	25
Married (separated)	7	14
Divorced	2	04
Admission to Hospital	*51*	*100*
Voluntary	39	76
Committed	12	24

The distributions according to sex, race and religion are fortuitous as we did not specify them as criteria. The minimum age for admission to the hospital is eighteen years but otherwise adults of all ages are admitted. We ended with a young-adult group probably because of the criteria for exclusion. However, an older-age sample of patients is mentioned in Chapter 10. The predominance of voluntary admissions may be a function of the clinical entity we were seeking.

The families of the ever-married group were relatively small. Of the 22 ever-married patients, only four had families of four or more children. Occupationally and educationally the sample had a distinct character.

Excluding the housewives, the patients were predominantly either in white-collar clerical and sales or in blue-collar occupations. A few were students. Educationally, 67 per cent of the sample were school dropouts at the high school or college level.

Procedures for Obtaining Behavioral Observations

In this research we aimed for a sample of the spontaneous and natural behavior of patients over a sufficient time-span. We did not put patients in test or experimental situations nor control behavior in any unusual manner. Observations of patients' behavior by the staff, the kind of observations required for the usual practice of the various disciplines involved, were the basic source materials of this research. We proceeded on the assumption that the staff that serves the patient could make valid observations of his behavior. This basis calls for specification of (1) observational periods, (2) observers, (3) a means for recording observations, and (4) a system of transcribing and organizing observations. An interview was used to elicit the behavioral data from the observers. Behavioral reports were mechanically recorded and then transcribed into individual protocols. All of these procedures are described in the sections that now follow.

1. OBSERVATIONAL PERIODS

Two observational periods were specified under the assumption that a large enough time-sample of the behavior of an individual patient is an adequate index of his psychological structure.

The *first* observational period was initiated not earlier than the beginning of the patient's third week and not later than the beginning of his fourth week in the hospital. The observational period then lasted for two weeks. We assumed that by the time the patient has been in the hospital two or three weeks he was going to be there for some time and had begun to settle down.

The *second* period was initiated at the time the patient and his therapist mutually decided that the patient was moving toward leaving the hospital. The second period was individually determined on the basis of this intent or actual activity. Observations continued for two weeks after initiation of the second period. We assumed that leaving the hospital stirred ambivalences in all patients, and therefore we would be observing the patients in a common stress situation.

During observational periods, drugs that might affect the ego-functioning of patients were not to be administered with the exception of small doses of very mild drugs like Miltown, Librium and hypnotics. Charts of patients were flagged for this restriction. We also stipulated that study patients would have to remain on the same Unit (8E) through two observational periods to qualify for our sample. Seventeen patients referred for study were dropped from the core sample because these conditions were not met; principally they were not on the Unit (8E) for two observational periods. Three were transferred to a closed unit; five eloped; one signed out; seven were suddenly discharged for varying reasons before the second observational period; one was placed on drugs. These will be further described in Chapter 9.

2. OBSERVERS

The professional and subprofessional staff who served the patients within the full field of the hospital observed and reported patient behavior over a two-year period from July, 1961, through September, 1963. The range of personnel included nursing staff (including aides), occupational therapists, activities leaders, vocational counselors, social workers and residents. Over a given observational period our model of coverage for nursing and occupational therapy reports is shown in Table 3.

TABLE 3. *The Observers*

	Number of Reports	
	Minimum	Maximum
Staff nurse during day	3	4
Staff nurse during evening	3	4
Psychiatric aide during day	3	4
Psychiatric aide during evening	3	4
Occupational therapist	1	2
Activities leader (when utilized)	1	1
Vocational counselor (when utilized)	1	1
	15	20

The average number of nursing and occupational therapy reports for the group of patients under study was 16.6, S.D. 2.8 for the observational period. The median and modal number of reports was 17 (reports, not different reporters). These figures are a testimonial to the unusual cooperation that the investigators enjoyed. Those members of the nursing staff who had the most consistent opportunity to serve the individual patient during observational periods were chosen by the supervising nurse and our research interviewers to report their observations of patient behavior. Over a period of time all staff on the unit had a chance to participate in the research program; no one staff person or group was ever singled out as the research staff.

In addition to the nursing and occupational therapy observations, we also obtained reports from the residents and social workers assigned to the patient. Their reports (at least one from each discipline, at most two for the observational period) included not only the patient's behavior as observed in their contacts but whatever data they had about the patient at the time of the observational period.

Although the reporting of usual practice observations required no modifications in the administration, program or supervision of staff, it did require cooperation and a substantial contribution of staff working time. The reporters participated in the project as members of the 8E staff serving the patients who were selected as study patients. In their role as research reporters, they were requested: (1) not to provide other staff with feedback from their own reports because we wished to avoid eliciting mutual decisions or consensus about study patients; (2) not to intervene with the patient in order to have something to report, averting induced responses for research purposes; (3) not to inform the patient that he was a study patient since we aimed for the natural behavior of the patient as he lived his life in the hospital. The staff strictly followed these three conditions designed to minimize contamination of behavior and reporting.

The participation of the administration and staff on 8E in this research program was notable for its consistency, constancy and quality. The reasons are numerous. The hospital was new and in a formative state; the administration and staff were young, dedicated to the purposes of the hospital and eager to contribute to molding the hospital into what it was meant to be—a research as well as a training and service center. The task of reporting observations of patients' behavior was natural to them in their practice. The experience of verbally reporting observations for research purposes served to sharpen their observational skills and ability to articulate and thus proved rewarding to the staff as well as the researchers.

Over the two-and-a-half-year period of observations of patients' behavior 84 different staff members participated in the research program. However, the nursing, occupational therapy and social work staffs were unusually stable.

TABLE 4. *Professions of Observers*

		Number
	TOTAL	*84*
Nurses		17
Aides		17
Occupational therapists		6
Residents		31
Social workers		9
Vocational counselors		4

Sixty-two per cent of the 84 participants were under 30 years of age. The youth of the staff was not characteristic of any one discipline. All nurses were females; one-half of the aides were males; the majority of the resident psychiatrists were males; the majority of those in the other disciplines were females. All of the nurses were registered, and the aides had experienced in-service training. Only three of the aides had not completed high school; several had attended college and several were college graduates.

3. RESEARCH INTERVIEW AND PROTOCOLS OF BEHAVIOR

The research interview was utilized to elicit from staff members their observations of patient behavior. Two highly skilled experienced social caseworkers conducted the interviews in an office located five floors away from the unit where the study patients lived. All reports were mechanically recorded. One interviewer followed through on a specified patient and obtained all staff reports on him.

The interview as used in this research was guided by transactional theory. The abstract interview model outlined the forms of interrogation devised to extract the mutual reciprocal processes experienced by several people in a given field (cf. Appendix II). Descriptions of patient behavior were sought in the context of what was going on at the time. Within each context the aim was to elicit: "What did the patient say? How did he sound? What did the patient do—how did he act? How did he look? How did he feel?" In addition to the abstract outline, interviewers had several other aids to guide the process. They had knowledge of the ego-functions framework into which the behavioral data were to be placed, and illustration of how behavioral data related to its content.

Interviewers were instructed: (1) primarily to conduct spontaneous interviews; (2) to probe for the facts of patient behavior, rather than for inferences about the patient; (3) to tap uncovered behavioral content that would relate to the ego-functions framework, but to avoid assiduously a stereotyped set of questions. On this basis no one interview could insure complete coverage. From these instructions it is clear that we wished to obtain spontaneous observations supplemented by questions that pressed only for what the observers could report. We emphasized the avoidance of interrogation that might tend to build in content and fictional creations. The interview was unstandardized; the interviewers' technique was flexible and was adjusted to what the respondent could give.

Maccoby and Maccoby (1954) in their discussion of interviewing for research in the *Handbook of Social Psychology* list the advantages of unstandardized interviews. In favor of unstandardized interviews they say: (1) they permit standardization of meanings rather than of the more superficial aspects of the stimulus situations; (2) they are more valid in that they encourage more true-to-life replies; (3) they are more flexible.

The role of research interviewers required that they engage positively in communication with the reporters (the staff), adjust the interchange to the role of the reporter in the hospital and adapt to his verbal capacities. It was the task of the interviewers to aid the reporter in contributing concrete observations and to encourage and sustain his participation over time.

It was necessary for the research interviewers to become aware of and manage their own potential involvements and biases. A few of the prohibitions that were inherent in the role of research interviewer in this situation were: (1) interviewers should not provide reporters with feedback from any source; (2) interviewers should not give help in understanding or dealing with patients, thus abstaining from any involvement in the treatment of patients; (3) interviewers should not select staff to interview for unique reasons related to the individual staff person, that is, to choose one staff person more verbally fluent than another; (4) interviewers should not make demands on staff that do not coincide with their role of research interviewer; (5) interviewers should establish no differential identifications with the various programs that serve the 8E patients or make public their position on critical, controversial events or forces in their 8E environment; (6) interviewers should not make unilateral observations of the patient nor prepare for interviews by reading patient records; (7) interviewers should not share the ego-functions formulations of the study with the reporters or with anyone else.

In summary, we aimed to set up a situation that would keep the interviewers completely outside of the observational field. It was our purpose to obtain uncontaminated observations of the natural behavior of the patient uninfluenced by the research process. We are confident that the conditions were meticulously followed since none of our behavioral reports suggested contamination.

The behavioral reports were transcribed and set up in protocols which were then assembled in two separate units for each observational period: Unit I consisted of all nursing and occupational therapy reports, each preserved as a separate entity and arranged in the protocols sequentially by date of the report; Unit II consisted of the reports of the residents and social workers. The separation was dictated by the intent to rate the reports from these sources separately. The reports assembled in Unit I constituted the richest source of behavioral data which we proposed to rate without contamination from the kind of information to be found in the reports of residents and social workers (cf. Appendix III).

It was our experience that our methods provided desirable comparable behavioral observations from the various reporters. The behavior of the patient came through clearly in 17 reports spanning a two-week period. The reporting was internally consistent since the wealth of evidence was never strongly contradictory. Bias in the form of positive or negative affect for the patient on the part of one reporter was spontaneously expressed in the interview. Bias of this kind on the part of one reporter was cancelled out by the reports of the other reporters.

We had seriously considered using Rorschach and TAT test data. We abandoned the idea for we reasoned that these tests would give data on inner phenomena. Internal events would not relate directly to the majority of the variables in our ego-functions framework. To use the test results the investigator would have had to be willing to accept a highly inferential set of data, difficult if discrepant, to reconcile with the external behavioral data. We anticipated little agreement between test data and observed behavior.

After weighing the evidence for the usefulness of the Rorschach technique in diagnosis by means of a careful analysis of the available data, Zubin et al. (1967) concluded that only when the protocols are regarded as interview material can any relationship be established between the Rorschach results and those of the clinical interview.

Process of Obtaining Ratings

The protocols of behavior were translated by coding the behavioral evidences according to the ego-functions variables and making ratings based on the coded evidence. This section describes the instrument used, the procedures for making the ratings and resolving disagreements, and the extent to which agreement was obtained in the ratings.

1. INSTRUMENT USED

The major instrument of this research was the Schedule for Individual Ratings of Ego-Functions (cf. Appendixes IV and V). The schedule was independently applied to the protocols of behavior by two raters. Many of the study procedures were set up to maximize and safeguard the use of this instrument. None of the staff who reported behavior ever had clues to the content of the ego-functions framework since the interviewing was focused on behavior.

The schedule consisted originally of 280 variables accompanied by a set of definitions. General definitions were abstract explanations of variables or words that were intended to set the boundaries and limits of meanings. The variables were divided among five major *sections* which were designed to measure attributes of the ego as follows:

    I. *Outward behavior* used as measures of *adaptation to reality,* that is, the adaptation of the ego to people, environment and tasks. Thirty-three of these variables entered into cluster and factor analyses.

   II. *Perception* used as measures of reality-testing, sense of reality and some cognitive functions. Fourteen of these variables entered into cluster and factor analyses.

  III. *Messages* used as measures of language capacity. Six of these variables entered into cluster and factor analyses.

  IV. *Affects and defenses* used as measures of object-relations, regulation and control of drives and defensive functions. Forty of these variables entered into cluster and factor analyses.

   V. *Synthesis* used as measures of capacity for problem-solving and organization. Six of these variables were correlated with the follow-up study (cf. Appendixes VI and VII).

Variables from sections I through IV entered into the cluster and factor analyses, and the variables of section V were correlated with the follow-up study. Of the 280 variables included in the original schedule, 93 spread across the four sections remained for analysis.

It is thus noted that the number of variables finally appearing in the analyses (93) is far lower than the number included for rating in the primary design (280).

Variables were lost for two reasons. First, in the process of relating the protocols of behavior to the ego-functions framework, it became clear that we were not getting the behavioral data to rate 75 variables that required estimates of the messages and affects of others in relation to the patient. For example, we did not find it possible to rate the tolerances of the patient for the affects of others since the behavioral data for the affects of others were not always sufficiently clear. Second, we lost 112 variables because data were missing for seven or more patients. (For 20 variables having a missing data-state of only one through six, estimates were made and used in the data analyses.) The majority of variables dropped for reason of missing data dealt with the patient's outward behavior, role behavior and affects in relation specifically to relatives and friends. The loss of these variables is not surprising. To expect that behavior in relation to relatives and friends would be observable for every patient was overly optimistic. In spite of the large attrition of variables, every section of the schedule was covered by multiple variables for data analysis.

2. RATING PROCEDURE

The ratings of this study are clinical assessments of behavior that have been systematized. Definitions provided the criteria for the ratings, but since judgment is involved, ratings were also relative to implicit norms of behavior derived from the raters' range of experience, knowledge of human behavior, and knowledge of the unit (8E) where the patients lived.

Variables ranged from a fairly concrete to a global variety and differing levels of inference were required. On conditions of sufficient evidence a low degree of inference was required from the evidence for those variables that represented small manifest behavioral units: most of the variables in *outward behavior*, some in *messages*.

Varying degrees of inference were required for other variables in accordance with the level of abstraction and the extent to which the variable estimated quantities and qualities of psychological processes: most variables in *perception*, some in *affects and defenses*.

Predictions were the most global assessments: some variables in *synthesis*.

We used a ten-point ordinal scale ranging from zero through nine. Points one through nine were thought of in triads: 1, 2, 3—low; 4, 5, 6—moderate; 7, 8, 9—high. The midpoints—2, 5, and 8—of each triad were operationally defined for each variable. Operational definitions were more or less concrete cues or illustrations of behavior calibrated for the ranges and modes of behavior known on 8E (cf. Appendix V). The scale was supplemented by several explanatory categories: NE, no evidence; IE, insufficient evidence. Several design decisions guided the rating process: (1) independent ratings would be made by only two raters; (2) in order to preserve data, disagreements would be resolved by a third rater. These decisions led to a two-stage rating process.

At the first stage two raters (with one exception, the four raters at the first stage were fully trained experienced social workers), working independently, processed the behavioral observations and rated the variables. Just as we had learned from previous research that nurses, aides and occupational therapists are better observers of behavior than psychiatrists and residents, so too we knew that judgment necessary for ratings required highly educated, skilled and trained professionals. In contrast to our procedure of using a time-sample of patient behavior in the hospital rated by professionals, descriptions of psychiatric rating scales currently in use (Lyerly and Abbott, 1966) typically fit one of two patterns: (1) professional interviews with patients conducted and rated by staff such as psychiatrists, psychologists, and social workers as interviewers and raters; (2) observations of patient behavior in the hospital with hospital personnel such as nurses, aides, occupational therapists as observers and raters.

At the first stage: (1) with the protocol of behavior (nursing and occupational therapy reports) and the definitions of the variables at hand, the rater read a single report. From the single report the rater selected the evidence that applied to individual variables and coded on the protocol the evidence by variable number, thus pegging the evidences to be used in making ratings. The protocols were set up so that evidence could be coded in a separate space for each of the four sections of the schedule (see Appendix III for an illustration). On the basis of the coded evidence, ratings were made. The procedure required that each report be coded and rated separately in the order they were set up. Reports were ordered sequentially by the date of report.

This detailed procedure: (a) insured full use of the behavioral data (relevant behaviors were rarely skipped over); (b) minimized what the rater had to keep in mind (an important condition when there are 280 variables to rate); and (c) provided a means for resolving disagreements. Having to code and thus to identify the behavioral evidence for every rating decision makes every decision explicit and public. When the decision is public, disagreements can be resolved with a minimum of bias.

(2) On completing the ratings developed report by report, raters were asked to make a final set of ratings, based on the total protocol that best represented the patient's profile. The final profile as symbolized in numbers was meant to characterize the patient in the ego-functions framework. The final ratings were a set of clinical assessments, not a mechanical averaging, of the ratings that had been made report by report. The paramount criterion for the final ratings was the extent to which they characterized the patient's pattern as it emerged over time. In making clinical assessments rather than an arithmetical average, the raters could eliminate the biased evidence in the reporting.

At the second stage the objective was to resolve disagreements of two or more steps. One step disagreements were usually automatically resolved by a mean of the two ratings; for example, a pair of ratings of 5 and 6 went into data analysis as a 5.5. The procedure for resolving two or more step differences was as follows:

(1) A review of the coded evidence of the two raters. One of the two original independent raters was supplied with the two coded protocols, and the sheets on which all pairs of ratings were posted in order to identify the disagreements. Differences in the use of evidence were traced to find evidence that was missed or inappropriately coded. Differences in the use of evidence accounted for some of the disagreement. The identified differences were reviewed jointly by the rater and a third independent person—one of the authors. A small number of resolutions in final ratings were immediately apparent on the basis of the review of the evidences and were made at this stage when the two people agreed.

(2) The disagreements that could not be easily resolved by the above review, which constituted a majority of the disagreements, were submitted to the senior author for resolution. He was supplied with a protocol, a set of paired final ratings and a statement locating in the protocol the coded behavioral evidences used to make the ratings. In resolving disagreements he became the final arbiter of the appropriate use of evidence for the variables and the application of evidence to scale points. The senior author not only resolved the differences but reviewed the total set of final ratings for the correctness of the level of the ratings and the extent to which they described the patient's profile. Also at this stage he made the synthesis ratings and wrote a brief impressionistic clinical statement about the patient.

The four independent raters were first thoroughly trained to do the coding and rating task. The training was designed to familiarize the raters with the entire process of coding and relating the behavioral observations to the ego-functions variables, and to give them practice in making the ratings using the definitions of the scale points. Their agreement with other trainees was checked, and their disagreements and questions discussed. Throughout the rating process they were encouraged to ask questions about definitions, scale-points and use of behavioral evidence for the variables. They were also given feedback about their use of behavioral evidences.

Assignment of protocols to raters was made in the order that the protocols were transcribed and available for rating; this was approximately in the order that patients entered the study. Assignments could only be made in this order, since the rating job was initiated one year before the total sample of behavioral observations was completely collected. The raters did not know the patients, or with whom they were paired, and in fact did not know each other. They worked independently in their own homes. Including the training of raters and review and resolution of disagreement, the total rating task took three years.

3. RESULTS OF THE RATING PROCEDURE

The data of this study rest on the assumption that an agreed rating of at least two raters who independently applied the same instrument to the same behavioral material plus resolution of disagreement by a third person who had access to all the materials including the behavioral evidences used by the two raters is more likely to be the correct rating than one made only by a single rater. In brief, two views are better than one. The point of view in the design of this study was that the method would yield data sufficiently free of the peculiarities or eccentricities of one person to identify with some confidence groups of patients.

The data on extent of agreement in Table 5 are based on 90 ego-function variables in the data analysis that were rated on a ten-point scale. Three variables in the data analysis were originally based on checks of categories. The categories were placed on a hierarchal scale for data analysis; only data that both raters checked were scaled.

A one-step difference means that when one rater chose a 5 the other may have chosen either 4 or 6; a two-step difference means that when one rater used a 5 the other may have used either 3 or in the other direction a 7. Only six per cent of all ratings (265 out of 4,137, a base which excludes occasions when one rater used no evidence and the other chose a scale point number) made on 90 variables were three or more steps apart. Ratings of more than a three-step difference were rare; of

TABLE 5. *Extent of Agreement and Disagreement for 90 Variables*

Two raters independently	N 90 Total Variables	N 33 Outward Behavior	N 13 Perception	N 6 Messages	N 38 Affects
Agreed exactly 33% or more of the time	71	26	5	2	38
Agreed within one step, 70% or more of the time	74	31	9	4	30
Agreed within two steps, 85% or more of the time	83	33	12	4	34

all three-step differences or more, over three-fourths (207 out of 265) were only three steps apart (cf. Appendix VIII for the detailed data on agreement for each variable).

The results presented in Table 5 compare favorably despite the different circumstances under which the ratings were made with those reported by Hamburg et al. (1958) at this Institute. They report an agreement for three affect variables rated on a 19-point scale. They found exact agreement on 33 per cent of all occasions, and they also found that more than 70 per cent of the paired ratings fell within one unit of each other. We obtained 33 per cent or more exact agreement for 38 affect variables on a ten-point scale, and on more than 70 per cent of the occasions paired ratings were within one unit of each other for 30 affect variables.

Resolutions of differences fell into three categories. In 61 per cent of the instances the third rater chose a rating of one of the independent raters. In 27 per cent of the instances a mean of two-step differences was selected as the resolution; for example, the resolution of a pair of ratings of 4 and 6 was 5. In only 12 per cent of the instances was a different rating made. These were predominantly one step apart from one of the independent ratings.

Of the patients admitted for the research, numbering 68 in all, 52 were voluntary admissions. Seventeen were dropped from the project for reasons stated on page 41. These are described later in our follow-up study. The final sample thus consisted of 51 subjects for whom data analysis was conducted on 93 variables.

We studied the protocols of the second observational period carefully to determine whether the time, effort and cost, all of which would have been considerable, were worth the possible result. The senior author concluded after reading each of the 51 second observational periods that sufficient change was not apparent and therefore these protocols were not rated. This also means that we could not demonstrate systematically the effect of discharge on ego-functions.

We attempted to rate Unit II containing the reports of psychiatric residents and social workers. After rating 20 of these protocols it was apparent that these professionals did not report sufficient amounts of observational data so that these ratings were dropped, leaving the 15 to 20 reports by personnel listed in Table 3. We also became convinced that the type of psychotherapy administered by the resident staff did not alter the behavior of the patients and therefore did not contaminate the research. Finally, not included in the original design was a study of the patients' family and a follow-up study, each reported separately in subsequent chapters.

Statistical Analysis

The next step planned in our design was a statistical analysis of our residual data composed of 93 variables for 51 subjects. We had anticipated that adequate methods for clustering variables in groups were available without realizing the complexities inherent in the numbers of variables and subjects involved. A search through the literature and discussions with a number of statisticians indicated that it seemed desirable to experiment with previous programs.

Fortunately we made contact with Herman Friedman and Jerrold Rubin of the New York Scientific Center of the International Business Machine Company who had been working on new methods for cluster analysis. They had tested out their procedures and programs in other fields and were interested in applying them to psychiatric data. The fortuitous fit of our two researches resulted in a clustering procedure to which a discriminant function analysis was applied.

CHAPTER 5 The Logic of the
Statistical Methods

HERMAN P. FRIEDMAN
and JERROLD RUBIN

The purpose of this chapter is to indicate on an expository level the logic of some of the major techniques of data analysis used in this study. The reader will be referred to appropriate publications for more detailed information.

CLUSTER ANALYSIS

Cluster analysis is the name applied to a variety of methods and procedures that deal with the problems of establishing categories of people or things. The need for a frame of reference within which to establish categories is common to all methods of cluster analysis and classification procedures. We establish this frame of reference initially by choosing a set of measurements to describe each patient. This initial choice is in itself a categorization which has no mathematical or statistical guidelines. The choice reflects the investigator's judgment of relevance for the purpose of the categorization. Another critical choice is the selection of the patients for study. This is especially important if the categories are to be useful for purposes other than a descriptive summary.

We begin our discussion with the fact that we have by some criteria selected n patients and for each patient have recorded p measurements. These are our basic data. The investigator's problem is to seek evidence in the measurements of the patients for the existence of a variety of different patients that could be organized into a coherent set of categories. From each of these categories the investigator might *define* prototype individuals. Thus, instead of describing the n patients individually, the investigators may reasonably speak of g types (g much less than n), within the framework of the measurement system, that express a clinically meaningful summary of the data. When the number of patients and the number of measurements are large, there is an enormous number of ways of organizing the data into categories, some of them more clinically relevant than others. When presented with two different sets of categorizations, an investigator may prefer one to the other, but may not be able to formulate precisely his criterion for selection. If he were to attempt to examine all possible organizations of the data in order to make his selection, he could not finish the process within his lifetime. The methods of data analysis used were designed to aid this process of exploration of the data. We will couch the problem in mathematical terms in order to explore the data in a systematic way; thus we will only present to the investigator those organizations of the data that we have decided, from a mathematical point of view, have some likelihood of being of interest to the clinician.

We now describe how we mathematically view the patients in the framework of the measurements. We assume that the measurements are quantitative. We think of n patients as points in a p-dimensional measurement space. The problem of exploration is to seek geometric evidence in the data themselves for the existence of groups in the measurement space. These groups of patients (represented as points) would appear as occupying well-separated regions of the measurement space. For example, if we only had two or three measurements the problem would be simple. We could use visual inspection. As soon as the number of measurements becomes large we can no longer look at the data in a simple way.

Thus we are faced with the problem of trying to characterize or describe group structure in p dimensions. To gain some insight into this problem, suppose we actually had three groups of patients with a single quantitative measurement on each patient. Let us denote the observations in group one by $x_1, x_2, \ldots, x_{n1}$, in group two by $y_1, y_2, \ldots, y_{n2}$, in group three by $z_1, z_2, \ldots, z_{n3}$. We have for each group the average measurements,

$$\bar{x} = \frac{1}{n_1} \sum_{i=1}^{n_1} x_i, \bar{y} = \frac{1}{n_2} \sum_{i=1}^{n_2} y_i, \bar{z} = \frac{1}{n_3} \sum_{i=1}^{n_3} z_i.$$

We also have the average of the total number of observations

$$C = \frac{n_1\bar{x} + n_2\bar{y} + n_3\bar{z}}{n_1 + n_2 + n_3}.$$

A measure of the total dispersion or scatter of the observations is given by

$$T = \sum_{i=1}^{n_1} (x_i - C)^2 + \sum_{i=1}^{n_2} (y_i - C)^2 + \sum_{i=1}^{n_3} (z_i - C)^2.$$

A measure of the scatter within each group is given by

$$W_x = \sum_{i=1}^{n_1} (x_i - \bar{x})^2, W_y = \sum_{i=1}^{n_2} (y_i - \bar{y})^2, W_z = \sum_{i-1}^{n_3} (z_i - \bar{z})^2.$$

The following is an algebraic identity: $T = W + B$ where

$$W = W_x + W_y + W_z$$

and

$$B = n_1 (\bar{x} - c)^2 + n_2 (\bar{y} - c)^2 + n_3 (\bar{z} - c)^2.$$

B is a measure of the dispersion between groups.

We now make the following observation. If the three groups had the same average value (that is, $\bar{x} = \bar{y} = \bar{z}$), then B would be zero. Hence T would equal W, meaning that all of the variation in the data would be accounted for by the within-group variation. The ratio T/W could be used as an index of the strength of separation of the groups.

Now suppose that we do not know precisely what the three groups are, but only think there may be three unknown groups of patients. We could plot the measurements on a line and look for visual evidence of "clustering." But if we are blindfolded and cannot resort to visual evidence, how can we decide on the groups?

In principle we can do the following. Consider all partitions (ways of organizing the patients into nonoverlapping groups) of the n patients into three groups and choose that partition for which T/W is highest. Since for a given set of n patients T is constant, we select the organization of the data into three groups that have minimum within-group dispersion and consequently maximum between-group separation. Thus in the ratio T/W we have a mathematical index of group structure that reflects our visual evidence in one dimension. What remains is to generalize this index to higher dimensions. This ratio has a nice property that we would like to preserve; a change in the scale of the measurement does not change the value of the index T/W. Group structure in one dimension is independent of the units of measurement.

Once we leave one dimension, the problem becomes more complex for a number of reasons. One reason is that with multiple measurements we have to consider the covariance of the measurements as well as the variance. Another reason is that the problem of weighting measurements becomes more crucial. That is, for one organization of the data into groups some measurements may be more important than others in distinguishing between groups, while in a different organization of the data into groups a different set of measurements may be dominant. Thus, until we know the groups we cannot determine the relative importance of the variables. The weights on the variables depend in a critical way on the variances and covariances of the measurements within each group. If we arbitrarily impose a set of weights on the measurements, then we will be restricting the structure of the geometry of the patients in the space. Thus, within the mathematical framework the investigator can, if he wishes, make a choice of weights of measurements reflecting his clinical opinion. In this study, the investigators decided not to exercise this choice and allowed the data itself, as reflected in the mathematical index which we now describe, to determine the weights.

Recall the algebraic equation for one quantitative measurement: $T = W + B$. This is a basic relationship that is used in the statistical methods known as the analysis of variance. For more than one measurement, there is a generalization of this equation that is found in the literature of methods of multivariate analysis of variance. We write this equation in the same way; namely, for each organization of n patients into g groups, $T = W + B$. Here, T, W, and B are matrices. They may be thought of as the total covariance matrix, the pooled within-groups covariance matrix, and the between-groups covariance matrix, respectively.

Since T, W, B are matrices and not numbers, we can no longer speak of minimizing W as in one dimension. There are several numerical criteria that one can derive from the matrix relation. These are discussed in the paper by Friedman and Rubin (1967). The one we used for this study is the ratio $|T|/|W|$ where $|T|$ and $|W|$ are the determinants of the matrices T and W respectively. $|T|/|W|$ is a generalized variance ratio that includes the effects of the covariance of the measurements within each group as well as the covariance of the measurements across the total n patients. Note that the determinant of a single number is just the number itself. Thus, in *one* dimension, $T/W = |T|/|W|$. This is one aspect of the generalization. Another is that the ratio $|T|/|W|$ does not change if the scales of the measurements are changed. There is an important restriction on the number of measurements in order to apply this criterion. The number of measurements p must be less than, or equal to, the number of patients n minus the number of groups g. If this constraint is not met, then $|W|$ will be zero.

We now return to the practical computational problem of evaluating all partitions of n patients into g groups in order to satisfy a given mathematical criterion. The number of partitions (organizations of the data) is enormously large. For example, the number of ways we can form two groups from one hundred patients is approximately 18×10^{29}. On the fastest computers in existence today the computation of the mathematical index for each of the ways of grouping the data and selecting the grouping with the highest index would take about 10^{17} years. For three and four groups, the amount of time is even longer.

We make the computational problem viable with a "hill-climbing" algorithm devised by Rubin (1967). In principle, this computer procedure attempts to examine only those organizations of the data for which the index is high, thus avoiding the problem of examining all possible groupings. A brief sketch of the procedure follows.

We start with any given partition into g groups. Consider moving a single object into every group other than the one it is in. If no move will create a partition for which the criterion is increased, leave the object where it is. Otherwise, move it so that the maximum increase in the criterion occurs. Using the partition thus created, we process the second object in the same way, then the third, etc. A "hill-climbing pass" is defined as the application of this procedure once to each object in some given order. After several hill-climbing passes, one must reach a point at which no move of a single object from the group it is in to a different group will cause an increase in the criterion function. At this point, we say we have found a "single move local maximum" of our criterion function. This rarely takes more than half a dozen passes. To try to rise above this, we apply some heuristic procedures; these are described in detail by Rubin. The objective of these heuristic procedures is to attempt to rise above the local maximum to possibly still higher values of the criterion. When it is found impossible to rise above the local maximum with these heuristics, the procedure is terminated. The computer then provides us with that organization of the data that had the highest value of the criterion. At this point in the process we can repeat the total procedure by randomly selecting a different partition with which to start the process. For data for which the group structure was known beforehand to be strong, this procedure was repeated 14 times, and in 10 out of the 14 times we recovered the proper groups. In the other four times we found a different organization of the data (the same each time) that was seen to be simply related to the other. This is reported by Friedman along with other examples.

With less well-structured data we have found that we do not always come back as often to the same grouping when we randomly restart. We never really know if we have the "best" answer with respect to the mathematical criterion, since we do not try all the possibilities. However, repeatedly coming back to the same value after perturbing the data gives us a strong feeling that we have a stable organization. The process of perturbing the data adds a qualitative dimension along which we evaluate the group structure in the data.

The following ways of looking at the process may prove helpful. Suppose that there were four well-separated groups in p dimensions, that is, four groups of points occupying distinct regions in some subspace of the measurement space (i.e., a space of smaller dimension where the dimensions are determined by weighted sums of the p measurements) such that if we could observe it we would see large empty gaps between the regions. The mathematical index $|T|/|W|$ would have a value for this partition. For other partitions of the patients, very different from the groups that are well separated in a subspace, the value of the index $|T|/|W|$ would be appreciably lower. Thus we might view a highly structured set of data such as just described, consisting of one large mountain peak with the value of the index representing this peak. The peak would dominate the terrain (the data). Different random starting partitions of the hill-climbing procedure would invariably find us climbing this peak. On the other hand, if there were no dominant group structure in the data we would expect this to be reflected in the values of the mathematical criterion by having a number of organizations producing local maxima that do not differ that much in value. We describe this by saying that we have a lot of hills in the data with no one hill dominating the others. Thus by randomly restarting the process we invariably will end up climbing different hills, which will result in the process producing different organizations of the data. To gain further insight into the mathematical criterion $|T|/|W|$ we discuss it in relation to the well-documented methods of discriminant analysis.

RELATION TO LINEAR DISCRIMINANT ANALYSIS (p DIMENSIONS, g GROUPS)

The procedure of linear discriminant analysis as described by Wilks (1962) utilizes the matrices W and B to determine a new set of coordinate axes by which to describe the observation vectors. In this procedure the groups are *given* a priori, whereas it is the purpose of the cluster analysis procedure to *find* the groups.

The observations originally described as vectors in a p-dimensional coordinate system are described as vectors in a t-dimensional coordinate system with $t = \min(p, g\text{-}1)$. For example, suppose we had four groups and 20 measurements; then the patients are initially described in a 20-dimensional measurement space. Each of the four groups has a center of gravity. (A center of gravity of a group is a point in space whose coordinates are the averages of the measurements taken over all the patients in the group.) These four centers of gravity lie in, at most, a three-dimensional space. On the other hand, if we had only two measurements and 20 groups, then clearly all patients may be described in a two-dimensional space. In general then, if we have many more measurements than groups, the procedure of linear discriminant analysis produces a reduction of the dimensionality of the space in such a way as to preserve the relation of within- to between-group separation. Thus if we had 20 measurements and four groups, the patients originally denoted by a vector of 20 measurements may be described after applying the procedure of linear discriminant analysis by a vector of three measurements where each of the three measurements is a *weighted sum* of the original 20 measurements.

It is further known that the coordinate directions in the $t = \min(p, g\text{-}1)$ dimensional subspace are the eigenvectors associated with the eigenvalues $\lambda_1, \lambda_2, \ldots, \lambda_t$ of the matrix $W^{-1} B$. Furthermore, the eigenvalue λ_i is the ratio of the one-dimensional between-group scatter to the one-dimensional within-group scatter as measured along the direction of eigenvector v_i associated with λ_i.

Also

$$|T|/|W| = \prod_{i=1}^{t} (1 + \lambda_i).$$

The eigenvectors determine the subspace in which we view the patients. The coordinates of the eigenvectors are the weights applied to the original p measurements that determine the weighted sums which are called discriminant function scores. The individual eigenvalues λ_i are actually one-dimensional T/W ratios of the patients' discriminant-function scores along the axis (direction in space of the p measurements) determined by its associated eigenvector v_i. The relative sizes of the eigenvalues λ_i determine the importance of the direction in space in reflecting the separation between the groups. In our procedure the main objective is to *find* the partition for which $|T|/|W|$ is maximal in the original p dimensions. We then apply linear discriminant analysis to the results of our procedure to provide a descriptive summary of the results. We add a note of caution: the usual tests of significance used in discriminant analysis do not apply because of our use of max $|T|/|W|$. Even if it is known that one had samples from g groups and computed $|T|/|W|$ from these samples, the value would be less than or equal to the value of max $|T|/|W|$ that one could get by reshuffling the sample.

This applies to all of our work in this study. We are using some methods borrowed from statistical methodology. However, we are using them in a purely descriptive and exploratory way. No probability statements are made. The relevant probability distribution theory needed to make statements pertaining to statistical significance requires further research.

In summary, then, we first *find* an organization of the data into groups using the methods of cluster analysis described previously. We then apply the procedure of linear discriminant analysis to the groups found from the cluster analysis taken as given. The effect of applying the procedure of discriminant analysis to the groups is to provide a graphical display which best illustrates the separation of the groups. The methods of linear discriminant analysis are nicely described by Rao (1948) and by Bartlett (1965). The methods are described in the context of psychiatric data in a paper by Eysenck (1955). These references are not meant to be exhaustive but are chosen for their importance, readability and adequacy in covering the necessary technical background to understand the methods used in this study. Another reference that is expository and treats other methods of cluster analysis as well as some of the reasons for defining categories is by Cattell et al. (1966).

PRINCIPAL COMPONENT ANALYSIS

The basic data of this study consisted of 93 measurements (ego-functions) on each of 51 patients. This presented a problem since the method of cluster analysis described here requires that the number of measurements be much smaller than the number of patients. The problem was how to reduce the dimensionality of the measurement space without throwing away much relevant information.

For our purpose of cluster analysis, relevant information meant the geometrical configuration of the 51 patients in the 93-dimensional measurement space. What we wanted to accomplish was to describe the 51 patients in a smaller space within the space of 93 measurements. The method of principal component analysis deals with the problem of fitting a subspace to a set of points in a higher-dimensional space. In an excellent paper by Rao (1964) on this subject it is mentioned that Karl Pearson defined a best fitting subspace as that for which the sum of squares of the perpendiculars to the subspace is a minimum. Such a subspace passes through the center of gravity of the points. The method of principal components utilizes the total scatter matrix T defined in our discussion of cluster analysis. The best fitting subspace of q dimensions is found by finding the q largest eigenvalues of the matrix T. The q eigenvectors associated with these eigenvalues define the subspace in question. The eigenvectors represent q orthogonal coordinate directions in the space of 93 measurements.

In this study we first normalized each of the 93 measurements so that they would have standard deviation one and average value zero over the 51 patients. Thus the center of gravity of the 51 points (patients) was the zero vector, and the matrix T in this case became the matrix of correlations of the 93 measurements taken over the 51 patients. We found the eigenvectors and eigenvalues of T (the total correlation matrix). Since there were only 51 patients there were only 50 nonzero eigenvalues. Fifty-one patients can always be completely described in at most a

50-dimensional space. In this study we kept the dimensions associated with the 14 largest eigenvalues. Thus we found the best fitting 14-dimensional space (in the sense of Pearson) to the 51 patients in the normalized space of 93 measurements. This subspace accounted for 70 per cent of the total variation of the larger space. The patients originally represented by 93 measurements were now represented by 14 measurements, where each of the 14 was a weighted sum of the original 93. These 14 measurements are called principal component scores. The 93 co-ordinates of each of the 14 eigenvectors associated with the 14 largest eigenvalues are the weights applied to the 93 measurements of each patient to determine the patient's 14 principal component scores. The measurement space in which we did the cluster analysis was the 14-dimensional space of principal component scores.

OUTCOME OF CLUSTER ANALYSIS OF 51 PATIENTS IN THE SPACE OF 14 PRINCIPAL COMPONENTS

A conclusion reached after performing the cluster analysis on 14 principal components for each of the 51 patients was that the data could be organized on a purely mathematical basis into four groups in a number of ways, with no one way strongly preferable over the other. In other words, we found some hills but no dominant peak. We include, for the sake of completeness, three of the organizations of the data along with relevant descriptive information.

TABLE 6. *Data for Organization A*

$$\log |T| / |W| = 5.374$$

MEMBERS OF GROUP A:
1   2   4   19   22   23   24   28   32   33   35   37   43   46   47   49   50   51

MEMBERS OF GROUP B:
8   10   11   20   27   30   36   38   39   41   44   48

MEMBERS OF GROUP C:
7   9   12   13   14   15   16   17   18   25   34   40   42   45

MEMBERS OF GROUP D:
3   5   6   21   26   29   31

WEIGHTED DISTANCE BETWEEN GROUPS:

FROM GROUP	TO GROUP A	B	C	D
A	0.0	3.4949	2.3528	4.8000
B	3.4949	0.0	3.0649	1.2808
C	2.3528	3.0649	0.0	3.9971
D	4.8000	1.2808	3.9971	0.0

EIGENVALUES OF W INVERSE TIMES B:

λ_1	λ_2	λ_3
12.9978	3.7405	2.2521

EIGENVECTORS OF W INVERSE TIMES B:

(1)	1.6166	−0.7707	−0.0697
(2)	−0.9064	−0.0513	−0.6568
(3)	0.8317	0.7916	0.0258
(4)	0.7815	−0.5248	0.1080
(5)	−0.2765	0.9493	0.9849
(6)	−0.8940	0.8478	0.2941
(7)	−0.7385	0.2859	−0.5352
(8)	−2.2798	−0.5910	0.0772
(9)	−0.1621	0.5265	−0.3969
(10)	0.6285	0.5906	−0.7718
(11)	0.3483	−0.3775	0.6154
(12)	0.7081	0.2628	0.3922
(13)	−1.1294	−0.5528	0.3850
(14)	0.5792	−0.2299	0.1517

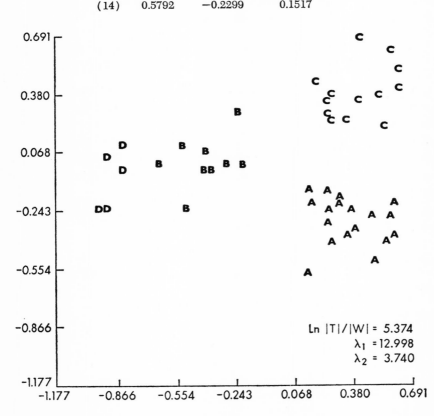

Figure 1. Plot of patients in space of eigenvectors 1 and 2. Selected partition based on clinical criterion (organization A). An A indicates 1 or more patients in Group 1, B in Group 2, etc.

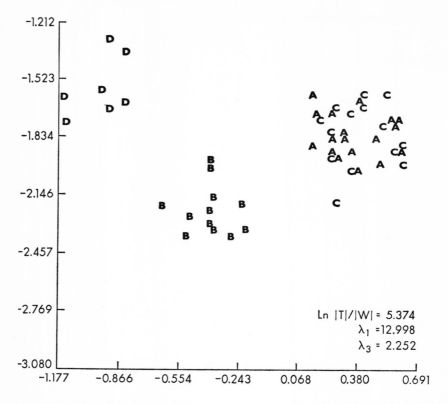

Figure 2. Plot of patients in space of eigenvectors 1 and 3. Selected partition based on clinical criterion (organization A). An A indicates 1 or more patients in Group 1, B in Group 2, etc.

TABLE 7. *Data for Organization B*

$$\log |T|/|W| = 5.578$$

MEMBERS OF GROUP A:
33 47 12 13 14 25 40 3 6 21 29 31

MEMBERS OF GROUP B:
1 2 19 22 23 32 35 46 8

MEMBERS OF GROUP C:
4 24 28 49 50 51 11 27 41 7 9 16 17 18 45

MEMBERS OF GROUP D:
37 43 10 20 30 36 38 39 44 48 15 34 42 5 26

WEIGHTED DISTANCE BETWEEN GROUPS:

FROM GROUP	TO GROUP			
	A	B	C	D
A	0.0	2.4560	3.1572	3.8980
B	2.4560	0.0	1.4370	4.2032
C	3.1572	1.4370	0.0	3.5143
D	3.8980	4.2032	3.5143	0.0

EIGENVALUES OF W INVERSE TIMES B:

	λ_1	λ_2	λ_3
	9.7652	6.7142	2.1864

EIGENVECTORS OF W INVERSE TIMES B:

(1)	1.1947	−0.0999	−0.5209
(2)	−1.4690	−0.3241	−0.0496
(3)	0.0303	0.6728	0.6004
(4)	1.7113	−0.4641	0.6999
(5)	0.0893	0.4469	0.7949
(6)	−0.5385	1.7344	0.0670
(7)	−1.1163	−1.0035	0.3294
(8)	0.1427	1.0484	−0.3734
(9)	1.0515	−0.0120	−0.5930
(10)	−0.4008	−1.0112	0.1064
(11)	−0.2040	−0.1308	−0.6547
(12)	0.4651	0.4882	0.3929
(13)	0.9244	−0.5286	0.2986
(14)	0.5521	−0.2457	−0.3786

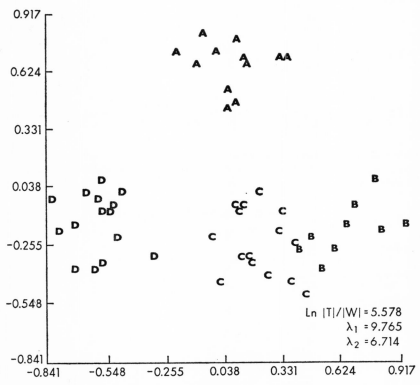

$Ln\ |T|/|W| = 5.578$
$\lambda_1 = 9.765$
$\lambda_2 = 6.714$

Figure 3. Plot of patients in space of eigenvectors 1 and 2. Alternative partition (organization B). An A indicates 1 or more patients in Group 1, B in Group 2, etc.

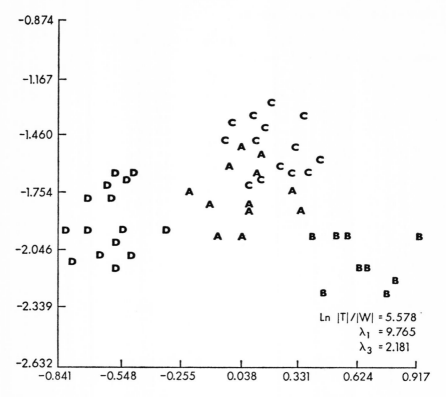

Figure 4. Plot of patients in space of eigenvectors 1 and 3. Alternative partition (organization B). An A indicates 1 or more patients in Group 1, B in Group 2, etc.

TABLE 8. *Data for Organization C*

$$\log |T|/|W| = 5.680$$

MEMBERS OF GROUP A:
33 47 41 14 40 3 6 29 31

MEMBERS OF GROUP B:
23 24 28 32 10 11 20 27 7 9 15 16 18 25 45

MEMBERS OF GROUP C:
37 43 30 36 38 39 44 48 13 34 42 5 26

MEMBERS OF GROUP D:
1 2 4 19 22 35 46 49 50 51 8 12 17 21

WEIGHTED DISTANCE BETWEEN GROUPS:

FROM GROUP   TO GROUP

	A	B	C	D
A	0.0	2.9239	6.9105	2.4962
B	2.9239	0.0	3.8309	2.6682
C	6.9105	3.8309	0.0	4.2583
D	2.4962	2.6682	4.2583	0.0

EIGENVALUES OF W INVERSE TIMES B:

	λ_1 16.4929	λ_2 4.6249	λ_3 1.9701

EIGENVECTORS OF W INVERSE TIMES B:

(1)	0.6087	−1.3320	−0.1090
(2)	−1.9747	0.6101	0.4182
(3)	0.6355	1.3053	−0.2284
(4)	1.1351	−0.0415	−0.6445
(5)	0.4985	−0.1818	0.2699
(6)	0.9070	−0.2645	0.8760
(7)	−1.5107	−0.5443	−0.2454
(8)	1.3198	−0.2026	0.7137
(9)	−0.5981	−0.3903	−0.5947
(10)	−0.7406	0.8039	−0.0848
(11)	−2.0862	−0.6257	0.0567
(12)	0.7127	0.2084	−0.3783
(13)	0.6492	0.0964	−0.3905
(14)	0.4861	−0.2995	−0.5042

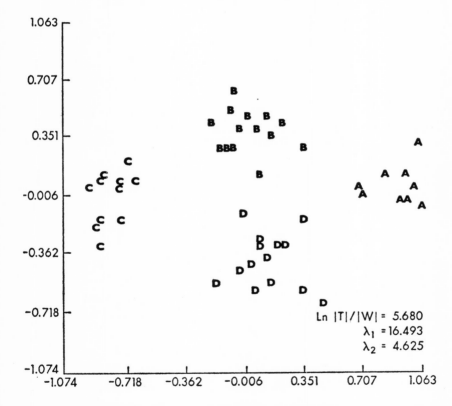

Figure 5. Plot of patients in space of eigenvectors 1 and 2. Alternative partition (organization C). An A indicates 1 or more patients in Group 1, B in Group 2, etc.

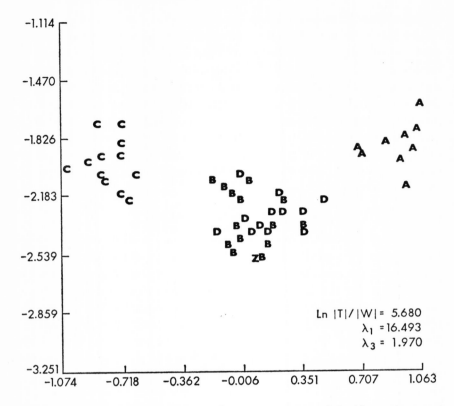

Figure 6. Plot of patients in space of eigenvectors 1 and 3. Alternative partition (organization C). An A indicates 1 or more patients in Group 1, B in Group 2, etc., Z indicates overlap between two groups.

DISCUSSION OF RESULTS OF CLUSTER ANALYSIS

In comparing the three organizations of the data we find that C has the highest value of $|T|/|W|$, while A has the lowest. However, if we look at the graphs of the different organizations they all seem to indicate evidence of group structure. If we look at the patients that group together in the different organizations we find them considerably different, although a goodly number stay together such as 3, 6, 21, 29, 31.

A glance at the eigenvectors of W inverse B shows that the 14 principal components are being weighted differently in each of the organizations of the data. The eigenvalues of W inverse B are also of interest since no three of the eigenvalues of any one organization dominates the eigenvalues of the others. Because of these findings we could not say there was strong evidence for selecting on a mathematical basis one organization of the data over the other. If a selection or definition of types is to be made it will have to be based on criteria or values external to data. To facilitate the interpretation of the groups so as to enable external criteria to be applied, it was necessary to do further analysis on each of the organizations of the data; namely, given the groupings in the space of principal components, we returned to the original basic data of 93 measurements in order to determine which of the 93 could be used to distinguish between the groups and to understand the correlation pattern of the ego-function measurements within each of the groups in the different organizations of the data.

STEPWISE DISCRIMINANT ANALYSIS

The procedure of stepwise discriminant analysis deals with the problem of selecting a small set of variables from a given larger set for the purpose of discriminating among a given collection of groups. The assumptions about the data are the same as those for linear discriminant analysis. A number of criteria for selecting variables have been discussed and compared by Weiner and Dunn (1966). The procedure we used is as follows: Select as the first variable the one for which the ratio $|T|/|W|$ is largest. Choose as the second variable the one that, together with the first, gives the highest value of $|T|/|W|$. Select as the third variable the one that, together with the two previously selected, gives the highest value of $|T|/|W|$. This procedure continues until the change in value of $|T|/|W|$ is smaller than some predesignated value, or until all the variables have been selected.

We applied this procedure to the groupings of data which the cluster procedures found in the space of principal components; that is, *we went back to the original basic data of 93 measurements to determine which of these measurements could be used to distinguish between the groups.* For all three organizations into four groups we found that with about 20 of the original measurements we were able completely to identify all 51 patients in their groups. For each of the three organizations of the data it was a different set of 20 measurements that played a role. This result gave us a little more insight into the differences between the organizations of the data which were elicited by the cluster procedures; namely, that different subsets of measurements were producing the different organizations into four groups. Mathematical procedures alone cannot tell us which of the subsets of the measurements are more meaningful. One empirical observation which was made about the data during the process of applying this procedure is worth mentioning. In all instances roughly 75 per cent of the patients were completely identified with only *eight* of the original 93 measurements. The other 10 measurements were necessary to classify the remaining 25 per cent of the patients. This empirical fact indicated to us that, even though the cluster procedure was producing partitioning (nonoverlapping groups) that placed each of the 51 patients in a distinct category, it might be more meaningful to define categories that overlap. That is, the hard core of each category may represent useful types or theoretical constructs, but not every patient in the sample could be definitely categorized as being of one type or the other.

Although from a data-analytic point of view we were happy with the fact that we could reproduce the categories with relatively few variables, the clinicians were not too happy because these few variables did not present enough of a "gestalt" for them to provide a rationale for the groups within the theoretical framework of ego-functions.

FACTOR ANALYSIS

Faced with four groups of patients with 93 measurements on each patient, we wanted to understand the different correlation pattern within the groups. There are $93 \times 92/2$ pairwise correlations of the measurements within each group—many numbers indeed. Also the sample sizes of each group were very small. Hence, we decided to extract only the first two principal components from each of the four separate correlation matrices. A varimax rotation (Harman, 1960) was performed for each pair of principal components. In essence, then, we did four separate factor analyses, one for each group of patients. The idea was that some striking differences in the four different correlation patterns of the 93 measurements might be reflected in the eight factors, two for each of the four patterns of correlations. As will be mentioned in Chapter 6, the differences in the factors of the four groups, viewed clinically, provided the major reasons for preferring one organization of the data.

DISCUSSION OF CLUSTER METHOD
USED FOR FAMILY DATA

Often one deals with binary data where each observation is not a number but rather the presence or absence of a trait. This is true of the family-background data described in Chapter 8. A technique somewhat different from the above was used to organize this data into a meaningful classification. The method relies on the definition of a coefficient of similarity between each pair of families. We define this simply as the fraction of traits on which the two families match. For example, suppose "present" were recorded for both families on 25 per cent of the traits measured, and "absent" recorded for both on 30 per cent of the traits; suppose, also, for the other 45 per cent one family had "present" and the other "absent." Then the coefficient of similarity for these two families would be .55.

As in the above technique, we define a mathematical criterion which purports to measure precisely how well organized into groups is a given arrangement of the families. We base the criterion on similarity coefficients. The attempt to optimize the criterion function, that is, to find that arrangement of families into groups which is most well organized (at least according to the chosen criterion), proceeds exactly as before —by trying out different groupings of the families, searching for the best arrangement. In fact, the computer program used to search for the optimum arrangement here is the same as that used for the criterion based on within-group covariance. The criterion function uses the concept of the stability of an object (a family) in a given classification. Stability is defined as the difference between the average similarity of the object to the group it is in and the highest average similarity of the object to any other group. Thus, if a family has traits much like those of families in group A, but its traits are different from the traits of families in groups B, C, D, then it will have high stability when placed in group A but low stability when placed in any other group. Given an arrangement of the families into groups, one can calculate the stability of each family in that particular arrangement and use the total stability (the sum of all stabilities) as a measure to evaluate the arrangement. The computer program constantly performs such evaluations while searching for the optimum arrangement (the one with highest total stability).

Example: Suppose we measured six traits on each of the four families as follows:

	Traits					
	1	2	3	4	5	6
Family 1	0	1	0	1	0	1
Family 2	0	0	0	1	0	1
Family 3	1	0	1	0	1	0
Family 4	1	0	1	0	0	0

The similarity coefficients would be

$$S_{12} = .83 \qquad S_{13} = 0 \qquad S_{14} = .17$$
$$S_{23} = .17 \qquad S_{24} = .33$$
$$S_{34} = .83$$

Then, for the following arrangement of the four families,

Group 1: Family 1, Family 2
Group 2: Family 3, Family 4

the stabilities would be

Stabilities

Family 1: $.83 - \left(\dfrac{0 + .17}{2} \right) = .75$

Family 2: $.83 - \left(\dfrac{.17 + .33}{2} \right) = .58$

Family 3: $.83 - \left(\dfrac{0 + .51}{2} \right) = .75$

Family 4: $.83 - \left(\dfrac{.17 + .33}{2} \right) = .58$

There are some additional complexities. For example, if a family had been in a group by itself, its similarity to its own group would be undefined. Modifications to the concept of stability are therefore necessary and for a detailed mathematical treatment the reader is referred to Rubin (1967).

REMARKS ON COMPUTER PROGRAMS

The family data were analyzed on the IBM 7094 using a computer program called "Optimal Taxonomy Program" by J. Rubin. This program uses only the criterion based on similarity coefficients. The data consisting of the 93 measurements were analyzed with an omnibus computer program that has been developed by H. Friedman and J. Rubin for the IBM 360 computer called "Cluster Analysis and Taxonomy System for Grouping and Organizing Data." This program incorporates the $|T|/|W|$ criterion, the criterion based on similarity coefficients as well as others. The stepwise discriminant analysis and factor analysis were performed on the IBM 7094 computer with the Biomedical Programs obtained from the University of California at Los Angeles, School of Medicine. The IBM programs are now available from the IBM Program Information Department, Hawthorne, N.Y.

6 Results of Data Analysis and the Clinical Interpretations of the Syndrome, Its Groups and Factors

The general objective of the research program—to throw light on the uncertainty and vagueness that pervade the borderline—led to three specific questions: (1) Is there a single borderline state that can be described and what are its boundaries? (2) Are there several types of borderline states that can be defined? (3) If there are several, in what ways are they alike and in what ways do they differ from each other?

The major purpose of the procedures of the data analysis was to seek evidence internal to the data, that is, the 93 ego-function variables, for assistance in answering the above questions. The procedures of the data analysis were as follows:

1. A principal-components analysis was performed, a procedure used to reduce the dimensions of the measurement-space from 93 variables to 14 components. As a result the 51 patients were described by 14 components which accounted for 70 per cent of the total variance in the data after the original data were normalized to zero mean and unit variance.

2. A cluster analysis was performed in the space of 14 components using the methods described in Chapter 5. The results of the cluster analysis showed that there were several equally good ways of grouping the data reflecting different weights on the 14 components. There was no statistical evidence for choosing one set of groups to reflect the dominant structure in the data. Based on the cluster analysis three ways of organizing the data into four groups were chosen for further detailed analysis.

3. A separate factor analysis of each group was directed toward finding meaningful dimensions of the multivariate domain to describe the separate groups internally. To obtain the initial factor structure for a group, a principal-components analysis was conducted using the 93 variables. A varimax rotation was then performed on the first two factors of each group. Only two factors were rotated because of the small size of each group.

One set of four groups was selected on the basis of the factor analysis. It is this set of four groups that will be discussed here, since it was based on the clinical viability of the groups reflected in the within-group correlation structure.

4. A multiple discriminant-function analysis was applied to the results of the clustering procedure as a means of locating the patients in space and providing an efficient basis for examining the differences among the groups (cf. Figs. 7, 8 and 9).

5. A stepwise discriminant function of the 14 components was aimed at identifying the minimum number of components that would predict group membership. Ten components accurately identified 49 of 51 patients.

6. A stepwise discriminant function analysis was carried out in the space of the original variables (rather than components) for the purpose of finding a minimum set of variables for predicting group membership. A set of 20 variables was found.

RESULTS OF DATA ANALYSIS
ON THE SELECTED FOUR GROUPS

The Groups and Their Location in the Space of Principal Components

The selected set of four groups contained varying numbers of subjects: Group I, 18 patients; Group II, 12 patients; Group III, 14 patients; Group IV, 7 patients.

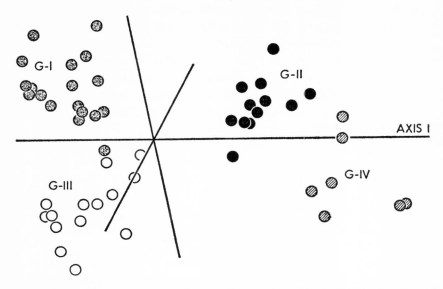

Figure 7. The four groups are shown in space, but principally the location of Groups I and III on the negative end of Axis I and Group II and IV on the positive end. (Representation model designed by N. Solhkhah.)

Once the groups were clustered, a multiple discriminant analysis was applied to obtain a graphic representation of the groups and to use as a basis for examining the nature of the difference among them. Discriminant analysis is a procedure for estimating the position of an individual on a line that best separates classes or groups. The estimated position is obtained as a linear function of the individual's scores. Since one "best" line may not exhaust the predictive power of the data in distinguishing among the classes additional discriminants, all mutually independent may be fitted. The maximum number of discriminants in the instance of this set of data is indicated by the number of groups minus one; that is, three axes could be fitted. The discriminant function transforms the individual ratings to a single discriminant score on each axis and these scores locate the patient in space.

In Figs. 7, 8 and 9 each patient is accurately represented in space by a spherical object. The planes of axes 2 and 3 are each perpendicular to the plane of axis 1. The weighted distance between the groups are presented in Table 9.

Groups I and IV, III and IV, and I and II are the most separate in space; Groups II and IV, and I and III are the least separated. However,

TABLE 9. *Weighted Distance Between Groups Based on 14 Components*

Distance From Group	To Group			
	I	II	III	IV
I	0.0	3.49	2.35	4.80
II	3.49	0.0	3.06	1.28
III	2.35	3.06	0.0	4.00
IV	4.80	1.28	4.00	0.0

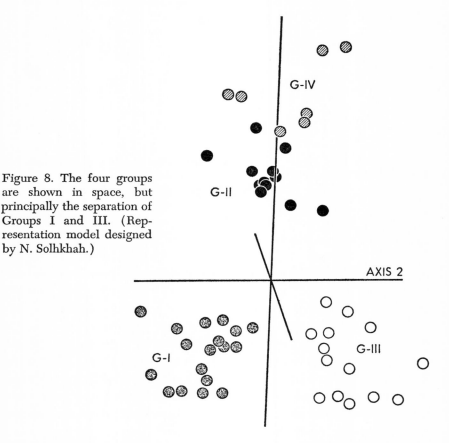

Figure 8. The four groups are shown in space, but principally the separation of Groups I and III. (Representation model designed by N. Solhkhah.)

as the figures and the data in the Table show, there is space between each group in relation to every other; each group is a distinct entity.

Figure 7 shows the role of axis 1—discriminant function 1—in locating Groups I and III on the negative end of the axis and Groups II and IV on the positive end of the axis.

Figure 8 shows the role of the plane of axis 2—discriminant function 2—in separating Group I from III. Group I lies on the negative side of the plane of axis 2 and Group III on the positive side.

Figure 9 shows the role of the plane of Axis 3—discriminant function 3—in separating Group II from IV. Group II lies on the negative side of the plane of axis 3 and Group IV on the positive side.

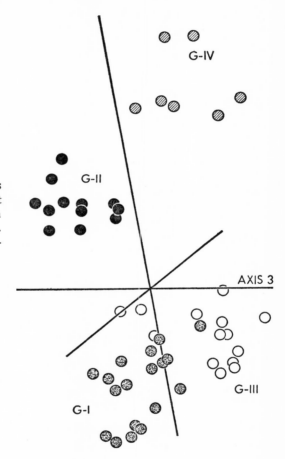

Figure 9. The four groups are shown in space, but principally the separation of Groups II and IV. (Representation model designed by N. Solhkhah.)

The Components and Their Group Means

Although 14 components were required to classify the 51 patients, in a stepwise discriminant-function analysis of the components, 10 of the 14 accurately predicted group membership for 49 of the 51 patients (components are factors made up of a number of variables that correlate with the factor). Table 10 shows the group means and standard deviations for all 14 components and specifies the 10 that predicted group membership for all but two patients.

TABLE 10. *Means and Standard Deviations of Components for Each Group*

| Components | Group Means | | | |
	I (N = 18)	II (N = 12)	III (N = 14)	IV (N = 7)
I*	2.43	−1.11	−0.49	−3.35
II*	−0.69	2.17	−0.92	−0.10
III*	−0.53	−0.45	1.51	−0.90
IV*	0.91	−0.57	−0.31	−0.75
V*	−0.82	−1.47	1.33	1.96
VI*	−1.05	−0.06	0.71	1.39
VII	−0.64	1.07	−0.09	−0.03
VIII*	−0.22	0.74	−1.41	2.11
IX	−0.53	0.55	0.37	−0.32
X*	−0.42	0.74	0.61	−1.42
XI	0.48	−0.83	−0.12	0.42
XII*	0.08	−0.67	0.52	−0.09
XIII*	0.15	−0.08	−0.73	1.21
XIV	0.31	−0.33	0.01	−0.25
	Standard Deviations			
I*	4.32	2.49	3.01	2.51
II*	2.70	3.81	3.22	2.24
III*	2.18	2.13	2.79	1.98
IV*	2.09	2.43	2.35	2.50
V*	1.70	2.04	1.39	2.53
VI*	1.87	1.25	2.26	2.24
VII	2.00	1.23	2.04	2.28
VIII*	1.13	0.89	1.74	2.17
IX	1.89	1.67	1.45	1.43
X*	1.41	0.90	1.47	2.55
XI	1.14	1.23	1.79	2.19
XII*	1.25	1.41	1.80	1.86
XIII*	1.28	1.22	1.60	1.50
XIV	1.64	0.96	1.48	1.28

* *Components that in a stepwise discriminant-function analysis accurately predicted group membership for 49 of 51 patients.*

The 10 components (cf. Appendix IX for variables and loadings) that predicted group membership for 49 of 51 are as follows:

Component I: Group I is different from all other groups on this component but most unlike Group IV, as shown in the group means in Table 10. Component I is a bipolar factor. Variables measuring adaptive reality-oriented behavior had positive loadings. Variables measuring negative behavior and affect had negative loadings. This component contrasts adaptive and unadaptive behavior and affect.

Component II: Group II is different from all other groups on this component but most unlike Group III (Table 10). Component II is made up primarily of positive loadings on negative affect and impulse-discharge variables, mixed with a few variables of adaptive outward behavior to staff and the environment.

Component III: Group III is different from all other groups on this component. Component III is distinguished by positive loadings on variables that suggest some tolerance for other people, principally female staff and male patients, as exemplified by such variables as tolerance for physical closeness to people, capacity for relationship constancy with males (not affect), investment in one other male and ability to communicate personal messages.

Component IV: Group I differs from all other groups on this component. Component IV is dominated by a set of relatively high negative loadings on the perceptual variables of speed and spontaneity of identification in relation to people and situations.

Component V: Groups II and IV are dissimilar on component V. The highest loadings on this component were positive loadings on impulse eruption, nonverbally acted in relation to situations, and positive affect for female staff, and negative loadings to hospital programs.

Component VI: Groups I and IV differ most on component VI. On this component the variable "confidence" has a relatively high positive loading, with which the intensity of free anxiety and the duration of depression are negatively correlated.

Component VIII: Groups III and IV differ most on component VIII which primarily describes somatic involvement and physiological impulse discharge. Variables that denote attention to other people are negatively correlated with the variables denoting somatic involvement. Component VIII has the highest weight in the discriminant function of all the components. In addition, in the stepwise analysis it is the first component to enter as a discriminator.

Component X: Groups II and IV differ most. Component X describes primarily positive behavior and affect for females, with negative correlation of behavior and affect for males.

Component XII: Group means on component XII differ only slightly; thus, it does not in itself differentiate any pair of groups. Component XII deals primarily with relationship constancy to staff; constancy with male and female staff were inversely correlated.

Component XIII: Groups III and IV are dissimilar. The component is made up of a few variables that are positively correlated, primarily perception of self (inner and outer) and capacity to delay impulse discharge.

The summary of the differences in mean values of the 10 most important components separating the groups shown in Table 10 is consistent with the relative spatial distances reported in Table 9. Groups IV and I stand out as most unlike all other groups. Group IV has an extreme position on 8 out of 10 components. Group I is marked off as different from all others on two components. All components operate together in forming the groups. Differences among the groups do not describe the within-group similarities which will be delineated by the factor analysis of each group.

We have stated how each component differentiates groups in a general statement not very useful for clinical diagnosis. The interpretation of the internal characteristics of groups and factors is presented in the second part of this chapter.

Minimum Set of Variables for Prediction

We now turn to a minimum set of 20 variables which predict group membership. These are presented in Table 11 with their means and standard deviations. In order to determine the importance of the means of each variable for group membership, each has to be compared with the means and standard deviations of the variable in each other group.

TABLE 11. *Stepwise Discriminant Function on the Original Variables—Group and Overall Means and Standard Deviations*

		Group Means			
	Total N = 51	I N = 18	II N = 12	III N = 14	IV N = 7
VARIABLES					
OUTWARD BEHAVIOR					
7 Negative behavior to male patients	3.38	4.06	2.75	3.79	1.93
11 Appropriateness of behavior to male patients	4.44	4.06	4.42	5.07	4.21
13 Appropriateness of behavior in groups	4.13	3.69	4.38	4.61	3.87
15 Positive behavior to the routine of eating	6.51	6.22	6.33	7.00	6.57
18 Positive behavior to organized programs	4.78	4.99	5.33	4.07	4.71
PERCEPTION					
35 Perception of self—outer	4.37	4.13	3.88	4.61	5.36
46 Patient's assessment of others in relation to self (trust)	3.32	2.84	3.38	3.25	4.57

	Total	I	II	III	IV
	N = 51	N = 18	N = 12	N = 14	N = 7

VARIABLES

AFFECTS AND DEFENSES	Group Means				
55 Positive affect to female staff stated verbally	1.52	1.08	0.25	2.14	3.57
57 Positive affect to female patients stated verbally	0.51	0.28	0.	1.11	0.79
64 Negative affect to male patients stated nonverbally	2.82	4.14	1.17	3.82	0.29
68 Tolerance for physical closeness to male patients	4.73	5.72	4.00	4.21	4.43
71 Relationship constancy for female staff	2.06	1.56	1.54	2.86	2.64
72 Relationship constancy for male patients	3.08	3.47	1.88	4.57	1.14
75 Investment in one male	2.50	2.53	1.04	4.07	1.79
77 Investment in more than one male	2.42	2.33	2.13	2.07	3.86
78 Investment in more than one female	2.36	1.89	2.13	2.43	3.86
79 Quantity of impulse discharge to people stated verbally	3.78	5.19	1.67	3.46	4.43
86 Quantity of physiological process stated nonverbally	1.97	1.06	1.58	1.71	5.50
89 Free anxiety—duration	2.56	1.17	2.71	3.39	4.21
90 Depression—intensity	3.80	3.06	4.42	3.25	5.79

	Standard Deviations				
OUTWARD BEHAVIOR					
7 Negative behavior to male patients		1.51	1.34	1.83	1.92
11 Appropriateness of behavior to male patients		1.00	1.08	1.27	2.08
13 Appropriateness of behavior in groups		1.07	1.88	1.14	1.15
15 Positive behavior to the routine of eating		1.09	1.65	0.83	1.02
18 Positive behavior to organized programs		1.21	1.37	1.36	0.70
PERCEPTION					
35 Perception of self—outer		1.16	1.48	0.84	1.11
46 Patient's assessment of others in relation to self (trust)		0.98	0.61	1.19	1.27
AFFECTS AND DEFENSES					
55 Positive affect to female staff stated verbally		1.98	0.87	2.22	2.82
57 Positive affect to female patients stated verbally		1.18	0.	2.04	2.08
64 Negative affect to male patients stated nonverbally		1.87	1.60	1.64	0.76
68 Tolerance for physical closeness to male patients		1.42	1.94	2.51	2.05
71 Relationship constancy for female staff		1.15	1.23	1.96	1.49
72 Relationship constancy for male patients		1.41	1.58	2.13	1.49
75 Investment in one male		1.76	1.30	1.98	2.38
77 Investment in more than one male		1.25	1.17	0.87	1.18
78 Investment in more than one female		1.24	1.17	0.98	1.18
79 Quantity of impulse discharge to people stated verbally		1.86	2.71	1.71	1.62
86 Quantity of physiological process stated nonverbally		2.48	2.94	2.56	2.66
89 Free anxiety—duration		2.31	2.92	3.15	2.60
90 Depression—intensity		2.65	2.86	2.38	2.25

When we search for the level of the means we can see that Group I has the highest means for nonverbal and verbal anger and negative behavior; Group II has more variability with no outstanding large means; Group III has highest means on adaptability and constancy; and Group IV has means indicating anger, anxiety, depression, trust and positive attachment to females. These differences, represented by the means of 20 minimum discriminating variables, have been sufficient for group differentiation but they are too few to be more than suggestive for diagnostic purposes. Yet they are meaningful since Group I shows the most anger and negative behavior, Group II vacillates, Group III is adaptive and Group IV has conflicting affects but positive relations and trust in others. It would not be expected that these few variables could be pathognomonic for clinical group membership. It takes a gestalt of many variables, including both those present and absent, to differentiate a syndrome or a subsyndrome clinically. It will be quite apparent that the variables mentioned so far are consistent with those characteristic of the groups and factors we are going to describe. These more numerous variables permit a more accurate delineation of the borderline as a whole —its groups and factors.

THE CLINICAL INTERPRETATION OF GROUPS AND FACTORS

The large ego-functions framework used in this study was broken down into many variables of describable behavioral traits. The variables were quantified and statistically analyzed. It is now our task to translate the statistical results into words and sentences that describe traits of behavior. The description of each group as a clinical entity will be derived from the interpretations of the two factors of each group. It is our hope that the four clinical entities so derived will assist clinicians in making discriminations among borderline patients.

These interpretations are not literal repetitions of the behavior traits with high loadings; they represent the clinical amplifications of what is present but also of what is absent. The total clinical gestalt which clinicians habitually use is composed of the raw data of behavior and extrapolated inferences and implications. Our clinical interpretations of groups and factors follow the pattern of clinical thinking in order to be of use to clinicians. It was this thinking in lieu of statistical evidence that enabled the investigators to select one set of four groups from the other sets of four produced by the cluster analysis.

GROUP I: THE PSYCHOTIC BORDER

Group I is characterized clinically by inappropriate and negative behaviors toward other humans, whether in individual contact, group activities or various hospital programs. These patients were careless in their personal grooming and slept and ate erratically. They did not take full advantage of the permissive and therapeutic milieu of the nursing unit. This outward behavior was congruent with their verbalizations. Measurements on variables relating to perception of self and others and of situations and events revealed deficiencies, and spontaneity was limited. These patients manifested essentially negative affects toward other patients and the staff, expressed both verbally and nonverbally with occasional angry eruptions in an impulsive manner. In addition, depression of recognizable duration was present.

TABLE 12. *Group I—The Border with Psychoses*

FACTOR I

VARIABLES	FACTOR LOADINGS°
OUTWARD BEHAVIOR	
13 Appropriateness of behavior in groups	−.71
14 Positive behavior to grooming	−.69
15 Positive behavior to the routine of eating	−.65
17 Positive behavior to freedom	−.79
18 Positive behavior to organized programs/situations	−.83
19 Positive behavior to informal programs/situations	−.66
20 Negative behavior to grooming	.65
24 Negative behavior to organized programs	.62
25 Negative behavior to informal programs	.64
26 Appropriateness of behavior to grooming	−.75
28 Appropriateness of behavior to sleeping	−.70
29 Appropriateness of behavior to freedom	−.79
30 Appropriateness of behavior to organized programs	−.94
31 Appropriateness of behavior to informal programs	−.83
PERCEPTION	
34 Patient's awareness of self—inner	−.69
35 Patient's awareness of self—outer	−.70
36 Patient's awareness of body qualities	−.82
39 Spontaneity of identification of others	−.70
41 Spontaneity of identification of situations and events	−.64
42 Speed/spontaneity—time/place	−.63
43 Speed/spontaneity—things	−.63

FACTOR II

VARIABLES	FACTOR LOADINGS[*]
OUTWARD BEHAVIOR	
5 Negative behavior to male staff	.68
6 Negative behavior to female staff	.68
7 Negative behavior to male patients	.70
8 Negative behavior to female patients	.70
MESSAGES	
53 Congruence of behavior with verbal messages	.68
AFFECTS AND DEFENSES	
58 Negative affect toward male staff stated verbally	.65
59 Negative affect toward female staff stated verbally	.65
60 Negative affect toward male staff stated nonverbally	.84
61 Negative affect toward female staff stated nonverbally	.84
62 Negative affect toward male patients stated verbally	.62
63 Negative affect toward female patients stated verbally	.69
64 Negative affect toward male patients stated nonverbally	.68
79 Impulse eruption to people stated verbally	.72
80 Impulse eruption to people stated nonverbally	.79
90 Depression—intensity	.62
91 Depression—duration	.62

[*] *A loading indicates the extent to which a variable correlates with a factor. A negative loading indicates that the variable is inversely correlated; that is, the higher the values on the variables with positive loadings, the lower the values on the variables with negative loadings.*

The two factors describing Group I indicate within-group variance in several traits. Factor I contains negative behaviors directed toward the *environment,* while in factor II the targets of negative behavior are other *human beings.* Factor I includes nonadaptive behaviors but no overtly expressed negative or positive affects toward other human beings—in fact there were no measurable object-relations. On the contrary, factor II includes variables of overt negative affect toward other human beings— real anger with hostile eruptions associated with depression.

The following is a summary of the clinical characteristics of Group I:

1. Inappropriate and nonadaptive behaviors.
2. Deficient sense of self-identity and sense of reality.
3. Negative behaviors and anger toward other human beings.
4. Depression.

Although the majority of Group I patients remained nonpsychotic, they are closest to disintegration when their behaviors over time are viewed (Chapter 9). We therefore infer that the patients constituting Group I are at the psychotic border of the borderline.

In follow-up only two patients were found in state mental institutions. These two are in the Group I cluster. They were diagnosed as schizophrenic during their stay at Illinois State Psychiatric Institute (ISPI), a diagnosis that was independently confirmed by the senior author when he reviewed their behavioral reports.

GROUP II: THE CORE BORDERLINE SYNDROME

Group II is characterized by a pervasive negative affect which was "acted-out" in various ways. The behavior of these patients was not close to the psychoses or neuroses, nor were they blandly passive in their adaptation. In fact, they seemed to know their own identities, yet they did not always behave accordingly. Scrutiny of the variables gives one a confused feeling which characterizes these people exactly. They were adaptive and acted-out negatively, they showed both positive and negative behaviors and negative affect, indicating at the very most a little "involvement" with others. They were depressed, but not if they "acted out." They participated in activities or rebelled against the environment, demonstrating inappropriate behavior.

TABLE 13. *Group II—The Core Borderline Syndrome*

FACTOR I

VARIABLES	FACTOR LOADINGS
OUTWARD BEHAVIOR	
3 Positive behavior to male patients	.73
5 Negative behavior to male staff	.81
6 Negative behavior to female staff	.81
7 Negative behavior to male patients	.79
8 Negative behavior to female patients	.79
13 Appropriateness of behavior in groups	.83
14 Positive behavior to grooming	.72
18 Positive behavior to organized programs/situations	.85
19 Positive behavior to informal programs/situations	.91
29 Appropriateness of behavior to freedom	.71
33 Negative behavior to tasks	.79
PERCEPTION	
36 Patient's awareness of body qualities	.72
40 Speed of identification—situations and events	.60
42 Speed/spontaneity—time/place	.63
43 Speed/spontaneity—things	.64
MESSAGES	
48 Quantity of patient's verbal messages—organized situations	.60

FACTOR I

VARIABLES	FACTOR LOADINGS
AFFECTS AND DEFENSES	
58 Negative affect toward male staff stated verbally	.67
59 Negative affect toward female staff stated verbally	.87
60 Negative affect toward male staff stated nonverbally	.82
61 Negative affect toward female staff stated nonverbally	.85
62 Negative affect toward male patients stated verbally	.84
63 Negative affect toward female patients stated verbally	.62
79 Impulse eruption to people stated verbally	.89
80 Impulse eruption to people stated nonverbally	.80
84 Impulse eruption to things stated nonverbally	.64
90 Depression—intensity	.64
91 Depression—duration	.60

FACTOR II

VARIABLES	FACTOR LOADINGS
OUTWARD BEHAVIOR	
9 Appropriateness of behavior to male staff	−.66
10 Appropriateness of behavior to female staff	−.66
12 Appropriateness of behavior to female patients	−.85
16 Positive behavior to the routine of sleeping	−.83
22 Negative behavior to the routine of sleeping	.60
23 Negative behavior to limits/regulations	.62
26 Appropriateness of behavior to grooming	−.73
28 Appropriateness of behavior to sleeping	−.75
30 Appropriateness of behavior to organized programs	−.60
MESSAGES	
49 Quantity of patient's verbal messages—informal situations	−.64
AFFECTS AND DEFENSES	
77 Involvement with more than one male	−.68
78 Involvement with more than one female	−.68
90 Depression—intensity	−.61
91 Depression—duration	−.65

Factor I is characterized by negative affect and behavior to all persons—staff and patients. Outward behavior was vacillating, as both positive and negative outward behavior toward male patients are positively correlated. There was evidence of participation in groups and formal and informal activities. Proper grooming and use of the freedoms of the hospital were characteristic. There was awareness of body qualities, and responses to situations, events, time and place were adequate. However, tasks were viewed negatively, and sometimes anger erupted toward people and things. Depression of some duration was apparent.

In factor II depression is inversely associated with rebelliousness against the environment. Behavior was contrary to limit-setting and regulations, such as refusal to retire at the proper time; inappropriate behavior was shown to organized programs and people.

Group II, or the core group of the borderline, is characterized by the following:

1. Vacillating involvement with others.
2. Overt or acted-out expressions of anger.
3. Depression.
4. Absence of indications of consistent self-identity.

GROUP III: THE ADAPTIVE, AFFECTLESS DEFENDED, "AS IF" PERSONS

Group III is characterized by bland and adaptive behavior. Notice that there was little evidence of negative behavior or affect; behavior seemed generally appropriate. But what is also missing is manifestation of positive affect—in fact there is no evidence of love for anybody or anything. Furthermore, there is no indication of a well-developed sense of self-identity. This group is like Helene Deutsch's "as if" persons.

TABLE 14. *Group III—The Adaptive, Affectless, Defended—"As If"*

FACTOR I

VARIABLES	FACTOR LOADINGS
OUTWARD BEHAVIOR	
1 Positive behavior to male staff	.85
2 Positive behavior to female staff	.74
3 Positive behavior to male patients	.67
4 Positive behavior to female patients	.77
10 Appropriateness of behavior to female staff	.78
11 Appropriateness of behavior to male patients	.60
12 Appropriateness of behavior to female patients	.79
13 Appropriateness of behavior in groups	.67
17 Positive behavior to freedom	.71
18 Positive behavior to organized programs/situations	.86
19 Positive behavior to informal programs/situations	.84
21 Negative behavior to the routine of eating	.60
29 Appropriateness of behavior to freedom	.88
30 Appropriateness of behavior to organized programs	.88
31 Appropriateness of behavior to informal programs	.88
MESSAGES	
49 Quantity of patient's verbal messages—informal situations	.72
AFFECTS AND DEFENSES	
67 Tolerance for physical closeness to female patients	.63

FACTOR II

VARIABLES	FACTOR LOADINGS
OUTWARD BEHAVIOR	
6 Negative behavior to female staff	−.72
8 Negative behavior to female patients	−.78
14 Positive behavior to grooming	.75
20 Negative behavior to grooming	−.90
22 Negative behavior to the routine of sleeping	−.67
26 Appropriateness of behavior to grooming	.77
27 Appropriateness of behavior to the routine of eating	.66
28 Appropriateness of behavior to the routine of sleeping	.61
PERCEPTION	
41 Spontaneity—situations and events	−.61
AFFECTS AND DEFENSES	
59 Negative affect toward female staff stated verbally	−.78
60 Negative affect toward male staff stated nonverbally	−.74
61 Negative affect toward female staff stated nonverbally	−.82
65 Negative affect toward female patients stated nonverbally	−.75
67 Tolerance for physical closeness to female staff	−.65
92 Defense, withdrawal (highest frequency)	−.66
93 Defense, intellectualization (second frequency)	.63

Factor I is characterized by generally adaptive and appropriate behaviors and attitudes. The hospital environment was conducive to typical well-being, but evoked little affect of any kind. In general these lives were structured according to the rules and regulations, and patients related complementary to the structure set by others, thereby indicating that they had not acquired a sense of personal identity.

Factor II also characterized adaptive and appropriate behaviors. There was little show of affect and indeed little spontaneity in response to situations and events. No evidence of a firm sense of self-identity was discerned. In addition, the patients of Group III demonstrated primarily or most frequent defensive behaviors of "withdrawal" and second most frequent defenses of "intellectualization," correlated in opposite directions. The 14 patients in Group III are those in whom defenses stood out most clearly, and their behaviors were most adaptive.

Group III is characterized by the following:

1. Adaptive and appropriate behavior.
2. Complementary relationships ("as if").
3. Little affect or spontaneity in response to situations.
4. Defenses of withdrawal and intellectualization.

GROUP IV: THE BORDER WITH THE NEUROSIS

Group IV was a small group containing subjects different from those in other groups, and each patient shows characteristics of both factors at similar levels. Unfortunately there were only seven patients in this group, indicating that the selection process tended to pass over this type since it was close to characteristic neurotic depressions. This group had the highest means on the variables concerned with positive affects which were directed toward female staff or patients, consistent with a childlike clinging depression. They resembled the men exemplified in our group of chronic hospitalized "depressions" described in Chapter 7.

TABLE 15. *Group IV—The Border with the Neuroses*

FACTOR I

VARIABLES	FACTOR LOADINGS
OUTWARD BEHAVIOR	
3 Positive behavior to male patients	.83
4 Positive behavior to female patients	.83
15 Positive behavior to the routine of eating	.70
18 Positive behavior to organized programs/situations	.77
20 Negative behavior to grooming	−.88
21 Negative behavior to the routine of eating	−.88
27 Appropriateness of behavior to eating	.86
30 Appropriateness of behavior to organized programs	.79
31 Appropriateness of behavior to informal programs	.85
32 Positive behavior to tasks	.74
33 Negative behavior to tasks	−.94
PERCEPTION	
39 Spontaneity of identification of others	.79
AFFECTS AND DEFENSES	
72 Relationship constancy to male patients	−.88
73 Relationship constancy to female patients	.75
77 Involvement with more than one male	.87
78 Involvement with more than one female	.87
85 Physiological processes stated verbally	−.86
86 Physiological processes stated nonverbally	−.74
92 Defense, intellectualization (highest frequency)	−.85

FACTOR II

VARIABLES	FACTOR LOADINGS
OUTWARD BEHAVIOR	
1 Positive behavior to male staff	−.71
9 Appropriateness of behavior to male staff	−.76
25 Negative behavior to informal programs	−.71

FACTOR II

VARIABLES	FACTOR LOADINGS
PERCEPTION	
37 Self-identity	−.84
45 Patient's assessment of self (self-esteem)	−.86
47 Patient's assessment of situations, events and institutions (confidence)	−.87
AFFECTS AND DEFENSES	
54 Positive affect toward male staff stated verbally	−.73
59 Negative affect toward female staff stated verbally	−.89
61 Negative affect toward female staff stated nonverbally	−.71
70 Relationship constancy toward male staff	−.78
74 Involvement with self	.76
75 Involvement with one male	.82
88 Anxiety—intensity	.68
90 Depression—intensity	.92
91 Depression—duration	.75

Factor I revealed positive behavior in programs and tasks. Although there are no indications of involvement with the staff, relationships developed with other patients, especially constancy with female patients. This group of patients became involved with people.

Factor II reveals little positive or appropriate behavior with the staff as a whole or with male patients. Salient features were anxiety and depression, with defects in self-esteem and confidence. This depression was not associated with anger or guilt feelings.

Group IV is characterized by the following:

1. Childlike clinging depression (anaclitic).
2. Anxiety.
3. Generally close resemblance to neurotic narcissistic characters.

OVERALL CHARACTERISTICS OF THE BORDERLINE SYNDROME

Four basic facts are derived from the total analysis of the data in the ego-functions framework: (1) Expressed more or less directly to a variety of targets, *anger* seems to constitute the main or only affect that the borderline patient experiences. (2) The borderline patient is characterized by a *defect in his affectional relationships*. These are anaclitic, dependent or complementary, but rarely reciprocal. (3) The third characteristic is the *absence of indications of consistent self-identity*, which seems to be linked to the lack of affectional relationship and consistency, with anger at closeness. This vacillating behavior is associated with a confused view of the self—"as if I were watching myself playing a role" and the frequent assumption of complementarity. (4) The fourth characteristic present most clearly in some factors is *depression*—not the typical guilt-laden, self-accusatory, remorseful "end-of-the-rope" type, but more a loneliness as the subjects realize their predicament of being unable to commit themselves in a world of transacting individuals. This depression is different in Group IV where it is more anaclitic in contrast to the depression that moves along with anger.

DIFFERENTIAL DIAGNOSIS
IN RELATION TO THE GENERAL SYNDROME

It was anticipated and hoped that included in the sample of patients originally admitted to the hospital for our research, based on the criterion of "not definitely psychotic, who on admission looked clinically unclear," would be control cases. We anticipated that a number of schizophrenics and typical neurosis would be included. Unfortunately, very few schizophrenics were selected, even fewer depressives or neurotics.

Actually the "natural" control group constituted the 17 patients admitted, observed, described and recorded in the first interview period; but these could not be followed for a second period because of untoward events. Some of them became disturbed and were transferred to a closed unit, and one was placed on heavy doses of drugs; both are reasons for rejection from the study. The majority of the 17 either eloped or signed out against medical advice shortly after admission. In this they contrasted with the borderlines who sought voluntary admission, thrived in the hospital and were reluctant to leave. A review of these 17 patients' records revealed that most of them could not be called borderline by the criteria subsequently elicited from our analysis. These patients were classified as follows: schizophrenic (5), psychopathic personality (5), depression (3), hysterical psychosis (2), post partum psychosis (1), and borderline (1). They are mentioned in our follow-up studies in Chapter 9.

For comparison we will refer to the vast amount of knowledge and experience well documented in the literature, utilizing what we know about the core processes or source traits of other diagnostic groups.

1. *Schizophrenia*

We begin with schizophrenia because it is the most frequent diagnostic term applied to the borderline. The specific type is either chronic undifferentiated schizophrenia or pseudoneurotic schizophrenia.

Some of our current knowledge about schizophrenia has been derived from the classical descriptions of Kraepelin (1912) and Bleuler (1950) as well as more contemporary authors. More recently other disciplines, utilizing their specific techniques, have contributed both to our knowledge and confusion. Sociologists and anthropologists focus on the sickness of society, in general, and the family, in particular; psychologists rely on test results; psychoanalysts focus on internal dynamics; and others concentrate on language and systems of communication. In addition to all these are biologists who study genetic factors, disordered biochemistry, autoimmunity and aberrant focuses of electrical discharges from the midline of the brain.

The clinical concept of schizophrenia, succeeding the term dementia praecox, is ancient, predating by far the systematizing activities of Kraepelin. Although some forms of this entity had been carefully described before, Kraepelin brought together the entire *complex* of symptoms under one heading which included several subtypes. Bleuler, on the other hand, viewed schizophrenia as a process involving affective and intellectual functions. Affective pathology including fixed or reduced emotional tone was primary and related to disturbances of the intellectual and associational processes and to excessive autistic fantasy life. Bleuler was always uncertain about what was primary and what was secondary in the symptomatology.

Subsequently thousands of publications have viewed the schizophrenic from various frames of reference. Only lately has interest centered on the family as etiology and/or a deeper concern with the basic or core problems or deficits. We have had closest contact with the work of Beck (1964) over the last two decades; we choose to refer to his work as an example of a study of the schizophrenic process because he attempted to discriminate types. Our particular interest is in the similarities or dissimilarities between his types of schizophrenia and our types of borderline.

Beck states that the most important disturbance occurs in the emotional and intellectual spheres, whereas fantasy, defenses and social maladjustment are secondary. For him schizophrenia is a survival process, an adaptation to inner data not suitable to the outside world. He states that the emotional push, the intellectual channelling, the fantasy that introverts and the defensive devices, all in interaction, constitute the individual. The individual is an adaptation that results from the transactions among the patient, his family and the culture in which he lives.

Beck's *core or dream* schizophrenics reveal serious disruption of intellectual functions leading to autistic and regressive thinking, primarily affective pathology of fixed tone or lability, and serious social maladaptation. On the other hand, his transitional type, although revealing much psychopathology in the form of emotional instability, excitement, turmoil, associational restriction and autistic regression fantasies, is balanced on the favorable side because there is still a powerful groping toward adjustment. The *sanctuary* type is rigidly accurate but coherent; the breadth of interest is narrowed and inflexible. This description, including the report of Andrew, is typical for the *borderline* case, although Beck is reluctant to use this term. In Beck's cases coherent thinking ranks high, and hallucinations and ego-disorganization rank low. His sanctuary type shows affective lability and some subtle associative disintegration. But these patients "know" the world of reality; they live with an even tempo and seem unruffled on the surface. Language is free from confusion; there is little disorganization of thinking, and errors of judgment are avoided. On the negative side are concrete thinking, hypersensitivity, poverty of fantasy, self-depreciation, self-absorption and restrictive and constrictive defenses.

Artiss (1966) described the schizophrenic's behavior operationally as (1) "too much" or "too little," (2) deficiency in social skills, and (3) odd and idiosyncratic use of language which seemingly bids for deviance. Artiss summarizes: "The schizophrenic's quandary results from a relative deficit in the connotative aspects of language." He rejects novelty and perseverates the old.

In summary, although we have not subjected schizophrenics to the same types of observations, descriptions, ratings and analyses, we can state that the borderline does *not* have (as does the schizophrenic):

1. Disturbances in intellectual associational processes.
2. Autistic or regressive thinking.
3. Characteristic family with "pseudomutuality" or "skewing."
4. Delusions or hallucinations.
5. Deficit in connotative aspects of language.

Nevertheless the patients in Group I reveal behaviors which are negative and inappropriate toward their environment, indicating a state "close to disintegration." If psychotic disintegration does occur it is transient, sometimes for only a few hours. On this basis Frosch (1964) terms them "psychotic characters."

The transient behaviors labeled as psychotic differ from those observed in the schizophrenic psychoses. They seem to be induced by quantities of rage unmanageable by the deficient defensive functions of the ego.

Dr. Reid (Chief of 8E, ISPI) has astutely pointed out that to the border-line patient these episodes are ego-alien. Important to the patient is the recognition that some disintegration is impending, and he voluntarily seeks help even if it can be obtained only through legal commitment. (Some evidence of this is the fact that 39 out of 51 patients in our sample were voluntary admissions.)

2. *Pseudoneurotic Schizophrenia*

Since Hoch and Polatin described this entity (1949), little information has been published further about its characteristics (Chapter 2). The three generalities—pan-anxiety, pan-sexuality and pan-neurosis—have been of little help in diagnosing or understanding the condition except after a psychosis has developed. The patients to whom this diagnosis is applied become psychotic less often than other schizophrenics. In some ways they may be mistaken for the borderline.

Weingarten and Korn (1967) have reported on 10 pseudoneurotic schizophrenics who comprise 11 per cent of 87 patients studied by a variety of psychological tests. They report the following results: (1) good social façade, appropriate behavior and well-kept appearance; (2) successful academic and occupational attainment; (3) underlying thought disorder involving primary-process thinking; (4) forced or contrived af-fectional responsiveness; (5) unabating states of tension, constant tur-moil; (6) ego-syntonic acceptance of thought disorder, ego-alien reaction to social maladjustment or academic failure; (7) profuse, unintegrated neurotic and psychotic defenses.

These patients, when decompensating into a psychosis because of external stress, internal tensions or injudicious reconstructive therapy, cannot be differentiated from other forms of schizophrenia.

3. *Depression*

In one factor of each of three patient groups depression was observed. Only in Group III, characterized by adaptation and absence of affect, was depression not characteristic. Unlike the erroneous dynamic stereo-type that depression is always the obverse of hostility, the two were sometimes correlated in a single factor. In factor II of Group I depres-sion was associated with verbally and behaviorally expressed anger. In factor I of Group II depression was positively correlated with negative behaviors and anger. On the other hand, depression was associated with anxiety in factor II of Group IV. Actually the depressed appearance which is basically loneliness (except in Group IV) contributes the most significant problem in differential diagnosis.

We turn back to review our studies of the phenomena of depression (Grinker et al., 1961) to compare the factors developed in that research. There was no similarity with the borderline in the factors of the pilot study. For example in factor A depression was associated with guilt and remorse not seen in any borderline. Factor B was involved with hopeful attachment to the external world with the idea that supplies and gratification were due these patients. These same criteria were characteristic of "feelings and concerns" in factor II of the main study. In this study, "feelings and concerns (factor IV), which was essentially anxiety, and factor V, which included traits of "unloved, clinging, angry" attempts to force others to give, were in combination as in factor II of Group IV borderline. In the study of "outward behaviors" in depression the isolation and withdrawal of factor I was like factor I of Group III borderline; factor I, including clinging ingratiating behavior, was like Group IV of the borderline. The combination factor patterns in the depression study was not similar to any of the borderline categories.

In general it can be stated that although depression as an affect is found in several of the borderline categories it does not correspond with that seen in the depressive syndrome. The borderline depression is a feeling of loneliness and isolation. The exception is Group IV (borderline on the neurotic) which is similar to the neurotic anaclitic depressive syndrome in which there is a great hunger for dependent gratification.

4. *Personality or Character Disorder*

Character disorders are relatively stable, ego-syntonic adaptations to a field of process in conflict. Character represents an adaptive synthesis (Gitelson, 1963). Only when this state of equilibrium breaks down does a psychoneurosis develop which is ego-alien and distressful. There are many nuances of character, some of which have been given names such as neurotic, erotic, compulsive, narcissistic and psychopathic character, and many others defined according to their predominating type of behavior. The borderline character or premorbid state is described in Chapter 10.

In many psychiatric centers what corresponds to the borderline syndrome is diagnosed as chronic severe personality or character disorder. Similar to chronic undifferentiated schizophrenia, this vague item in our nosological classification is used, not only because the borderline syndrome has not been defined and differentiated, but also because it does not exist in our nosological classification.

Unlike the temporary disintegrations the defenses of the borderline are characterological and correspond to those employed by psychoneurotics. This is the borderline's adaptive overlay acquired over many years; they become ego-syntonic. They probably become intensified as the first reaction to specific strains, especially the threat of closeness. For this reason withdrawal, intellectualization and denial are so frequent; these are techniques that increase interpersonal distance.

During their hospital stay so little stress was impinged on these patients that extraordinary coping strategies were not necessary. It was only in the period between decision for discharge and the actual discharge that the patients showed stress responses.

On the other hand, sexual acting-out and alcoholic excesses occurred on passes away from the hospital. These were easily detected and reported within our behavioral observations. They may have constituted defenses against anxiety and/or substitute gratification without the danger of involvement. These were not the antisocial or asocial behaviors characteristic of the so-called "psychopathic personality." Within the hospital several factors revealed compliant conforming adaptive behavior. These may be termed defenses in the sense that they serve to maintain distance—the good patient need not be given too much attention. Partially this was initiated by the staff's demand for adaptive behavior, but the fact that some could comply and others could not indicates that the capability for conforming and "as if" behavior was a salient characteristic of a type of borderline.

The diagnosis of "schizoid personality" is often applied to borderline patients. According to our current definitions, the schizoid avoids close or competitive relations. However, they are shy and sensitive, and experience considerable autistic thinking. Also, they rarely express open hostility or ordinary aggressive feelings. Finally, they may, and frequently do, develop overt schizophrenic psychoses.

A recent interest in deaf adults mistakenly kept in state mental hospitals with the diagnosis of schizophrenia has introduced diagnostic difficulties. Once communication is established with the patients, the diagnosis of schizophrenia may be untenable. They have been called "primitive characters." However, they strongly resemble the borderline as delineated in Group II. Their early-life deficiencies in communicatory input may be an important etiological factor.

Man has a limited number of behaviors in the service of defenses or adaptation. When cornered he can use "flight or fight," and neither is easy or without punishment in modern civilization. Therefore, his fight or flight, his magical rituals, and his thinking-through or withdrawals are universals found in a variety of situations and related to a variety of intrapsychic conflicts. The core nature of the borderline illness is thus not in symptomatic adaptive defenses, a mixture of which is found in all psychoses, neuroses, personality disorders and varieties of health, but in the basic defects in maturation and early development expressed in ego-dysfunctions.

CHAPTER 7 Individual Patients

with EDWARD WOLPERT

Behavioral items which we observed in our research delineated disturbances of ego-functions of the borderline and were statistically analyzed into groups and factors. The resultant scientific skeleton requires the flesh and blood of recognizable symptoms to become useful for clinicians.

The syndrome or borderline class of patients has difficulty in achieving and maintaining affectional relations; they have trouble in controlling aggressive impulses and rarely achieve a consistent reliable and satisfying identity. Ego-alien, short-lived confusional or paranoid-like psychoses may occur, as well as temporary states of loneliness, appearing as depression without guilt, and depression of the anaclitic clinging type. Absent are evidences of cognitive disturbances, looseness of associations, or hallucinations or delusions.

In this chapter we present vignettes of borderline patients who are members of the four large groups obtained by means of clustering analysis. Our protocols contained descriptions of behaviors from a large number of observers suitable for the rating of items derived from an ego-functions framework. Hence it is not possible to utilize all these transcribed data to delineate typical clinical "cases." We have therefore chosen to fill out the clinical gap with descriptions of each of our four large groups, condensed from the protocols of several patients, other individual case reports and a previous experimental study.

It should be kept in mind that statistical analyses are procedures for the study of numbers of subjects, traits or symptoms. The identified individual patient will naturally not have all the traits or symptoms characteristic of the group. A syndrome or a subsyndrome is an idealized category, stereotype or diagnostic entity into which a patient's symptoms or behaviors make the best fit.

In this chapter we amplify the general clinical characteristics of each group already outlined in Chapter 6, to which the reader should refer.

GROUP I: THE BORDER WITH PSYCHOSES

Case 1 (Dr. Wolpert)

At the time of admission to Psychosomatic and Psychiatric Institute (P & PI) the patient was a 30-year-old mother of two who was separated and who had been living with her parents in Chicago while her children were in the custody of her husband in California. On admission she was confused as to the reasons for admission, saying, "I don't know whether I should be here or not. My father wanted me to come." In this way she disclaimed responsibility for her treatment but would accept the facilities of the hospital, ultimately taking advantage of the hospital for room, board and social life.

Anamnesis revealed that her difficulties had begun some four years previously. On the surface she had been doing well with her husband and two children. However, she resented his seeming lack of interest in her sexually; he had taken a job as a traveling salesman, which kept him away from her a good deal of the time. As her resentment increased she accepted, without understanding why, a dinner invitation from friends she knew her husband would resent. For the entire day before the dinner and while at the dinner she felt an aimless dread but had no insight as to why she should feel so upset. Nothing unusual occurred, however, and she returned home, going to bed without incident. Early the next morning, however, she was awakened by pain in her left shoulder radiating down the arm to the fingers, associated with difficulty in breathing. She feared she would die, awakened her husband and was rushed to an emergency room where she was told that she only had "nerve trouble" and needed some counseling.

For the next two years the patient received intensive psychotherapy from a younger male psychiatrist who saw her three times a week, ultimately decreasing to once a week. At one point during her therapy she became "suicidal," and although she had made no suicidal attempt she was hospitalized for three months, being allowed to sign out then against medical advice. Toward the end of the therapy she developed strong erotic feelings for her psychiatrist, characterized by sexual daydreams, dressing in a seductive way for her sessions and beginning an affair with a neighbor. At about this time her husband became more attentive to her. She felt things were going well and terminated the treatment although the psychiatrist felt she needed more. For four months she felt relatively well, but when her lover moved to another part of the state, depression set in and she sought further psychiatric care from a second but older male psychiatrist who concurred with her own desire for electric shock treatment.

Following the second course of treatment, she told her husband of her recent affair, and the marital relationship deteriorated. He began to drink, she began to drink and use drugs, and soon they separated. From time to time she would be visited by her lover, and during such periods she would feel well, but at other times she was quite depressed. Her ability to take care of the home and children deteriorated. One year before admission to a hospital her elder child was hit by a car and suffered a brain concussion. Following the child's recovery she granted her husband a divorce, took a second lover and became depressed after he asked her to marry him. Six months before admission she took an overdose of sleeping pills, planned so that her lover found her unconscious, and she was hospitalized for a second time. While in the hospital the court granted custody of the children to her husband, and upon discharge the patient moved in with a girl friend. At that time she was unable to do more than drink and be isolated in the house.

The patient's family then persuaded her to return to Chicago where she saw a psychiatrist once a week but remained isolated in her parents' apartment. Because of increasingly severe depression and drinking, her parents forced her psychiatrist to place her in a hospital where she stayed for one month. Almost immediately upon admission the depression dissipated and she began to function with the patient group as if she had been a long-standing member. She had two affairs while in the hospital—one with an attendant and one with a nurse from another hospital. All in all, she felt more relaxed and more comfortable in the hospital than ever before. Because of her improvement she was discharged; once home with her parents interminable arguments and drinking began. After an argument she took some pills, slashed her wrists superficially and was readmitted to the hospital.

The patient was born and raised in Chicago. She is the elder of two children, having a brother six years younger. When asked about her early life she remembered that when she was about three or four her parents lived near her grandmother's home but she was always left out of the communication between mother, father and grandparents. While her parents were always "terribly devoted to each other," she felt, "I never belonged. Maybe that is why I felt a wall around me. I can't feel." Although she said she was always "mother's and daddy's little girl who never wanted for anything because of the type of family I lived in," in the next breath she would say she was always unsure of herself.

In high school when she was elected secretary of the senior class she noticed that the other girls who were elected officers seemed to be experiencing strong emotions, including crying and exuberance, while she herself could feel nothing. In fact, she reported that she could not feel anything except when she took drugs.

The patient is aware of how angry she sometimes becomes and how her angry outbursts often jeopardize her relationships. One such example occurred in elementary school. Mother said to her one day that if it was 40 degrees outside the next day the patient wouldn't have to wear leggings. The patient was pleased because that meant she might not have to wear the hated clothes. The next morning mother said that the patient had to wear her leggings. The patient became angry and decided to leave home to go to her grandmother's house. She remembered walking very slowly because she was frightened, and she kept looking back over her shoulder, hoping that someone would come after her.

"This is kind of what I do when I make suicidal attempts, hoping someone will save me. Finally my father did overtake me and took me home. I was glad. I was really quite relieved. When I was in California recently I told my folks over the phone that I felt like killing myself, that they did this to me. I also called my mother to tell her that I'd kill myself but what could she do about it. I guess I just wanted to hurt her. And I told my husband about the affair to shock and hurt him, and tell him how bad I really was. I guess I've always done things to be cruel, to hurt other people."

The patient dated a neighbor's son, T., for a couple of years while in high school. Finally she broke up with T. and started dating W. and D. Subsequently T. asked her out again, and instead of refusing as her other girl friends had encouraged her to do she went out with him immediately. For a period of several years she dated T., W. and D. interchangeably. She didn't particularly have a preference except for the boy that she was with at the moment.

Comment

This patient represents a prototype of Group I of the borderline. In her own statement she has never considered that she "belonged" and says very clearly that she cannot feel. Her early role assignment was that of an object of mother's narcissism; mother's concerns were of appearance and behavior, not of feelings. Having no help with her feelings, they were taken as signs of her badness and she developed a self-image of worthlessness. When she attempted independence and self-reliance, she was inhibited by mother's controls.

Now she shows she is unsure of herself; her self-image is that of an inferior person who must anxiously attempt to meet standards of others. She has difficulty in feeling anything except when she is comfortable in the hospital where there are relatively well-defined roles, or when she is under the influence of alcohol or of drugs. In order to get a feeling of belonging and identity, the patient must attach herself to someone, living an almost parasitic relationship. Information regarding her high school boy friends indicates that she didn't have a preference except for "the boy I was with at the moment." Her elopement was an impulsive desire to hang on to someone. Inward attachments, in order to be of significance to her, in view of her lack of ability to experience feelings, take the form of violent feelings, either hurting herself or hurting others. Thus, her relation with others may be quite intense but is very unstable. In this sense she is like a tabetic who has to stamp the ground to feel; to feel, the relationship must be violent.

In a vain attempt to resolve her loneliness and need for attention, the patient gradually acquires the role of the sick person; her conversion symptoms, alcoholism, drug abuse and hospitalization being the signs of this newly developed role.

Thus we see a patient unable to form stable affectionate relationships, to control aggressive feelings, or to develop a coherent self-identity, vainly trying to escape from depression by promiscuity, drugs, alcohol and hospitalization.

Case 2

A 32-year-old female entered the ISPI unit, expressing anger at the entire environment. She was so outspoken that negative reactions were evoked from everyone. Nevertheless, she had to have things her own way—right or wrong. At times she was so loud that she had to be controlled from inappropriate gales of laughter. When her husband called and left a message that her sick daughter was feeling better, she evidenced no response and acted as if she had not heard. Her appearance was that of a dishevelled person who did not care about the environment, nor was she insulted when criticized. The patient was well aware of the time schedules of various activities yet always shuffled in late. She monopolized group meetings with loud talk. She broke the rules concerned with proper dress and frequented the male section which was off-limits. When intensely angry she seemed to get further and further away from reality. There were no evidences of positive relations to anyone.

Summary

Patients in Group I in general do not achieve a sense of consistent identity and have great difficulty in establishing positive relations with others. They apparently have given up actively trying to develop object-relations and withdraw more or less from the scene. Yet they are lonely, depressed and enraged at the environment and other human beings. It is this rage that has many behavioral outlets, but these are not sufficient to protect the ego from transient and mild dissolution of the function of reality adaptation. Hence the transient psychoses superimposed on inappropriate, nonadaptive and negative behaviors (cf. Appendix III for an additional case from Group I).

GROUP II: THE CORE BORDERLINE SYNDROME

Case 3 (Therapist's Report)

This 22-year-old female was a school dropout, sometimes alcoholic, occasionally a drug-user, promiscuous and had one illegitimate pregnancy and abortion. Her psychotherapeutic sessions have been filled with accounts of vacillation between Joe and Larry, always breaking up with one or the other. No evidence of any affectionate relationship was ever found, not even to a dog she bought and permitted to die, and there were no transference manifestations in the therapy. However, the subject is stable enough to hold a job and live alone in an apartment through her own earnings. The partial contents of the 28th psychotherapeutic session reveal in the subject's own words an intellectual understanding of her hate and lack of affectional consistency.

She seemed to have a great deal of difficulty in beginning the session. She looked up at me, smiled, and in a warm, clear voice expressed that she was having difficulty starting. She said, "I don't know what to say, but I guess there's enough that happened to me that I should." She smiled. After about three or four minutes I asked her why she felt that she was having such difficulty today and she said, she didn't know. After another several minutes she said that she was going with Joe again. "I saw Joe on Friday night; he called me. We went out on Saturday and then again yesterday we went to a movie. He didn't take me to the usual bar and I asked him thinking that I was right, if he didn't want to be seen with me. Joe agreed. Not out loud, but I could tell it was true." She began talking about Friday night—Larry and Sally seeing her, and how they came up to see her; I was somewhat confused and told her that I didn't understand whether Larry and Sally had come up to her apartment to visit. She said no, that Larry came up alone and seemed to want to talk to her about what had happened. The word had gotten around that if Joe catches Larry he's going to really beat him up. Larry said that Joe could do this if he wanted to but he wasn't going to stop talking to her. She said, "Larry actually came up to explain and apologize to me that all this trouble had come about because of me. Then on Sunday I gave Joe a call and he said, let's go to the show, so we want to the show." I said, "All these things are events, things. What about your feelings, and thoughts and fantasies?" She gave a short laugh and said, "Well, I was mad all weekend. I just seemed to have so much hate. I don't know what the hate was about but it was there. I seem to hate everybody. I certainly hate Joe and Larry and yet, I need them too." I asked what she needed them for. She said, "Well, I don't want to be alone. I'm just disgusted with the whole thing. I don't really want to go back and yet I find that I am. It's like watching, waiting to see what I'm going to do next. It's almost like a play and I have a certain role and I look to see what's going to happen in the next act." I asked her if she felt like a director or a spectator, and she laughed and said, "I wish I were the director but I sort of feel like it's all happening to me and I don't have too much of a say."

She said, "I'm so disgusted, I just feel that nobody cares." I asked if that includes Joe and Larry. She said, "Yes." I said, "It seems that you would like to have closeness and concern and yet, when it's within your

grasp there's something about it that seems to make you flee from it."
After a long silence she said, "Yeah, I know that's true. I can see that now.
But what do I do about it?" I asked her what there was about the closeness that forced her to break it off. She said, "Well, I don't know." She
thought for a while, and then said, "Well, when you get into a relationship like that you get trapped. At first it's fine. But then you start getting
in a pattern. You have to do what the other one wants you to do." I said,
"You mean you feel obligated?" She said, "Yeah, obligated. And you've
got to do whatever the other person wants. Then I'm just completing a
pattern. It's like when I sleep with a boy for a few months. At first it's
exciting and fun. And then after a while, I just have to keep going. Not
'cause I want to any more. Then I want to be free. I want to get out of
the relationship, and I don't know how to do it. So then I have to start
creating little incidents so that the other one will have to break up with
me. I want my freedom then, but then, when I have my freedom I just
feel lonely again." I said to her that a close relationship entails, to her,
meeting the other person's needs. I wondered if she was saying that when
she starts meeting the other person's needs that she kind of loses herself.
She said, "Yeah, and then I don't know how to break it off." There was
a prolonged silence and I asked what she was reflecting about and she
didn't answer. I waited a little while longer and then finally said to her,
"You seem to see a close relationship as resulting in your total submission
to it. I'm wondering why you should feel that that's the only way?" She
said, "The ideal relationship to me would be a two month relationship.
That way there'd be no commitment. At the end of the two months I could
just break it off. The relationship would just evaporate and I'd be fine.
But the only criterion for this would be that there would have to be
someone else around so that I wouldn't get lonely." She said she seemed
to see these relationships as just transient episodes which protected
against loneliness. And she added, "It would be fine as long as that's the
way it was. But then again," she said, "I wouldn't mind totally submitting
to a relationship or losing myself or meeting someone else's needs if it
was someone that I liked. But it never is." Then she thought for a while
and then finally said, "I guess the ones that I could totally submit to,
like Larry, would be the ones who would never permit it."

Comment

In capsule form this sector of a therapeutic session reveals all the
characteristics of Group II: vacillating involvement with others, overt
or acted-out expressions of anger, varying degrees of lonely depressive-
ness and failure in achieving her own identity.

Case 4

A 22-year-old, single, male clerk complained of many problems, one of which was the suddenness with which his feelings of well-being would disappear. For example, when his girl friend seems to accept him and tells him she wants him to take care of her, all the world appears good; when she is impatient with him, all the world is bad. However, he is very unsure of his feelings toward her. At times he feels he loved her and needed her, at other times not. When she would tell him she loved him, he would have no feeling or response whatsoever. However, when he would return to his room, he would develop a strong longing for her which would disappear when he was in her presence. This patient reveals difficulty in achieving and maintaining affectionate relationships.

Summary

Patients in Group II still actively search for companionship and affection from others. They are involved but in a vacillating fashion. They move toward an object but soon become anxious and angry and retreat only to become lonely and depressed. The resultant confused picture is often labeled as "ambivalent," but in reality there is little real affection, only anger and loneliness. They do not become psychotic although the to and fro movements in relationships to objects are confusing to the ob-server.

GROUP III: THE ADAPTIVE, AFFECTLESS, DEFENDED— "AS IF"

Case 5 (Nurse's Report)

I got in touch with him about two or three weeks ago about coming to patient activity meeting. He was sitting at the desk in his room read-ing. He was very pleasant, but didn't say much. He said that he couldn't consider coming down and that he wasn't ready to do anything yet. There was really no affect at all, including no sign of annoyance. At the end of the week I contacted him about getting started with some activity and about the activity meeting. He said that he wasn't able to tolerate this group, there were too many people. I mentioned several programs such as morning recreation, O. T., and men's recreation. He was aware of these things going on. I asked him about the morning recreation program and he found cheer in the fact that he could come and observe, but he wouldn't participate. I invited him in to sit on the sidelines in the gym; he refused. He watched the entire period, leaving a short time before the group. I also talked to him about coming to O. T., and he let me know that he was assigned to work with the group and knew what it was. He said that he didn't know yet if he would be able to come, but he promised me that he would try; however, he did not appear. I asked him about any particular interests he had had before coming into the hospital. He said that he had particularly enjoyed bowling. He knew that we did go bowling, but he wasn't ready to do this. He didn't look directly at me, but he did turn somewhat toward me. This he doesn't always do. I had the feeling that the information that he volunteered, which was more than I really expected, was an effort to get things over with so that he wouldn't have to tolerate the contact any more than possible. He didn't look really depressed; he was more withdrawn. There was no real affect. I have gone in his room to talk with his roommate Mr. S. and they are both there, but there doesn't seem to be any communication. He does leave the ward quite a bit, but he's always by himself. He seems to plan his trips to the canteen when it isn't crowded, because he is always alone. He seems to have some expectation that this is just a period that he had to go through and at some point it will be over and he'll feel better and that's it.

He will come out and watch one TV program, then he will go back in his room and read. Then he might come out and watch another one later. Then he'll go back again. He was having a pretty hard time making an adjustment to having a roommate. Whenever his roommate was in the room, he was out. When the roommate was out, he was in. Now he is able to sit with his roommate in there. How much they talk I don't know, but at least he is in there with him now. Once he told me that he was sleeping during the day because his roommate snored at night and he couldn't sleep. Most of the time he reads in his room.

His father visited with him Saturday evening. They went to the canteen. His father came in and went straight to his room. I was in the dayroom. When they were ready to go to the canteen his father was with him and the patient asked: "Is it all right if we go to the canteen?" I told him sure. I have never seen his expression change. It's like someone who just doesn't care about anything. He has this sort of vagueness. It's always the same. I have never seen him smile. He and Mr. S. had a date to play pool. Mr. S. went in his room and reminded him. He told him, "When I get ready, I'll let you know." Mr. S. was under the impression that he was going to be ready that evening. The pitch of his voice never changes. He just says what he has to say and that's it.

Comment

This patient is a quite withdrawn person who attempts to maintain isolation from other human beings. He conforms very well to the ordinary rituals and seems to have a desire to please. He eats well, he shaves himself every day, and he dresses appropriately, but he avoids people. His isolated attitude becomes somewhat grotesque in that he will pretend to read without sufficient light or with the book upside down in order to avoid conversing with others. With some of the personnel his conversation is in a jocular form but without any real feeling. There's a certain teasing element in the relationship. He has a hunched-over posture as if he's trying to crawl into a shell. He doesn't smile or laugh or become angry, and his eyes remain cast down. His conversation is about sports and he does follow the sports page in the newspaper and knows a great deal about the details of baseball affairs.

Apparently large groups of people, conversation within the group, and noise create a confusion in him. He gradually was able to assert himself to some degree in that he admitted his dislike for the hospital food and began to eat downstairs in the canteen, and he has a choice of television programs. He is shy and doesn't make friends easily. Overt violence and aggressivity apparently disturb him a great deal.

This is a patient whose relationships and behavior outwardly toward people are quite bland, and he does not appear to be either anxious or depressed nor does he overtly express anger or annoyance. He simply isolates himself and has a kind of bland communication but mostly withdraws from contact with people. One could hardly ascribe any affect to him. There are no apparent hallucinations or delusions, and one can only consider him as having a defect in his total affective system in that he is unable to relate himself meaningfully to any other human being, except father.

Summary

Patients in Group III are isolated and withdrawn without even negative affect or behavior. They await cues from others and attempt to relate by assuming complementary roles. In this maneuver they constitute "as if" characters who behave as expected and often appear to be involved. Yet their role vacillations depend on the other person to whom they facilely adapt. This is how they live in a world in which they feel no personal identity.

GROUP IV: THE BORDER WITH THE NEUROSES

In our laboratory we have studied a group of adult male patients who were hospitalized on a state hospital ward for chronic patients. They were erroneously considered to be suffering from chronic depressions (Oken et al., 1960).

The depression which constituted the major symptomatic complaint of these subjects had a characteristic quality. Little deep sadness was evident. In place of a sense of heartfelt sorrow and misery of the sort which stirs an empathic response, these men communicated a dull dejection and bland loneliness and hopelessness; they seemed defeated, discouraged, and cowed, apathetically accepting their state. There was little in the way of spontaneous self-remonstrance or abnegation. Rather, they were free in blaming their manifest failures or lack of "breaks," maltreatment, and misfortune; they "never had a chance." Their own part in their difficulties was minimized, rationalized away, or blandly glossed over in a very facile manner. Only when pressed in this particular area did they show any sign of tension or anxiety, losing some of their composed resignation and becoming irritable and whining. Here, too, their response took the form of evasion and denial. They took no firm stand in their own defense; mobilized aggression was weak and diffuse. Shifts of mood occurred readily in response to changes about them. They were quite responsive to a display of interest or concern. But this, too, was devoid of force or enthusiasm. The general picture was one of resignation, *lack of involvement*, and marked passivity.

The anamnestic data were very much in keeping with these findings. All these men gave evidence of long-standing markedly limited adjustment, frequently traceable back to early childhood. The typical pattern was of a moderately stable adjustment with restricted function in a relatively protected environment, usually involving a relationship with an older woman. The relationship then broke up (or the situation somehow changed), leading to the necessity for a new adjustment. Of the six men who had married, only one was living with his wife at this time, and he gave a history of a previous divorce. In six of the group the precipitating factor was clearly the loss of the key relationship. Rarely was this break initiated by the man himself. When it was, it followed upon his becoming unable finally to bear remarkably intense and long-standing abuse and exploitation. Whatever the precipitant, the new adjustment called for never could be made. A passive deterioration of function ensued. Jobs became less frequent and less skilled, and finances deteriorated. Alcohol was used as a periodic balm but there were few true binges. Overt homosexual activity sporadically occurred in many, but without enthusiasm or the development of any continuing relationship. Often this was used as a device for obtaining money.

During the latter period some symptoms appeared, chiefly in the form of depression with suicidal thoughts (but uncommon attempts), feelings of hopelessness and confusion. Any frustration called for a response of avoidance, denial, withdrawal, and flight, or when these were impossible, passive-aggressive acceptance. Solace was obtained by mutual sympathy from those similarly afflicted. Daydream fantasy was frequently used. This was of a simple wish-fulfillment type, in which they saw themselves with their troubles at an end without any intermediate steps or efforts on their part. Exacerbations, associated with periods of diminished gratification, led to deepened depression, irritability, more-or-less developed ideas of reference and also some anxiety which at times was represented as fears of going crazy or "something terrible happening to me." During such periods hospitalization was readily sought and usually resulted in rapid improvement. But there was no great urge for discharge; they had "found a home." When release was arranged they "dragged their feet" but then accepted it passively, adding it to their list of injustices. It was difficult to make a diagnosis in almost every one of these cases.

Case 6 (Nurse's Report)

This female patient spends most of her time with Mrs. S. She may be sitting with someone else at dinner, or watching TV with someone else; but she does spend the majority of her time with Mrs. S. I was curious as to how she was going to handle this after the patient meeting. Was she still going to stick with Mrs. S. or seek other patients? Today I noticed she is still spending the same amount of time with Mrs. S. that she did before. This morning she and Mrs. S. were laughing outside the office. Mrs. S. was laughing, scolding her for not stealing some bacon off the breakfast tray for her. Mrs. S. didn't come out for breakfast because she had her robe on and didn't want to get dressed. All the patient could say was, "I forgot. I forgot." The patient's reaction was one of real passiveness. She did seem angry and disgusted—she looked at me and rolled her eyes, like, "Oh, me . . . ," but she couldn't express it. She doesn't seem to object to anything that I can recall on the ward. I noticed they were watching TV. She was watching a story or something Sunday afternoon. She got up to go to her room, and when she came back the fellows had changed it to the baseball game. One of them said, "Oh, I didn't realize you were watching the story you left. We could turn it back on. I just wanted to see how the game is going." She said, "No. You watch it. That's all right. I'll watch anything." I thought she would have been interested in the story because she had been watching it for about a half-hour. I know in the evenings when they vote on the programs they are going to watch she doesn't want anything special—whatever the group wants. When she eats lunch she always eats with Mrs. S. They sit at the same table across from each other in almost the same chairs every day. She looks depressed to me sometimes, but not when you are talking to her and when she's with somebody. If you happen to find her by herself, maybe watching television, she isn't really watching all the time. She does look depressed then. On the outside someone might just think she's being thoughtful. I can't think of any incident where she has initiated something. She sits there with the group and she will talk, but nothing really spontaneous occurs. I think she is well accepted by the group. She's very nice to everybody. If someone is out of cigarettes and she's going downstairs, she will offer to get them for you. From how I've seen her act with the group, I think she adapts to the situation. When she's questioned she'll voice what she has to say. She isn't aggressive to the point of initiating anything though. She spends time mostly in the dayroom. She isn't in her room too much. Her affect is always appropriate. I've never really seen her upset. When you approach her she quite readily becomes very friendly. She goes to the gym and plays well. She goes on the patio.

I feel that I don't get through to her because she just won't let me. I sense a definite need for dependency relationships, not in her relationship to me necessarily but in her relationship to this other female patient. This need for dependency still seems pretty evident perhaps because if you push her—make her feel that she's needed or wanted at a certain time—she will come. When she didn't attend the baking group last Thursday, for instance, I'm sure if I'd waited until she'd combed her hair, she would have come.

"There are a lot of people that I like, but I can't say that I love them." She was also trying to point out to Mrs. S. that everybody isn't alike. They seem to seek each other out, but they can't stand each other for long.

Comment

The outstanding characteristic in the behavior of this patient is her clinging, and need for a dependent relationship. This is demonstrated in her relations with another female patient. Otherwise the patient is adaptive and unobtrusive. Outstanding, in contrast with her needs, is her inability to love any other person or to maintain interpersonal contact for long.

Summary

Group IV patients are frequently misdiagnosed as depressives because they attach themselves to others and react with whining, crying sadness when their dependent needs are not satisfied. Thus they reveal more overt seemingly positive affect than any other borderline patients. Yet they still lack a consistent identity and have no capacity to give to others. Their clinging is not object-focused but satisfaction-oriented because they have little capacity to love.

The six patients presented in this chapter, observed and described in different settings, clearly belong within the borderline syndrome as derived from our investigations. More than that, the vignettes demonstrate the fact that between-group differences are clear enough so that the clinician can diagnose the subcategories of the borderline. The sharpness of these differences permits a specific diagnosis from history and anamnesis without the necessity of long periods of observation or depth interviews. The recognition of a patient's membership in a particular group of the borderline may in the future have practical value even if now not apparent. At any rate, the classification opens a vast area of research for possible biological, psychological and sociological correlations.

CHAPTER **8** The Family
Background

THE TREND TOWARD FAMILY STUDIES

Since psychoanalytic theory demonstrated its heuristic value and psychoanalysis or some of its modifications became the American therapeutic method of choice in psychiatry, at least until recently, the focus of interest in etiology has been on deviance from the supposedly healthy path of development according to theoretical time-specific phases. This is the so-called genetic frame of reference. Experiences in early life focused especially on the mother-child relations to the point where some rejecting mothers were called "schizophrenogenic" and "Momism" was a perverted term publicly applied to a maternal attitude of overindulgence.

During the last decade, as a result of the pragmatic appeal for psychiatrists to do more for more people, community psychiatry has become a popular public health concept, group therapy is widely practiced, and focus on the individual is decreasing. In addition on sound theoretical grounds a few pioneers concerned with etiology began to study the families of psychiatric patients (Ackerman, 1958). With some exceptions these began with investigations of families in which one offspring was schizophrenic. According to Wynne and Singer (1963): "These studies have suggested that intrafamilial communication and relationship patterns can be linked in considerable detail to forms of personality organization, including styles of thinking, in offsprings who have grown up in these families."

The role of the family in furthering the development of the child is summarized by Goldfarb (1955) who states that the presence of family rewards and gratification are the source of the child's social emotions. Deprivation of sensory and emotional stimuli is the precursor of psychopathology. To quote a summarizing statement of Lidz, Fleck and Cornelison (1965):

> Man's biological make-up requires that he grow up in a family or a reasonable substitute for it, not simply for protection and nurturance during his immaturity but in order to assimilate the techniques he needs for adaptation and survival. It requires that he grow into and internalize the institutions and instrumentalities of structured social systems as well as identify with persons who themselves have assimilated the culture. He acquires characteristics through identification but also by reactions to parental objects and through finding reciprocal roles with them. His integration is guided, in part, by the dynamic structure of the family in which he grows up, which channels his drives and guides into proper gender and generation roles, and provides a space relatively free from role conflict in which the immature child can develop and feel secure. His appreciation of the worth and meaning of both social roles and institutions is affected by the manner in which his parents fill their roles, relate maritally, and behave in other institutional contexts.

THEORIES ON FAMILY PATHOLOGY

Mischler and Waxler (1966) have recently written an analytic essay on the theories of family interactional processes and schizophrenia proposed by the three groups headed by Bateson, Lidz and Wynne. In brief the Bateson group proposes a theory based on processes of communication, including the famous "double bind." Bateson states, however, that this is really not a theory but more like a new language. Lidz deals with content of interactions among members of the family according to psychoanalytic theory. For example, the male schizophrenic evolves from a dominant mother ("skewed" pattern) and the female from a seductive father ("schism" pattern), and the entire family is seen as pathological.

Wynne uses sociological theory viewing the family as a unit whose roles are ambiguously structured under a façade of "pseudo-mutuality" and isolated from the extended social environment by "rubber fence" protective devices. These theories are in agreement that the family structure is a mode of defense, and that the schizophrenic member is a scapegoat whose illness is necessary for the family's stability.

In spite of defects in each of these theories, they focus on the family as a unit implicated in etiology, and are fruitful for the derivation of hypotheses that can be empirically assessed. In his discussion of the review Spiegel (1966) expresses our own views in somewhat different language. He states: "Little progress in theory-building can take place without better articulation of the paradigmatic models among themselves." This we have discussed under the title of Systems in Chapter 10.

THE BORDERLINE FAMILY

Few references to the specific characteristics of the borderline family can be found in the literature. Singer and Wynne (1966) state:

> Those patients who, in the global, over-all ratings are classified as borderline schizophrenics have not been clearly psychotically disorganized, but may have a questionable history of a transient psychotic episode, and on examination may show similarities to schizophrenics in their styles of thinking. However, even when they are temporarily quite nebulous or fragmented in their thinking, when one follows these patients in the sequences of their thoughts and actions over a period of time, they are seen to "recover" point and meaning. Their thinking seems disjunctive only when observed in isolated portions of behavior. On over-all view— crucial to adequate evaluation—there is evidenced both to these patients, themselves, and to observers, an underlying connectedness and coherent, meaningful pattern in their thinking and in their lives. Such persons may be highly conflicted, disturbed, and disturbing, but they are not basically schizophrenic.

Singer and Wynne have some evidence:

> Suggesting that clear-thinking fathers can reduce the impact of even very disturbing mothers. Sometimes the contribution of the less disturbed parent is not an active one, but rather a passive collusion and acquiescence with the style of the more disturbing parent.

Wolberg (1952), without specifying the number of her cases or the methods she used in her study, states that the borderline comes from a disorganized family. The mother is unable to plan and to conceive a functioning social unit for which she is responsible; or she thinks of her current family according to the culture and society of her own past. As a result the patient has no stable relations to any family member except accidentally to a member of the extended family. He finds the outside culture different and confusing. Wolberg classifies the mothers of the borderline patients as (1) obsessive, (2) narcissistic-masculine, (3) paranoid, and (4) passive-schizoid. Thus they may repudiate femininity, desert family responsibility for a career (the child becomes an obstructive monster), communicate distrust of the hostile world, or just "not be there" but withdrawn from the child into fantasy.

Beck's (1964) studies of the families of his six schizophrenics contrasted careful interviews by psychiatrists and social workers of the parents of sick children against similar interviews with parents of neurotic and healthy children as controls. From the 106 traits which he utilized, four categories each with three modes were used in the analyses. The parental attitudes elicited included rejecting, attacking, coercing, indifference and coldness. The parents of schizophrenic children showed considerable psychopathology with symptoms similar to their children. In general he states that the family as a unit moved a lot, was unstable, and that the father was weak and the mother dominant. Since this was really not a study of the family unit per se such as Wynne and Singer (1963) published, but of the parents, it was not unexpected that the families of neurotic children were not much different. On the other hand, the families of healthy children were not at all similar. These parents were ambitious for their children, often coercing, but they placed great emphasis on achievement which they rewarded.

There are other references to the families of the borderline patient in many individual case reports but they were not systematically studied. There seems to be no doubt that the family of the borderline is unhealthy but how specifically does it differ from the schizophrenic family or any other type is not known. Furthermore, many clinicians think that when they describe the mother or father they are focusing on the family. In truth, the family is a system which should be studied as a unit greater than its component parental parts (Zuk and Nagy, 1967).

THE FAMILIES OF THE RESEARCH PATIENTS

Our purpose in conducting this limited investgiation of the families of our research patients was to describe in some manner their functioning as families, in other words, as a social system. The main question for investigation was, "At what level does the family function as a system over time?" It was our premise that the major functional task of the family—the nuturant care and enculturation or socialization of children —is a time-limited process. The family must maintain its integration through its allotted life-span. When the children are adults they should be ready to distribute themselves into new families, which initiates a process of disintegration of the family of origin.

The question of how the family functions were divided into four parts:

1. How does the family function in relation to the patient's illness and hospitalization as a family crisis?
2. How does the family maintain its integration?
3. How does the family resist the natural process of disintegration?
4. How does the family function in relation to other systems, for example, the community and the larger social system?

A *check list* of 69 family traits was organized in relation to questions 2, 3, and 4, and *narrative statements* were required for question 1. The major source material for completing the check list and the narrative statements was the record of information obtained in the course of usual practice by the social workers assigned to the Nursing Unit on which this study was conducted. A social evaluation of the patient and service to families are prime responsibilities of the ISPI Social Work Department. The department uses a standard format for recording the social evaluation. Included in the outline are: (1) the worker's assessment of the informant, usually a member of the family, which covers how the informant views the patient's problems and hospitalization and his attitude toward the patient and the illness; (2) background information which is basically a descriptive picture of the patient as he developed within his unique social, economic and cultural setting, covering the patient's pertinent experiences within the family and broader environment and the nature of interpersonal relations within the family. Supporting data from the psychiatric resident's summary were also used. We did not use any family data reported only by the patient. The data used were provided by one or more family members (cf. Appendixes X and XI).

A psychiatric social worker on the staff of the Department of Social Work who had never worked on the unit on which this research was conducted completed the check lists for 47 families of origin of the sample of 51 patients; additionally separate check lists were completed for the few nuclear families of which the patient was a spouse in the sample. The worker had had no contact with the patients in the sample or with any other aspect of the research. Information about the family of origin was not available for four patients (two patients born illegitimately had no families, and two other families lived far from Chicago so that social service had no contact with them). The social worker was trained to use the check list by filling it out for 15 patients who were not in the sample of 51. She and one of the authors (B.W.) independently checked the lists for the 15 patients and compared and discussed the results. For the core sample the check list was filled out only by this one part-time staff worker, who had been trained to use the check list; further, the worker was required to write a brief statement of evidence, a sentence or two for every check representing the presence of a trait. This procedure insured that the factual basis for every check had been given consideration and thought.

FAMILY FUNCTIONING IN RELATION TO THE PATIENT'S HOSPITALIZATION

On entry into the hospital, more than half (27) of the patients (single, never married) had been living with their families of origin. Both parents were present in the majority of these homes; however, some patients (11) did come from homes where one parent, usually the father, was absent. Thirteen patients entered the hospital from intact nuclear families (either a husband or a wife was the patient), and a few patients came from broken nuclear-family homes. The remainder, including several separated or divorced and several single, never married, were living independently in the community. The heads of families were primarily in occupations classified as clerical, craftsman, operative and service, and a few were receiving public assistance.

The family's functioning in relation to the patient's illness and hospitalization was described by three variables: (1) the family's involvement on behalf of the patient, for example, keeping appointments, providing patient with needed articles such as clothes, and planning for discharge; (2) the family's attitude toward hospitalization; (3) the relevance of the patient's illness to the family.

Since these questions were not precategorized but answered narratively, all of the categories being reported were derived from the data itself. Although family involvement on behalf of the patient ranged from minimal or none to intense, most frequently some member of the family, usually the mother and/or spouse, cooperated with the social worker on behalf of the patient.

TABLE 16. *Family Cooperation on Behalf of the Patient*

	Total 47	Per Cent 100.0
1. Minimal or no family involvement	15	31.9
2. Family cooperated on behalf of patient	20	42.6
3. Family member cooperated on behalf of self	2	4.2
4. Family involved	10	21.3

The attitude of the family toward the patient's hospitalization was rarely indifferent. The family responded in one of five ways (see Table 17). There is a qualitative difference between categories 4 and 5— category 4 implies acceptance of the fact of illness and hospitalization without much understanding of the illness and the need for hospital care.

TABLE 17. *Attitudes of the Family toward the Patient's Hospitalization*

	Total 47	Per Cent 100.0
1. Family indifferent	2	4.2
2. Denial of illness and need for care	12	25.5
3. Discomfort or anger	9	19.1
4. Acceptance of the fact without understanding of the need	7	14.9
5. Perceived patient behavior and need	17	36.3

Half the families tended not to connect the patient's illness to any factor. Some attributed the illness to a variety of people or forces other than themselves; a few attributed the illness to their behavior; usually this kind of attribution was made by mothers who blamed their own past behaviors or child-rearing practices.

TABLE 18. *Family Theory of Etiology*

	Total 47	Per Cent 100.0
1. No connection made between illness or any factor	23	49.0
2. Attribution to people other than self or external forces	15	31.9
3. Some connection between patient's illness and self	9	19.1

The question of how the family functioned in relation to the patient's illness and hospitalization can be described only for the group as a whole, since none of the three measurements of the family's functioning in relation to the patient's hospitalization were associated with the patient groups. All of the categories were found scattered among all the patient groups.

On the whole, these families displayed a range of functioning in relation to the patient's illness. It would be unwise to infer levels of family pathology from these descriptive categories since there is no single desirable standard of family functioning in relation to the mental illness of the family member, except that some family involvement and access to family are generally considered desirable.

FAMILY TYPES

The original check list of 69 traits minus a list of 29 was used to cluster the data for 47 families of origin. Traits were deleted for reason of infrequency of occurrence (five or fewer) in the group as a whole. On this basis all traits dealing with the question of how the family functions in relation to other social systems were discarded.

The 40 remaining traits were analyzed by a clustering program designed to handle dichotomous data developed at the New York Scientific Center of IBM by Jerrold Rubin (1965, Chapter 5). The criterion function which is used to measure the structure of a grouping of the data is based on a similarity coefficient, which is a measure of the number of matches between two subjects on the traits under study. The presence of a trait for both of a given pair of subjects is a match, and the absence of a trait for the same two subjects is also a match. Hence both the presence and absence of traits enter into the measure of structure.

The 40 traits resulted in six family clusters (families of origin) present among the four patient groups as shown in Table 19.

TABLE 19. *Family Type and Patient Group*

Family Type			Patient Group			
			I	*II*	*III*	*IV*	*Total*
		Total	*17*	*10*	*13*	*7*	*47*
I			4	6	9	—	19
II			3	—	3	—	6
III			6	—	—	3	9
IV	Residue		3	2	—	2	7
V	Residue		—	1	1	2	4
VI	Residue		1	1	—	—	2

Type I families were found more frequently among Group II and III patients than among Group I and IV patients. There is no one kind of family associated with one kind of patient group. Family types I, II and III are different from each other and from the 47 families as a whole.

Clusters IV, V and VI should be considered residues. The small clusters V and VI separated out as misfits with any of the others. Cluster IV was unique in that it was primarily formed by the nonoccurrence of the traits under study. This cluster of families matched each other, with one exception, on the absence of the traits studied. The one exception was the presence of overdevotion on the part of the father. This result is of interest since the patients whose families were in this cluster were females (5 of 7).

Family Type I—19 Members

This group of families clustered on the presence of a set of traits which describe the pathological way the family maintained its integration. The occurrence of the traits shown in Table 20 was more frequent among this group of 19 families than among the remainder of the sample.

TABLE 20. *Family Type I*

	Frequencies		
	Type I	Total	
Trait	$N = 19$	$N = 47$	*Chi-square**
1 Marriage is highly discordant	18	30	11.04
7 Family relationships marked by chronic overt conflict or competition	17	28	9.85
9 Family is not a mutually protective unit	19	25	24.24
15 Outright rejection of parenthood or excessive conflict over parenthood	16	27	7.60
25 Mother-child relationships are problematic	15	28	3.71
37 Quality of mother's affect was predominantly negative	7	7	9.39
47 In general, communication may be characterized as confused	12	19	5.35

* *Adjusted by Yates' correction.*

Here and for the remainder of the discussion of family types the chi-square is presented to give the reader an index to the difference in the proportion of the trait present in the specific family type compared with the proportion of the trait present in the remainder of the sample. For example, the proportion of trait 9, "Family is not a mutually protective unit," present for type I was 19/19 compared with 6/28 for the remainder of the sample. The P values usually associated with the chi-square test of significance are not shown, since to show them would be misleading. The P values usually associated with the chi-square assumes under the null hypothesis that the groups were random samples from the same population. The groups produced by the clustering procedure were not selected at random but according to a criterion that maximized the difference between them (Chapter 5).

As trait 9, "Family is not a mutually protective unit," was present for all 19 families of this type, it serves as an anchor point of description of type I families in contrast with the other family types. The other traits on which family type I clustered are consistent with trait 9 as the anchor point: discord, conflict, role rejection and confusion. The nonoccurrence of traits also contributes to clustering; type I families also matched on the absence of traits that describe any resistance to the process of family disintegration which, we will now see, characterized type II families.

Family Type II—6 Members

This group of families clustered on the presence of a set of traits that describe how the families resist the natural process of disintegration, a polar opposite kind of pathology from type I families. Trait 10, "Family is excessively protective," was present for all six members of family type II, in contrast to the anchor trait for family type I. The remainder of the traits for family type II consistently describe the smothering, suffocating static family. The occurrence of the traits shown in Table 21 was more frequent among this group of six families than among the remainder of the sample, and they were not found at all in type I.

TABLE 21. *Family Type II*

| | | Frequencies | |
| | Type II | Total | |
Trait	N = 6	N = 47	Chi-square*
5 Parents and/or spouses are deficient in achieving reciprocal role relationships	5	16	5.14
10 Family is excessively protective	6	17	9.18
39 The quality of the mother's affect was overdevotion	6	14	12.59
45 Contact among family members is excessive and intrusive, very involved	6	24	4.54
50 The family has not set eventual separation of parent and child as a goal	6	13	14.08
52 Static state of the family is due to self-interest of one of the parents	6	16	10.17
54 Static state of the family is due to overinvolvement with children	6	17	9.18
57 Self-identity of children has been submerged by the family	6	14	12.59

*Adjusted by Yates' correction.

All six of the patients whose families are described by family type II were unattached males. We found in follow-up that none of the six were ever married, a testimonial to the resistance of the families to disintegration.

Type III—9 Members

Type III families are described by a few traits that occur more frequently for them as a group than for any others. The anchor point of contrast with types I and II is trait 8, "Family life marked by denial of problems." These families are also characterized by the absence of discordant marriages and the dominance of extremes of parental affect;

TABLE 22. *Family Type III*

Trait	Frequencies Type III N = 9	Total N = 47	Chi-square*
8 Family life marked by denial of problems	6	9	12.66
35 The quality of the mother's affect was mixed	7	18	5.42
36 The quality of the father's affect was mixed	7	20	4.01
57 Self-identity of children has been submerged by the family	6	14	5.22

* *Adjusted by Yates' correction.*

there were no checks for either parent of overdevotion or predominantly negative affect. The absence of these traits is consistent with the denial of problems and the presence of mixed affect, defined as the existence of both positive and negative affect with neither one nor the other being dominant.

In conclusion, it is possible to say that our sample of borderline patients came from three varying types of pathological families, differentiated from each other but unassociated significantly with the four patient groups.

NUCLEAR FAMILIES

Data were available for 20 nuclear families, 16 of whom had children. Traits are presented in Table 23 for the 16 families that had children of their own. Over one-half of the patients from the 16 nuclear families came from type I families of origin. None came from type II families of origin, since none of the patients from type II families of origin were ever a party to a nuclear family. It thus comes as no surprise that the traits in Table 23 more closely resemble the profile of type I families, marked by the trait, "Family is not a mutually protective unit." The nuclear families were predominantly marked by discord and conflict, the hallmarks of type I families.

TABLE 23. *Sixteen Nuclear Families with Children*

Trait	NUMBER
1 Marriage is highly discordant	14
7 Family relationships marked by chronic overt conflict or competition	13
15 Outright rejection of parenthood or excessive conflict over parenthood; family does not provide adequate nurturant care for children	12
37 The quality of the wife's and/or mother's affect and emotionality in this family may be characterized as predominantly negative	12
3 Partners unable to achieve a mutuality of purpose in major areas of living; conflicting demands remain unresolved	10
9 Family is not a mutually protective unit	10
38 The quality of the husband's and/or father's affect and emotionality in this family may be characterized as predominantly negative	10
2 Partners engage in mutual devaluation and criticism	8
5 Partners and/or spouses are deficient in achieving reciprocal role relationships	5

It can be seen clearly that, in addition to the fact that more than half of our patients on admission had never married, 16 of the remaining patients who had married and had had children experienced great difficulty in achieving a satisfactory union. Even more important than the discordant marriage and the overt conflict between spouses was the negative attitude toward children when they existed. In other words, the borderline marries infrequently and when he does he is an inadequate spouse and a poor parent.

DISCUSSION

It is apparent that the family's functioning in relation to the patient's hospitalization (question 1) was not specific for the borderline or, for that matter, any mental or physical illness. The family was sometimes involved and sometimes not. The highest per cent cooperated on behalf of the patient. Some denied the patient's illness and need for care; others perceived the patient's needs. Few families connected the patient's illness with the behavior of a member of the family; most made no connection between the illness and any internal factor and attributed the fault to others or external forces.

Forty of the available traits were utilized to discriminate family types which were then arranged in frequency of appearance in the four patient groups described in Chapter 6. Family type I occurred most frequently in patient Groups II and III. The traits of family type I indicate that the family is not an integrated protective unit; overt conflict and discord were present, the mother's affect was negative and there was outright rejection of the children. The patient Groups II and III were respectively the "core borderline" and the "adaptive, defensive" patients. The two groups stemming from this family type are sufficiently differentiated from each other so that the family type cannot predict the type of borderline patient, just as the family's functioning is not specific for the borderline altogether.

Nevertheless the family types I, II and III are clearly differentiated. Type II is static (resistive to healthy abandonment of control), dominant and generally intrusive. Although patients stemming from this type did not belong to a specific patient group, all were males and never married. Clearly they preferred to remain attached to their family of origin probably held by the family's domination and intrusiveness.

Family type III was characterized by denial and mixed parental affects. The patients from this type were in greatest number among Group I, the sickest and closest to psychotic.

It must be emphasized that the study of the family was an afterthought, not included in our original design. We neither interviewed the family directly nor observed the family interaction with the patient. Therefore we were dependent on data derived from routine psychiatric social workers' observations. The data available were adequately rated and statistically analyzed. Significant differences isolated three family groups, but none was specific for a patient group nor were the family functions and attitudes specific for the syndrome. We cannot, therefore, utilize family data from which to draw etiological conclusions except to state that all the families were "sick," which is no surprise in view of the sickness in at least one of its progeny. Furthermore, as spouses and parents in their own nuclear families, the patients carried on the deviant behavior.

As Fleck (1966) has stated, we would wish to relate specific family constellations to specific psychiatric entities—in this case the borderline —but this is not possible with our present concepts and methods applicable to family functions. If as Birdwhistell (1966) states, culture communicates information and devices for coding messages around a central theme, direction and order, then we as yet do not know the code.

9 The Follow-up Study

PURPOSES

Clinical investigations are incomplete when they are limited to the observations and descriptions of symptoms, behaviors or functions at one time. The natural history of disease is important, and the longitudinal course and outcome of any diagnostic entity are necessary data for a comprehensive clinical study. In our own design we obtained descriptions of our patients' behaviors about two weeks after admission and later when discharge from the hospital was imminent. The data obtained from observers of this second period were not much different from the first period and rarely (only eight cases) required re-rating despite the fact that these patients could be returned to their communities. The median length of stay in the hospital for our study patients was 5 months, the range 2 to 9.5 months.

After our primary study had been completed we therefore decided to follow our patients and ascertain their subsequent status. The observations of patient behavior had required 2.5 years (July, 1961, to December, 1963). The follow-up study was conducted between February and September of 1965. The time that elapsed between the patient's discharge and our follow-up varied from 1.0 to 3.5 years. The median length of time between discharge and follow-up was 2.5 years.

Another reason for the follow-up study involved our curiosity regarding the effect of treatment during hospitalization. The treatment program can be described as belonging to the vague and indefinable category of "milieu therapy." This defines a warm and accepting climate, yet structured by limits. It is a demonstration of reality-oriented behavior on the part of the staff. There are weekly activity, action and planning meetings, many informal patient groups, formal group therapy involving 4 to 8 patients at a time, and a "bridge group" preparing patients for reentry into the community. In addition, individual therapy is administered by psychiatric residents under supervision.

At the time that the staff reported patient behavior they were specifically interrogated about the future of the study patients. "Will he make it?" The basis for prognosis used by the staff and the director of the unit is the same and holds for patients of all types. If the patient can talk about his feelings and problems, look honestly at his own behavior, and survey the resources available to him, the prognosis is better. If he does not involve himself in the milieu program but instead engages in denial of his problems and withdraws, the prognosis is poor.

The chief, Dr. Reid, predicted that, as a result of the regime utilized on this ward, most of the borderline will not be rehospitalized, at least not soon, and that only a relatively small number of borderlines were untouched by the therapy. Whatever was achieved by the treatment, it can probably only be attributed to some effect from the milieu and the emotional climate of the ward. We could not ascribe much positive results to the brief individual therapy applied by inexperienced students. Neither can we consider that the regime was planned or directed specifically for the borderline.

Fortunately within our rating procedures we had included a separate short-form labeled "Synthesis" (Appendix VI). One item on this form was predictive in that it required a rating of the patient's "capacity to carry on usual life processes" on a four-point scale. This was not a dynamic prediction based on situational social or personal variances. We could not predict on the basis of "if this occurs" or "if that person does." Certainly all predictions of therapeutic results are contingent upon future happenings in real-life situations, and the normally expectable rarely occurs. Our predictions were global and based on the "state" of the patient as known to us through his behavior during our study.

The final reason for the follow-up study was to determine whether the outcome differentiated the groups in the criterion sample of patients and in the sample of patients who dropped out. Thus we followed the 51 criterion patients who had remained in the hospital on the open research nursing unit for the time required to obtain two observational periods. We also undertook to follow the 17 patients who were lost to the study due to transfer, elopement, discharge against medical advice, or whose behavior required the use of large doses of tranquillizing drugs.

METHOD

Our first approach to the study subjects was a letter which the director of the hospital wrote on official hospital stationery indicating our interest in how they were doing and suggesting that an appointment be made by telephone with a part-time assistant assigned to interview the subjects. When subjects did not respond to the letter in a reasonable time, we attempted to establish contact with them by telephoning for an appointment. Not more than six letters were mailed at one time to avoid long-time lags between the initial letter and our follow-up telephone call. Dealing with a small number at a time facilitated the objective of reaching subjects and flexibly setting appointments.

Some of the study subjects were readily available since they were continuing therapy in the out-patient clinic. Of the 44 subjects that we located, the majority (23) responded to the letter sent by the director and graciously made an appointment to come to ISPI to be interviewed by the psychiatric social worker. Five interviews were held in homes of the subjects. Since several lived outside of Chicago, six were interviewed by telephone and one communicated by letter. Two subjects were located in hospitals, one was visited in jail, and finally the psychiatrists attending five of the subjects were interviewed in lieu of the subjects themselves. Only three of the subjects ever mentioned that they thought that our contact was concerned with a research objective. All three had been college students. We are certain that when the behavior of the patients was being observed and reported in the hospital, they did not know that they were study subjects.

We obtained data on 44 of the 51 patients in our criterion group, 41 of whom were living in the community at the time of follow-up. The

TABLE 24. *Status of Patients at Follow-up*

Status at Date of Follow-up	Number of Patients				Per Cent in Other Studies Brown-Kosterlitz*
	Males	Females	Total	Per Cent	
TOTAL	28	23	51	100	100
Living in community	23	18	41	80	66
Living in mental institution	1	1	2	4	11
In jail	1	—	1	2	—
Unknown	3	4	7	14	21
Died in community	—	—	—	—	1
Died in state hospital	—	—	—	—	1

* Data from study conducted by Julia Brown and Nancy Kosterlitz, "The Social Adjustment of Psychiatric Patients Following Treatment in a Therapeutic Milieu," N = 76. (Publication pending.)

seven subjects for whom we do not have follow-up data had moved and could not be traced by any means known to us. We attempted to find out if these seven differed in any way from the others. Actually two fell in each of Group I and III, three in Group II and none in Group IV; thus they virtually occupied almost the whole range of the borderline.

One patient who had been paranoid and megalomaniac with an underlying depression had returned to his native land in Europe. Another continued her depressed, angry and impulse-ridden behavior with alcoholism, drug addiction and wrist-scratching suicidal gestures while under the care of a private psychiatrist. She had to be hospitalized several times, and on return to her new home in another city again entered a psychiatric hospital. The protocols of the other five patients were restudied for differences. Without going into detail we can summarize by stating that to greater or lesser degrees they fit into the borderline syndrome. In addition, this small group of seven displayed no social characteristics that differed markedly from the group as a whole.

Our principle data which were derived from a factual picture of the social functioning of each subject were obtained by means of a semi-structured interview conducted by a psychiatric social worker. The interviewer completed the schedule immediately following the interview; when necessary she took notes. The interview was geared to the instrument (Appendix XII) which the interviewer had memorized, but the interview was free enough to encourage the subject to say what he could about his social functioning. As a result, the interviewer recorded considerable information in discursive sentences which added much to our knowledge of the subject's functioning, feelings and behavior. The factual information elicited was internally consistent. The semistructured interview has the advantage of eliciting data systematically but freely enough to provide an integrated picture. The interviewer was instructed to conduct a research interview and not to offer advice, or attempt to provide help or referral. Interviews took about one hour.

In addition to the interview, records of the central files of the Illinois Department of Mental Health were cleared to ascertain the subsequent state hospital history of the subjects. The nine patients who had subsequent state hospital experience, according to the central files, also reported these hospitalizations to the interviewer.

We defined social functioning, the major content of our follow-up, as the individual's adaptation to his responsibilities and his relationships with people. We did not attempt to assess the extent of psychopathology at follow-up. Social functioning was the information sought on the assumption that the recovery level of the former psychiatric patient is reflected by the adequacy of his social adjustment. The follow-up interviews investigated, not only the current functioning of subjects, but also the course of their experiences between discharge and follow-up and the major modifications that took place with reference to living arrangements, use of leisure time, relations to family, friends and coworkers, marital status, children, employment, education, post-ISPI psychiatric care. We attempted to tap not only the factual picture of social functioning but also the subjects' satisfaction with their own functioning.

POST-HOSPITAL PERFORMANCE

Post-Hospital Psychiatric Care

A major goal of the staff of a psychiatric hospital is to enable patients to leave the hospital and remain in the community at a level of occupational and social performance that is comparable to that of other adults in the community. Consistent with these goals are the two criteria used by Freeman and Simmons (1963) in a detailed study of the post-hospital experience of discharged mental patients.

The first criterion is the ability of the former patient to avoid rehospitalization. Of our 41 subjects in the community at the time of follow-up, 13 had had a post-ISPI hospital experience of 14 days or more; the median subsequent hospital stay was 2.5 months. However, only about one of six patients was rehospitalized within one year after discharge from ISPI; the remainder of the rehospitalized patients (6 of the 13) had been in the community more than a year before their entry into the hospital again. The majority of the subsequent stays were at Chicago State

TABLE 25. *Success and Failure in Remaining in the Community Post-ISPI Hospitalization*

	Male	Female	Total	Per Cent
TOTAL	*23*	*18*	*41*	*100.0*
Succeeded in remaining in community	16	12	28	68.3
Failed to remain in community	7	6	13	31.7

Hospital. Our ratio of one rehospitalization within one year out of every six subjects compares favorably with the ratio of a little over one of three reported by Freeman and Simmons for patients who had non-organic psychotic disorders.

Five of the thirteen rehospitalized patients in our study had also had psychiatric hospital experience prior to ISPI. For these, "in and out" of the hospital may have become the way of life. Ten of the twenty-eight who remained in the community post-ISPI had had prior psychiatric

TABLE 26. *Post-ISPI Psychiatric Care*

	Number	Per Cent
TOTAL	*41*	*100*
Out-patient care only	17	41
ISPI–OPD	10	
Michael Reese Clinic	5	
Private psychiatrists	2	
Hospitalization	13*	32
No post-ISPI care	11	27

* *Seven were hospitalized within one year after discharge from ISPI.*

hospital experience. Seventeen of the twenty-eight had post-ISPI out-patient psychiatric care ranging in duration from less than six months to more than two years; 11 had no post-ISPI psychiatric care at all.

Perhaps more important than the ability to stay out of the hospital is a second criterion—the former patient's performance as a community member. Residence in the community and participation in its activities are accorded high value in our society. Adequate occupational and social performance is at least one of the ways that the healthy and sick are differentiated. Well people work and sick people must work to become well.

Occupational Adjustments

The role most generally expected of adults in our society is probably instrumental performance with reference to work. For adult men this usually means regular employment in a gainful occupation, and for adult women either gainful employment or responsible management of homemaking activities.

The extent to which our subjects fulfilled their social roles occupationally was measured by a five-point work-performance scale modified from Adler (1955). A score of five was assigned to the best performance and a score of one was assigned to those who were not able to work at all. Fifty-four per cent of the 41 found in the community on follow-up were performing occupationally at the two top levels.

TABLE 27. *Work Regularity between Discharge and Follow-up*
(*Classified on a 5-Point Scale*)

	Male	Female	Total	Per Cent
TOTAL	*23*	*18*	*41*	*100*
Score				
5 Regularly employed, regularly attending school, or both employment and school attendance (if housewife), managed household alone	11	8	19	47
Frequent job change				
4 Without substantial periods of unemployment	3	—	3	7
3 With substantial periods of unemployment	5	4	9	22
2 Employed occasionally	1	4	5	12
1 Employed not at all	3	2	5	12

At the time of their admission to ISPI less than one-third of the patients were employed in white-collar occupations and had at least completed high school. Most performed in occupational roles that required limited interaction with people and limited initiative. From admission to follow-up there were no changes in the general level of their educational and occupational status and consequently in the amount of interaction and initiative required of them in their work.

Educationally these patients were predominantly a group of school drop-outs. Thirty-seven per cent had entered but not completed college; 29 per cent had entered but not completed high school. At follow-up four were attending night school with the aim of getting a college degree. At follow-up the median age of the males was about 25 years; the females 30 years. All in all movement upward occupationally could not be expected of these people. Although gainfully employed and largely self-sufficient economically, the facts suggest that the group was occupationally and academically static at a fairly low level.

Social Participation

A five-point scale based on the one originated by Adler (1955) was used to measure social participation. On this scale, we measured the use of leisure time and the extent of contact with friends and people other than the family with whom the patient lived. We were forced to use only this dimension, since there was no evidence that these patients participated in voluntary associations or the activities of the larger community.

TABLE 28. *Social Participation of Former Patients Based on Use of Leisure Time and Contact with People*

	Male	Female	Total	Per Cent
Total in Community	23	18	41	100
Score				
5 Very active social life involving much contact with people	2	4	6	15
4 Active social life involving contact with people	1	—	1	2
3 Leisure-time activities limited, involving transient contact with people	8	7	15	36
2 No leisure-time activities, evidence of minimal social contact with people	4	2	6	15
1 No leisure-time activities, no friends, and no evidence of social contact with people	8	5	13	32

Our findings suggest gross deficiencies in their use of leisure time and in their social relations. Only 17 per cent were found at the two upper levels. The modal group is described by limited leisure-time activities involving transient contact with people. At the two lower points on the scale the patients live in virtual isolation. One can only conclude from these results that the strong emphasis in the milieu therapy program on developing skills in interpersonal relations did not carry over into the community lives of these subjects. But more than half of the total group (24) had had transient post-ISPI contact with their former fellow patients; few sustained contact with former patients over time. There was no evidence of deep and abiding relationships formed from the ISPI experience. One can infer that social participation constitutes a more problematic area of adjustment for this group than occupation, since there is no involvement in formal social activities and very little in informal social activities.

Family Relations

Males and females of the same age at the time of follow-up differed significantly with respect to marital status. Less than 30 per cent of the females but 70 per cent of the males had never married. Although the marital status of males and females differed significantly within our group, the incidence of single, never married, of both sexes in our group is higher than in the general population of the *same age* in the Chicago area (according to the 1960 census). That relatively fewer psychiatric patients have ever married is not surprising; it is a fact commonly found in studies of psychiatric patients.

TABLE 29. *Marital Status at Follow-up*

	Male	Female	Total
TOTAL	23	18	41
Ever Married	7	13	20*
Married to same spouse as during hospital stay	3	1	4
Married since discharge	—	3	3
Remarried since discharge	—	3	3
Divorced prior to hospital stay	—	2	2
Divorced since discharge	1	2	3
Separated	3	2	5
Single, Never Married	16†	5†	21

* *Of the seven subjects not found on follow-up, four (2 males and 2 females) had been married and three had never been married up to the time of hospital admission.*
† *Chi-square adjusted by Yates' correction = 5.48, P < .02.*

The majority of the subjects were living in a family setting, defined as a household, containing either a parent, spouse, child or cousin. The unattached males predominantly lived with their parents and the females

TABLE 30. *Living Arrangements at Follow-up of 41 Patients Living in the Community*

Living Arrangements	Number of Patients Male	Female	Total	Per Cent
TOTAL	23	18	41	100
With family	18	14	32	78
With one or both parents	14	3	17	
With spouse	3	7	10	
With children	—	3	3	
Other	1	1	2	
Alone	5	4	9	22

with spouse and/or children. Only nine of the total group were living alone. But between discharge and follow-up, the group had not necessarily been residentially stable. Some of the single males tried to live alone in various places before settling down with their parents.

Relations to family were coded on two bases: (1) how well the subject claimed he was getting along with spouse, children and/or parents; (2) the emotional strains the subject experienced in getting along.

TABLE 31. *Family Adjustment Scores*

	Male	Female	Total	Per Cent
TOTAL	23	18	41	100
Scores				
5 Gets along well with central family figures; more comfortable with a formerly conflictual relation	1	5	6	15
4 Gets along with central family figures but expressed some emotional strain	6	2	8	19
3 Managing to get along; emotional strain present but not serious	5	2	7	17
2 Expressed serious reservation about relations with central family figures	5	1	6	15
1 Does not get along, isolated, little or no contact	6	8	14	34

Nearly one-half of the subjects experienced serious reservations about their relations to central family figures or were isolated from their families. The unattached males tended to gravitate toward their parental homes which may account for the frequency of the claims that they were getting along or were managing to get along with their families without serious strain. The stresses of living with parents had to be tolerated, or they would have been forced to adopt another way of life.

We have considered the subject's post-hospital performance from three vantage points: (1) his occupational adjustment, (2) his social participation and (3) his family relations. We will summarize the results by comparing the means of the three measures. When we tested the hypothesis that the mean scores of the three measures were equal, we found that they were not alike (analysis of variance, $P < 0.01$). The difference was clearly accounted for by the higher mean for occupational adjustment compared with social participation and family relations. However, those who scored low on occupational adjustment also tended to score low on the other two dimensions, but those who scored high on occupational adjustment did not necessarily score high on social participation and family relations. In identifying occupational adjustment as the performance strength of these patients, we should be reminded of the static occupational status of the group at a relatively young age.

Subject's Estimate of His Psychological Health

We asked the subject about his view of his psychological health. If he claimed to feel better since discharge, we asked him to specify the improvements, if worse, to describe the setbacks. In this manner we obtained the pros and cons of the subject's self-assessment of his psychological condition.

TABLE 32. *Patient's Assessment of His Psychological State*

	Male	Female	Total	Per Cent
TOTAL	*23*	*18*	*41*	*100*
Score				
3 Feels well; expressed improvement	2	4	6	15
2 Feels better; expressed qualifications	4	4	8	19
1 Feels some change, but considerable qualification	12	2	14	34
0 Feels no change or worse	5	8	13	32

The subjects were modest and seldom described an unqualified state of well-being. Sixty-six per cent expressed considerable qualification or claimed they were no better or even worse. If we take the subject's assessment of his psychological condition as given, we can conclude that self-perception is an ego-strength of these people. Few of them claimed either the use of drugs (6) or excessive use of alcohol (4); only one subject reported smoking marihuana. It is surprising in view of their conservative estimates of their psychological well-being that relatively few were resorting to drugs and alcohol.

When males and females giving themselves low estimates on their psychological condition are compared with respect to work performance, as expected the males differ significantly from the females in the direction of a higher level of performance (chi-square, exact probability, $P < .05$). In this respect the males strive to perform the culturally assigned role in spite of their subjective complaints.

None of the performance measures—occupational adjustment, social participation, family relations or estimate of psychological health—differed by patient group or family type.

Overall Assessment Scores

In addition to coding the three discrete performance levels and the patient's psychological self-estimate, we also scored the status of each patient on four major dimensions, which include the previously described performance levels, but in categories that are more broadly defined (modified from Hunt and Kogan, 1950).

1. *Environmental circumstances:* This category includes living situation and attitudes and behavior of other people toward the patient.
2. *Adaptive efficiency:* This category includes leisure-time activities, ability to get along with other people (marital partner, children, parents, friends, coworkers, employers), employment, efficiency in running a home, acquisition of new skills, education and evidence of overt competence in any area.
3. *Attitudes and understanding:* This category includes attitudes toward self and others, attitude toward accepting help (for example, therapy), understanding of relation between present behavior and feelings and events in the past, and patient's goals. This category also includes understanding and attitude toward hospitalization, the hospital experience, and hospital friends, and response to being approached by ISPI follow-up investigator.
4. *Disabling habits and conditions:* This category includes psychological and physical health, social conflict and use of drugs and alcohol.

The senior author of the project coded each dimension on a scale that ranged from -1 through $+4$. The zero point meant that the subject's status was no better than being hospitalized; the minus point meant that the patient appeared to be deteriorated; the positive points represented an ascending order of functioning. The sum of the four was taken to represent a total follow-up score for each patient. The minimum total score possible was -4, and the maximum was $+16$.

The three discrete performance levels and the subject's psychological self-estimate were coded independently by a different coder. The sum of the four codes was also taken to represent a total follow-up score. The means of the two sets of scores arrived at differently and independently with the use of the same basic data were compared. There was no significant difference in the means of the two sets of follow-up scores.

One of the major purposes of doing the follow-up study was to determine if the groups were differentiated at follow-up. To examine this question the sum of the scores of the four broadly defined dimensions was related to the four patient groups. Table 33 shows the mean follow-up score by patient groups and a comparison of the means.

TABLE 33. *Mean Follow-up Scores by Patient Groups and Comparisons between Groups*

Patient Groups	Number	Mean Follow-up Scores	Comparisons between Groups			
	44*				*t* Values	Exact Proba-
I	16*	9.44	Groups	d.f.†	Obtained	bilities
II	9	9.33	I and III	26	1.698	0.05
III	12	12.92	II and III	19	1.632	0.06
IV	7	9.57	IV and III	17	1.227	0.11

* *Includes the three subjects not living in the community.*
† *Degrees of freedom.*

Since the follow-up data are data that were not used for clustering, rather than a test of the null hypothesis, the *t* levels are viewed as an index of some differentiation between groups in relation to the mean follow-up scores (total overall assessment scores) as an external criterion. A *t* value that exceeds the 10 per cent level offers some evidence of group differentiation in relation to the mean follow-up score as an external criterion. Group III patients, who were the most adaptive in the hospital, appeared to maintain their adaptive behavior in the community according to our follow-up scores. Yet it is not clear from these studies whether each group warrants specific types of therapeutic interventions, especially since there is within-group variability.

RELATION OF PREDICTIONS TO FOLLOW-UP

As mentioned early in this chapter, we obtained a set of separate concluding summary ratings on every patient, labeled "Synthesis" (Appendix VI). One of the questions on the form was an assessment of the patient's capacity for problem-solving assessed along five dimensions:

1. Delays action appropriately in pursuit of solutions to problems.
2. Weighs and selects among the demands of social pressures and influences.
3. Applies his thoughts to a problem.
4. Foresees consequences of decisions and actions.
5. Chooses realistically among alternative courses of action.

A second question was stated as a prediction: "To what degree is the patient able to carry on his usual life processes?" The ratings on these two questions—"problem solving capacity" and "capacity to carry on usual life processes"—were assessed by the senior author on the basis of the protocols of the behavior of the patients observed during their hospital stay. Ratings were made on a four-point scale, ranging zero, low, moderate, and high. When the predictive ratings were related to the total overall assessment scores, it was found that the mean follow-up scores for those who were rated zero and low and those rated moderate and high on capacity to carry on usual life processes differed significantly in the expected direction (one-sided t test, $P < .05$). We may conclude that the predictions were supported by the follow-up.

THE DROPOUT SAMPLE

Seventeen patients were dropped from our study sample when we were unable to obtain a second observational period for several reasons. We

TABLE 34. *Reasons for 17 Dropouts*

TOTAL	*17*
Transferred to closed unit	3
Discharged	
Against medical advice	5
By resident without advice	2
Eloped	5
Signed 30-day release	1
On drugs	1

attempted to follow these 17 patients but were unable to find more than 7. The others had moved, leaving no forwarding address. Forty per cent of the dropouts were successfully followed, as contrasted with 86 per cent of the criterion subjects who thus responded twice as frequently. This fact in itself is a differentiating characteristic of the two samples.

Dropouts Not Located

It seemed important to restudy the protocols of the 10 dropouts who were not located on follow-up to establish the clinical diagnosis. Only one was a borderline patient according to our investigations. He could not maintain affectionate relations which he craved; he did not trust people. He was sarcastic, angry and depressed and made a suicidal attempt on the ward because life was so difficult without close contacts. The others were typical schizophrenics, reactive depressions and psychopathic personalities.

Successful Follow-up of Dropout Group

Seven patients who were dropped out of the final sample were found and interviewed. There were three schizophrenics, one post-partum psychotic, one hysterical psychotic, one impulse-ridden hysteric and one agitated depressive.

SUMMARY

The follow-up study provided data which enlarge and amplify our picture of the borderline as a diagnostic entity. The follow-up as an external criterion provides at least moderate evidence of patient group differentiation. With one exception the patients (17) dropped from our criterion sample did not belong to the borderline category. Any improvement in one way or another in our research sample at follow-up was not associated with improved adaptation to the community or better skill in interpersonal relations. Milieu therapy did not carry over strongly into the lives of these patients in the community. They remained socially awkward.

10 Etiology

The explanation for any syndrome or disease of man is no longer even apparently simple. As medicine has extended its understanding of the multitudinous factors involved in health and illness only rarely do we encounter statements implicating single causes, even for infectious diseases.

Nevertheless "schools" of psychiatry will implicitly approach problems of etiology from narrow frames of reference or ideologies and perpetuate useless controversy. Strauss et al. (1964) have observed that clinical psychiatrists can be classified as somaticists, psychotherapists and sociotherapists who view patients' problems and prepare solutions in accordance with their personal ideologies. In contrast to these practice models, *investigators* have been increasingly involved in multidisciplinary research recognizing that explanations for functions and dysfunctions must be multifactorial.

We may be able to grasp the range of possible causes of the borderline better if we first focus on the functions that are disturbed and ask to what degree are various possible etiological factors contributory. To be specific we recapitulate the general characteristics of the syndrome as follows:

1. Anger toward a variety of targets.
2. Defect in affectional relationships.
3. Deficient sense of identity.
4. Depression usually experienced as loneliness.

The first obvious question concerns the relation of these disturbances to each other. Are they separate and independent dysfunctions or do they interact? Secondly, to what degree are constitutional defects responsible? Thirdly, if the borderline syndrome represents a developmental defect, what deficiencies or traumata are involved and when is the critical period at which these hypothetical pathogenic forces act?

THE INTERACTIONS

What is the relation or interaction between two fundamental traits of the borderline—anger and the incapacity to achieve or the inconsistency in maintaining affectional relations? Perhaps anger is a reaction against early deprivation. Or perhaps it is primary as an hypertrophied or quantitatively exaggerated drive which leads to rejection by others.

The work of Lorenz (1963) on lower animals is most pertinent to the problem of anger. He considers that aggression is a drive which functions for the preservation of the individual and species in all animals. It cannot be bred out by eugenic planning because aggression is not only preservative of life but it is also a component of personal friendship and the basis of all productivity or creativity.

In an avowal of optimism, however, Lorenz suggests that human beings could learn to displace aggression in its primal form to substitute objects, to sublimate and to develop friendship—even concepts of friendship with all mankind. Furthermore, aggression can be channeled into art, science, ideals and humanistic causes, which are worth serving in the modern world.

In a similar vein Menninger (1963), who terms the ego the guardian of the vital balance, considers five orders or phases of dysfunction or regression. Actually these are all related to increased activity of aggression, destruction and self-destruction, and associated with weakening of ego-defenses. In the borderline the aggressive component is related to defects of ego-development rather than regression. It has long been the Menninger preachment that only love can neutralize aggression. Likewise all religions include prayers for more love of one's fellow man.

Unfortunately these directions, which include displacement, sublimation, neutralization of aggression with libido and expanded ego-ideals, according to psychoanalytic theory are impossible without sufficient quantities of libido. In common-sense terms the lack of sufficient amount and constancy of affection prevents the control of aggression.

Some types of borderlines, however, do attempt to shield themselves from situations that provoke anger. It is likely that the search for a mother figure (Group IV patients) who is remembered as rejecting evokes anxiety, not only because of the expected danger, but also because closeness serves as a signal that this is a situation in which large quantities of anger will be aroused. Furthermore, the transient psychotic ego-disintegrations may be caused by an overwhelming anger which exceeds the ego's capacity for binding.

We have no good evidence to qualify the early mother-child dyad. To speculate about various forms of deprivation is not good enough. All we can say is that an adequate affectional system has probably not developed in the earliest years. Borderline patients have little or no capacity for object-relations, object-constancy, or transference capacities. They often search for objects but quickly withdraw or assume complementarity or demand dependent gratification. But they give little or nothing in the form of affection.

Patients in Group IV sought out peers; one or another was equally satisfactory, or they could replace another within a matter of moments. In this search there was no anxiety, only rage at slights or rejection. When, however, they searched for maternal objects in an anaclitic depression to avoid "starvation," they were extremely anxious as if the closer they moved toward a maternal object the more they were invading enemy territory.

In the hospital these patients correspondingly had wide mood swings within a few minutes. Their dependency could be described as voracious gobbling with abrupt cessation. It seemed as if their defenses were directed toward achieving interpersonal distance. In fact they tolerated failure more easily than closeness.

The deficient *sense of identity* seems to be a natural corollary of the two characteristics we have just mentioned, excessive anger and deficient love. The capacity to identify with another human being is dependent upon affectional, albeit somewhat ambivalent, relations with others. The memory images of external objects with whom the developing child transacts are integrated internally to become deposited in a repertoire of roles available for future adaptation in a wide range of situations (Grinker, 1957). The borderline apparently is successful only in achieving primary identification evidenced in his complementary relations.

Depressions of two types are observable. In Group IV depression was the anaclitic type, initiating an anxious search for a mother figure. Except for these subjects in Group IV the frequently occurring depression was in actuality loneliness. Frieda Fromm-Reichman (1959) ascribes this to a childhood taboo on tenderness, an early separation from mother resulting in a love-shy child who fears intimacy. Later, reality-testing is not adequately taught. Loneliness is a secret feeling, difficult to communicate, and it is terrifying. It is not like depression which accompanies preoccupations with relationship to others and with characteristic defenses. It is so frightening that patients must have contact even while hating the human beings to whom they cling.

We can now speculate on the movement of borderline patients in Group II toward and away from others and the transient psychoses. Separation from others results in loneliness and depression too painful to endure for long. Movement toward others ensues with mounting fear and rage which, if excessive, results in temporary confusion until distance is again achieved. The back-and-forth movement may persist—"anger when close, loneliness when distant." Adaptation and fixation in one position may ensue especially in Group III. Group I patients are too angry; Group IV patients are still hopeful that a symbiotic relationship is available. Patients in Group III give up all identity and peaceably try to be like the others—"as if." In a depth study (case 3, Chapter 7) early life indicated frustration and rejection from both parents (it may be possible that in some cases the father is imagined to be a duplicate of the unmotherly mother by displacement). Nevertheless this patient had access to each parent temporarily before rejection was experienced. Her life was a back-and-forth existence typical of patients in Group II.

An attempt at answering these crucial interactional questions has been unsuccessful. Important, not only for diagnosis and prognosis, but also for prevention and rehabilitation they have taken us far away from our own raw data. In fact to determine the meaning of the borderline syndromes we must also make inferences from subtle cues and extrapolations from experiments or observations on infrahuman animals in addition to clinical studies. In a sense, then, we are moving away from scientific statements and more toward philosophy. We see no objection to this shift in thinking as long as it is clearly stated that its purpose is to develop hypotheses.

CONSTITUTIONAL FACTORS

Attributing causal significance to constitutional factors is often used as an escape hatch when nothing else is available to blame. In the prepsychodynamic era of psychiatry constitution was blamed for almost every psychiatric entity, from psychopathic personality (constitutional inferiority) to schizophrenia. Today studies of constitution and the genic components of disease are becoming increasingly scientific after lying fallow for decades. As yet only studies on schizophrenics among the major psychiatric clinical entities have yielded suggestive results.

Yet there are constitutional differences in infants observable at birth, particularly in motoric behavior, degrees of awareness or apathy, irritability and capacities to nurse adequately. In a speculative formulation with no evidence Kernberg (1967) states that the borderline has a constitutional lack of adequate primary autonomy, low tolerance for anxiety and excessive development of agressive drives.

At some clinical centers what corresponds to the borderline is diagnosed as "anhedonia." This certainly describes the painful quality of loneliness and the incapacity to enjoy human relations. The modern neurophysiologists who have found "pleasure centers" in the brains of experimental animals could very well hypothesize a constitutional defect in the borderline patients' neural apparatus for experiencing pleasure.

CHILDHOOD EXPERIENCES

Only few child psychiatrists have described their patients as borderline and then verbally only with a brief sketch of a single case. It is understandable that observers of disturbed children in diagnostic interviews or in the process of treatment are less concerned with formal classification which often cannot be accomplished until the subsequent course is known. Only recently has a classification been proposed for psychopathological disorders in childhood (Pavenstedt, 1964). It does not include the borderline syndrome.

Pavenstedt (1964) describes the behavior of children with damaged egos who hunger for fantasied mothers to give them love. Pavenstedt watched how these children in a "skid-row" seek attention but then give a superficial response as if they were not separate individuals. They are obedient and have little direct expression of anger and avoid conflict. They have difficulty in coming to grips with reality. They function as extensions of mother or teacher and have little self-regard. Their mothers do not anticipate or guard against accidents, but in fact encourage the children to hurt themselves. Similarily Knowlton and Burg (1955) conclude from detailed studies of borderline children that their mothers have been guilty of "errors of omission" in mothering.

Several investigators have studied children who have been in traumatic situations in an effort to determine the possible effects in later life. None of these experiences, however, according to the available follow-up data was causal to the development of a borderline state.

Erikson (1963) has divided development into eight phases: Basic trust vs. mistrust, autonomy vs. shame and doubt, initiative vs. guilt, industry vs. inferiority, identity vs. role confusion, intimacy vs. isolation, generativity vs. stagnation and ego integrity vs. despair. Only two apply to the clinical characteristics of the borderline who (1) have role confusion and lack of identity evidenced clearly in adolescence, and (2) are isolates and lack the capacity for intimacy or affiliation and love, revealed when the adult role should have been attained.

Erikson's epigenetic stages are conceived as parts of a general system of development:

> Each successive stage and crisis has a special relation to one of the basic elements of society, and this for the simple reason that the human life-cycle and man's institutions have evolved together. . . . We can do little more than mention, after the description of each stage, what basic element of social organization is related to it. This relationship is twofold: man brings to these institutions the remnants of his infantile mentality and his youthful fervor, and he received from them—as long as they manage to maintain their actuality—a reinforcement of his infantile gains.

Do then the causal factors related to the development of the borderline syndrome reside in failures during adolescence and in the first attempts at intimacy thereby crushing further development? Or do they revolve about failures in earlier phases during which basic trust or confidence does not develop because of the poor quality of maternal administration of nutriment or love? We have no clinical evidence for this differentiation.

On the other hand, there have been sufficient reports indicating that the borderline syndrome appears frequently in childhood. When described, their behaviors are similar to that seen in our sample of adult patients. In sum this evidence indicates that the borderline syndrome even though not overt begins in early childhood.

How far anterior or how early the preparation is not clear. These questions are difficult to answer from our data derived by observations on behavior. They are likewise unanswerable at present by the use of any other method including psychoanalytic depth studies of intrapsychic processes or reconstructions of past experiences. Anamnestic data of early child-rearing practices impinging on the infant disclose only the general statements of deficient mothering and disturbed families.

Either before hospitalization or after discharge some of our patients seemed to cling to their families. Characteristically the family of type II as a child-rearing system did not disintegrate when the children became adults. The attraction was bilateral in that the family wanted the patient to return and reached out its octopus arms for him. On the other hand, very frequently no matter if advised to leave the family and live separately and even if arrangements were made for this goal the patients seemed pulled home by the magnetic attraction of the family. There the back and forth search and retreat resumed their monotonous cycles. Some females fared better if they had married or could remarry a husband who served as a less dangerous maternal figure.

PSYCHOANALYTIC RECONSTRUCTIONS

In our overview of the literature in Chapter 2 many reports by psychoanalysts referred to facets of early childhood experiences in etiological speculations. We cannot designate these as scientific reports nor were they based on systematic studies. It is not necessary to repeat again that most speculations about meaning of psychoanalytic data are not hypotheses about causes.

Greenson (1955) attributes a defect in the development of basic ego-functions in the borderline to a disturbance in early object-relations and early identifications. These dysfunctions are most likely due to very early traumata, especially massive sexual overstimulation in the first year of life, in flooding of the ego with excitation and an inability to postpone discharge. In contrast to this specific hypothesis other psychoanalysts have made general statements about the causes of a variety of neuroses and psychoses; among these are parental, physical, or mental illness and death, or broken homes. More generally they have used the all-inclusive phrases: "internal or external trauma" in infancy or "lack of early pleasurable experiences" leading to fixation on the "alimentary axis."

Gitelson (1958) has presented the psychoanalysis of an adult borderline case in great detail, describing the ego-defect as a distortion which holds at bay the patient's overwhelming instincts. Through a variety of neurotic and psychotic devices he manages to escape a breakdown. Gitelson's conclusions about the etiology of the borderline are as follows:

Outstandingly, the patient whom I described, and other such patients, have encountered unusual stress in relation to their original objects, particularly the mother. The consequences are seen in pregenital disturbances in the economy of libido and aggression, in defective superego development, and in compensatory internal and external adjustive and adaptive accommodations of ego functions.

The mother as the center of the infant's earliest environment plays a crucial role in the sucessful development of the ego. Therefore, the significant historical determinant of the borderline psychopathology is sought in disturbed mother-child relationships. The relationship may be traumatic for many reasons. There may be a limited amount or a complete lack of spontaneous affection from the ambivalent or rejecting mother. The intrusive, overprotective, possessive, or seductive mother hinders separation and differentiation. All these, but especially the destructive mother, produce intense rage that is inhibited by the fear of annihilation or by threats to the child's need for closeness. Thus, the borderline child is supposedly deprived, unloved, kept dependent, exposed to excessive sexual stimulation, or consistently threatened, beaten, humiliated, etc.

Margaret Little (1966) contends that there is not enough differentiation between id and ego in the borderline but enough to avoid psychosis. As a result of early negation the patient cannot take survival for granted and fears annihilation. The ego is patchy, uneven and unreliable as a whole even though there are some adequate ego-nuclei. Searles (1966) is more conservative when he considers identity as a threat to mother-child symbiotic relationship fought against by both partners. Mutual murderous feelings (ambivalence) maintains identity diffusion.

In 1957 Grinker wrote:

> I have observed several so-called 'borderline' cases as they became temporarily psychotic and then gradually became re-integrated. The psychosis usually developed abruptly with very little warning. Then they behaved like angry and frightened undomesticated animals indulging in cannibalistic and soiling behaviour. Gratifications in lying curled up, in being dirty and unresponsive except to their own fantasies were accompanied by infantile fears of a strange confusing world. As this behaviour was abandoned and the patients seemed more adult—they dressed, ate naturally, maintained cleanliness and responded verbally—they identified the surrounding patients, nurses and physicians as actors who played parts corresponding to their most painful memories and only occasionally to some pleasant ones. Despite the actual kind and understanding roles of the nurses and doctors, they were constantly misinterpreted so that a 'corrective emotional experience' was ineffective. This is the most important

point I wish to make here: that such a patient cannot understand a good human environment because his earliest transactions have imprinted 'badness' on him which is constantly in flux with those outside of him. Bad self cannot understand a good not-self until stronger boundaries are reconstituted and illusions accepted. Thus even after a psychotic regression, primary identifications usually remain immutable.

In Chapter 2 we cited Kernberg's (1967) suggestion that the ego of the borderline patient is split which may be the result of pathology of internalized objects. His psychoanalytic reasoning can be summarized as below:

1. Gratification and moderate frustration gives rise to differentiation of self-images from objects. Too much gratification retards differentiation. Excessive frustration results in repression of self and object-images.
2. The good and bad images based on affectional and aggressive drives undergo a process of integration.
3. The borderline, however, has a constitutional lack of adequate primary autonomy, low tolerance for anxiety, excessive development of aggressive drives, and experiences a reality producing an excess of frustration.
4. Although the borderline as contrasted with the schizophrenic has differentiated ego-boundaries and good reality-testing, he cannot synthesize positive and negative introjects and identifications. As a result the ego splits to preserve the good self- and object-images and the external good objects from the bad.
5. The ego-splitting weakens the ego's other functions as does the failure of neutralization of aggression. Both reinforce each other.
6. The results are as follows, indicating dysfunctions and defenses: abrupt reversal of feelings about others and the self, sometimes primitive overidealization of others, primitive forms of projection of identification and aggression, denial of emotional linkages between two vacillating states; submission to idealized external objects covering over grandiose, omnipotent, oral greed but no real love, no real depression with feelings of guilt or regret—rather feelings of defeat and impotent rage at projected superego; paranoid distortions create images of dangerous mother and father—hence both sexes are dangerous. As a result of lack of sexual identity, pathological condensations between pregenital and genital drives lead to polymorphous sexual perversions.

Kernberg's hypothetical statements "explain" the borderline's deficient image of self and identity diffusion, lack of depth in emotional relations, but otherwise firm ego-boundaries. In a sense, then, Kernberg's dynamic reconstructions correspond to what is observable in our behavioral studies. Yet whether we view the constellation of symptoms from within or without, the causes and mechanisms are not yet clearly elucidated.

We have certainly not exhausted the possible frames of reference from which to view the etiology of the borderline. Unfortunately little empirical data could be accumulated or correlations made with reference to an ill-defined concept as contrasted with a well-defined syndrome. Recently exciting new insights are being achieved from viewing mentation as a system of information processing which may suggest explanations for dissociation in the borderline, disturbances in affectional relationships, control of anger and the preservation of secondary-process logical thinking except under unusual conditions.

Barnett (1966 and 1967) has considered that knowing or cognition, concerned with meaning, constitutes a vast interdigitating continuum or field extending from sensory to linguistically structural experiences continually expanding and developing. Character is, then, a behavioral and cognitive reflection of durable organization of experiences in an individual's life. Take, for example, the devastating effect of early social deprivation or early infantile diseases. These may lead to internalized traits called character, leading to suspiciousness of others and inability to trust, which cannot be extinguished in later life. Barnett attempts to differentiate certain psychiatric categories with reference to the cognitive continuum. Thus, in hysteria and impulse disorders there is an "explosion of affect" before integration can occur. Internalization or "implosion of affect" disorganizes cognition, keeps informational data inside, contains affect and binds syntax as in obsessives and depressives. From this point of view the borderline extends over the continuum in that some groups "explode" whereas other "implode."

There seems to be no doubt that human learning extends beyond the primary identifications or mimicry of other animals. Human beings can use secondary identifications or internalization as a more complicated higher form of learning. In addition according to Shands (personal communication) humans not only behave like all animals but in addition they can describe their behaviors to others and to themselves. They can adapt under conditions of deprivation or trauma by internalizing or withdrawing. Only if they are relatively tolerant of anxiety are they able to learn.

From these relatively new forms of scientific thinking we may view the borderline apart from drives, motivations or internal conflicts as a defect in cognition based on developmental disturbances in the processing of information.

PSYCHOPHYSIOLOGICAL STUDIES

Many clinical conclusions infer that maternal behaviors or attitudes impinge on the developing child to influence its subsequent character, personality and health. Reconstructions are heavily one-sided, leaning on the recovered memories of adult or child. As a result we have had the "schizophrenogenic mother" as a stereotype. Often we are informed that the mother was cold, frustrating, hostile, rejecting, or that the father was weak and dependent. For these conclusions there is little evidence. In any case no one has explained how these so-called causes have produced their effects. It could be expected that such early severe stress on the maturing infant should also influence physiological symptoms and facilitate so-called psychosomatic disorders.

Grinker (1953) stated:

> The central core of the psychosomatic problem is the period of differentiation from total hereditary to individual learned patterns and their integration into a new personal system . . . the intermediate process of development between the undifferentiated whole functional pattern and the integrated matured process.

Greenberg (1957) and his colleagues embarked on a program of research to develop methods with which to study maternal personality and behavior in relation to infant behavior. He utilized a variety of physiological recordings under natural conditions of mother-infant behaviors during change (feeding, holding, rocking) in healthy pairs and in foundling-home infants. This is an on-going complicated multivariate system of observations with serious problems of data analysis. His purpose is to identify variables in maternal behavior that are pathogenic, variables in infants representing early forms of atypical behavior, and to determine how each set relates to each other. Follow-up studies can then specify the type of later psychopathology related to the form and content of maternal-infant transactions. As yet these studies are still in process. From them we may be able to specify, for example, in the borderline case what actually are the sources of damage to the ego-functions.

In stress interviews of borderline patients in our own laboratory, responses occurred only to threats of dissolution of their central defensive system. Once this had been accomplished and denial was no longer possible they responded with elevated heart rate and blood pressure, and increased plasma adrenocorticoid excretion. All responses occurred later, were less intense and lasted for shorter periods of time than in the acutely anxious or anxiety-prone. The threat of discharge from hospital to the "outside world" in these patients stirred more anger than anxiety or depression (Oken et al., 1960). Parenthetically, these middle-aged men remained chronically disabled for decades but were not biologically "burned out." We relate this fact because our current research sample contained patients so much younger and their long-term course could not be determined.

Since we had previously studied the response of acutely ill psychiatric patients in a similar stimulus, data were available for comparison. The responses of the borderline subjects were distinctive in that they were sharply delimited to the stress-period, whereas the acutely anxious group came to the situation already somewhat aroused and manifested a response which persisted beyond the stress stimulus. The focal nature of the observed response is quite compatible with the characteristic of the defensive structure described. Apparently there is no interference with the capacity to respond but rather an extraordinarily efficient exclusion of stimuli which might excite response. This hyperconstricted type of defensive organization represents an opposite pole of the too open and overgeneralized responses of the anxious group.

ANIMAL EXPERIMENTATION

There is now a vast literature derived from studies on early experiences of experimental animals which seem to confirm the concept that deficiencies during critical periods of development have profound and lasting effects in behavior. On the one hand, Levine (1956, 1957) has shown that early handling of infantile rats results in more rapid psychophysiological maturation and greater emotional stability. On the other hand, early maternal deprivation of rats has produced characteristic long-range deleterious effects on adult behavior.

Probably the most important experimental work applicable to our study of the causes of the borderline syndrome has been carried out by Harlow (1962, 1966) over many years. He has divided the affectional systems in their order of development, although there is considerable overlapping into five phases:

1. Infant to mother.
2. Infant to infant, age-mates, peers.

3. Sexual-heterosexual.
4. Mother to infant.
5. Paternal.

Harlow has studied the development of monkeys under varying experimental conditions from infancy to sexual maturity and has described the various stages of dependency of infant on mother ultimately leading to separation. The security of a real mother as against that of a surrogate (terry-cloth) mother facilitates the infant's ability to explore the physical world and the social world of its peers. The age-mate or peer affectional system of interactive play is followed by aggressive play which decreases gradually in adolescence and adult life. An absent mother and/or social deprivation greatly impairs the age-mate social interaction depending on the age at which the deprivation occurs and its duration. Serious behavioral deviancies resulted from surrogate mother experiences. Adequate peer-group experiences only partially made up the deficiencies in socialization. Both normal mothering and infant-infant socialization interact in a segmental manner and are necessary for adequate socialization, heterosexuality and parenthood in adult life. Not only is the subsequent heterosexual stage not reached, but artificially impregnated monkeys who fail to develop affectional systems in the first year of life are ineffective, inadequate and brutal mothers. They reject, kick and crush their offsprings.

Harlow (1962) states:

> I believe that the concept of multiple affectional systems can help us in understanding emotional problems. It can free us from a compulsion to trace all neurotic and psychiatric behavior back to infancy. It can also free us from the necessity of explaining all emotional ills as originating in psychosexual maladjustment. In my view, psychosexual maladjustment can be a result, not a cause, of affectional maldevelopment in nonsexual systems. That psychoanalytic theory is correct in tracing many ills to parental relationships in infancy and early childhood cannot be challenged. That individuals can become fixated in their psychosexual development at infantile and childish levels also cannot be challenged. I would ask especially that psychoanalysis look with unbiased eyes to the affectional relationships that develop between peers, for in the peer affectional system as I conceive it I believe lie the origins of many emotional problems that come to the analyst's couch.

To summarize: We have attempted to piece together the fragments of information available to us in order to elucidate the causes of the borderline syndrome. Study of adults and children by psychoanalytic and psychiatric techniques, study of the family of origin, psychophysiological studies and animal experimentation all contribute some, but little, information. At best we are only able to hypothesize by extrapolation from research on mother- or peer-deprived monkeys who as adults have deficient affectional systems and uncontrollable aggression against their own kind. These two characteristics are specifically what we found in borderline patients.

This is not to mean that we think we have the clue to the specific cause of the borderline. Other causes may be found by other methods of investigation or empirical observations when focused on the problems of the borderline. These may range from primary genic* to cultural influences. To clarify the possible relations of such a wide variety of causative factors we turn now to more general considerations of a general systems approach to etiology.

A GENERAL SYSTEMS APPROACH TO ETIOLOGY

That many factors are involved in the ontogenesis of personality, "normality" and illness is a twentieth-century conclusion which is opposed to by several schools of psychiatry who contend they possess all the information necessary for causal explanations and therapy. Against these ideologies there has developed a reactionary interest in "unified" and global theories of human behavior sometimes called "holistic" or "biopsychosocial."

Unfortunately global theories are great abstractions so far removed from experimental and empirical data that they have no external referents and serve only as umbrellas for other subtheories. Yet they are fruitful in that they attempt to connect in some fashion the several levels of discourse characteristic of the subtheories and to bring behaviors of many types viewed by appropriate disciplines within the boundaries of real or conceptual systems.

Biological, psychological and sociological researches have progressed without much concern for each other. They seem competitive rather than in some complementary relation. Bertalanffy (1952) developed a global theory under the title of "General Systems Theory." He attempted to counteract still current concepts which considered the living organism as a summation of its parts, by calling attention to the whole. Inanimate systems were contrasted with living systems by the fact that the latter are open. They have attributes of primary action instead of reaction, are

---

* We refer to genic as a biological constitutional process primarily emanating from the function of the genes (although modifiable by the environment). The term genetic has been usurped by psychoanalytic psychology to indicate the effect of experiences and environments on the process and results of development (phenotype).

dynamic instead of static, and develop by progressive differentiation. Bertalanffy attempted to establish living "isomorphisms" and to develop principles applicable to all living systems at levels from the cell to the whole man. His system is thus a huge "complex of components in mutual interaction."

Progress in biology, psychology and sociology during the nineteenth and earlier years of the twentieth century was essential before unitary theories could be formulated. The problem is how to bring the diversity of living systems now subserved by specific disciplines under the umbrella of a unified theory and relate them to each other by means of a common language.

We need not pursue the attributes of general systems theory but we would like to view the borderline as a special system ontogenetically derived from many phases of life experiences. We attempt to formulate how the system functions in the present and the nature of its future outlook.

When we discard the concept of a single cause for the development of a particular syndrome or disturbance or disease and accept the assumption that many factors enter into the attainment of health, or conversely illness, we are confronted with the problem of their functional and temporal arrangement. Should we conceive of a linear system of causes, of levels and/or hierarchies or of a system of transacting, reverberating cause-effect-cause relations within an identified field?

There are many ways to arrange a field or a system of processes, depending on the purposes for which an analysis is made, the position of the observer or investigator and his theoretical approach. In our research we have been anchored on the behavioral side in that we have observed, described and rated actual behaviors within the social structure of a nursing unit in a mental hospital. The changing general conditions grossly consisted of admission to the unit, milieu therapy within the unit and preparation for discharge. These conditions included a wide variety of interpersonal transactions among patients and staff.

Behavior as an expression of ego-functions, the final common pathway of a wide variety of psychological processes, led us to make inferences which were anchored to the raw data of behavior and not based on preconceived biases or dynamic stereotypes. Yet we were faced by the question of how what we think is an increasingly frequent psychiatric condition developed. How did the patient get that way?

Our records contained historical information from both patient and family; we knew something about the structure and functioning of the family and our follow-up studies told us the fate of the patient after discharge. Study of the scientific literature disclosed little information directly applicable to the borderline but there are suggestions from other approaches utilizing a variety of methods.

We, therefore, decided to consider the borderline as a system composed of parts or subsystems from the frame of reference of *causal factors*. These we will enumerate and describe in the context of the methods employed and their results as far as we know them today (Grinker, 1967).

1. The Invariable Factors (General or Universal)

a. The *genic or constitutional* basis for any psychiatric syndrome is not known. True, there are suggestions that the incidence of schizophrenia is greater in monozygotic twins than in the general population. Studies on twins reared entirely separately are important to exclude the factor of a common family environment but enough of these has not yet been studied. Genic studies have not yet been made on the borderline and if so they have been done under the diagnosis of schizophrenia. For schizophrenia there are reports of deficiency in certain enzyme systems affecting brain function but again not for borderline cases.

Perhaps more valid are repeated observations on the activities of neonates indicating that there are wide variations of early motor activities (Escalona and Heider, 1959). The amount of activity, crying, or early skill at nursing and other observations that any mother can easily make indicate that infants vary greatly. These may be indications of precursors of differences in the autonomous ego-functions and strengths of the drives. The capacity to endure frustration, to displace anger, and the degree of comfort evidenced very early in life may indicate basic genic differences in drive-ego relations. These become important as the foundation for adaptation, compromise and resistance to later-life stresses. Knowing the clinical picture of the borderline syndrome we may ask: Are there genic deficiencies in quantity of libido or excesses in quantity of aggression?

b. *Society and Culture* in general are also invariable factors in that their influences affect every phase of maturation, development and function. We do not include the subcultures and relatively isolated specific social grouping which are more directly involved in specific maternal, paternal and family processes. There is very little information available on how our changing society influences the health of the growing child and what is available consists of generalities and cliches. For example,

Meerloo (1954) writes about recent "technicizing," "psychologizing" and "glamorizing" the American family. Keniston (1960) writes about the dilemmas built into American life. Langer (1964) places the responsibility on modern science which has imposed a technological civilization in which culture lags (Chapter 11).

Certainly the incidence of the borderline and severely constricted and restricted personalities seems to have increased the world over and it would be helpful if we could ascribe this phenomenon to shifts in Western culture. Whatever these may be they should be anchored to specific changes in child-rearing practices and related to specific other conditions since everyone is not affected. Why are some borderline, some not, or some schizophrenic? These influences whatever they may be are generalized and invariant. Nevertheless they like any aspect of the environment influence all the components of the system under consideration.

2. The Development Variants

We will not take these up in detail; some information concerning development of the borderline has been considered previously. In recent years a huge literature has ensued from the child development specialty, some of which is summarized by Hoch and Zubin (1955). For the psychiatrist there is still a vast gap in understanding the relationship between emotional reactions in childhood to various neurotic and psychotic disturbances in adults, or between methods or contents of child care with adult personality. We may state, however, that normal development arises from a dynamic interaction between organism and environment at every temporal stage.

Development has been studied systematically from several points of view. Gesell and Armatruda (1941), for example, have utilized a "psychomorphological" approach. Spitz (1950) has made direct observations on the child-mother unit and attempted to correlate "psychotoxic" diseases with specific maternal attitudes or defects. Separation from the mother according to Bowlby (1952) results in poor ego-development and/or depression. Fries (1937) utilized the transference relations with children for her technique. Mead (1947) correlates character and psychosomatic types with variations in culturally imposed habits of feeding and elimination in nonliterate cultures. Piaget (1951) has utilized observation, experimentation and verbal communication with the developing child. Escalona and Heider (1959) have utilized the observation and quantification of maturation to correlate with later development.

Infant-mother relationships are transactional in that both influence each other. The child needs and/or demands, so does the mother. Each has a threshold of endurance before irritability, rejection or anger ensues. The mother teaches expressive roles and requires compliance. The child teaches maternal roles and also demands compliance. Various permutations of these transactions are fundamental to subsequent ways of adapting to the human situation.

Benedek (1938, 1956) states that the prerequisite for the developmental process, which is a biological-psychological continuum, occurs from the transformation of primary narcissism (an objectless state) through the reciprocal interactions of ego-object relationship by means of learning, including work, achievement and creativity. The general pattern is (1) attention to a need-satisfying object which (2) gratifies the aim of the drive and (3) returns to the self a sense of identity. As a result confidence develops in the child as a sort of emotional shelter protecting him against fear and orienting him to his environment.

Both mother and child are receptive to each other, the mother because of her temporary regression, and in their symbiotic unity each lives in a phase of primary narcissism. But the infant eventually hatches out of his symbiosis becoming separate and individual. The return of the self fuses the object of satisfaction and the situations under which it occurred. Thus depending on the degree of satisfaction and the object's attitude toward the self the self-image becomes good, bad and somewhere in-between.

As a result in a healthy infant confidence is projected in good expectations and extends to mastery of the inanimate world. Through a series of positive feedbacks, achievements enlarge the span of personality organization, especially in the development of regulatory structures such as the ego-ideal and super-ego.

When we consider the fact that the developing child has individual constitutional needs and hence perceives special qualities of its environment which it introjects, we also touch on the problem of varying sensitivity to deprivation. As Bowlby (1958) puts it, experiences occurring at critical plastic periods of phases of development have effects different from those at later more rigid periods. Since basic needs are considered instinctual, the ethologists have been helpful in formulating scientific concepts of instincts. Tinberger (1951) has conceived of primitive social responses evoked by simple perceptive stimuli as built-in ready-made responses awaiting innate releaser mechanisms (I.R.M.). Once these responses are released, further learning occurs by association with more differentiated stimuli. Thus children, with all due reference to hereditary differences, have a readiness to respond with love relation to a parental figure.

Later experiences with peers and as members of the community's schools and churches, and experiences as adolescents, including the age-specific crises and experiences as young adults, are probably all significant in the transition to the borderline personality and syndrome. At present, however, for the borderline, or, for that matter, any psychiatric entity, we cannot indicate which are crucial.

A vast literature concerning these experiences indicates their importance as significant facilitating or destructive influences on personality. Some experiences often as crises may severely damage hard-won integration or serve as nodal points from which profound constructive changes may be derived. The borderline character or syndrome may encounter any or all of these experiences but the effects have not been studied except in retrospect.

3. The Characterological Attributes

Under this heading are various deviations not severe enough to call sickness. Yet they are often reported in retrospect by the borderline or his family once he has become a patient. These include:

1. Low self-esteem.
2. Poor affectional relationship with little consistency.
3. Relations largely complementary.
4. Confusion regarding one's identity.
5. Poor capacity to organize behavior consistently.

These personality or characterological qualities arising from the borderline system are derived from the system's attributes. They become intensified due either to inner processes at critical periods and/or environmental pressures acting on a susceptible system. They, in part or together, may be termed the life-style which characterizes attitudes which have been molded into chronic automatic personality characteristics (Shapiro, 1965).

Among the characterological aspects of the borderline personality or the overt syndrome are the defenses which constitute one aspect of their life styles. In our study withdrawal and intellectualization were most frequent. The former reduces the amount of information accepted from the world, and the latter denies the inability to respond affectively. Painful feelings of lonely voids are defended against or substituted by alcohol, drugs and transient body closeness in promiscuity. In Group I brief episodes of confusional states may be an escape from the dangerous self-destructions of rage, and in Group III adaptation and complementary —"as if"—may defend against lack of identity. The characterological phenomenology of the borderline constitutes a significant component of its clinical symptomatology.

4. The Current Behaviors

Current behaviors constitute the symptom complexes of the border-line syndrome as described in Chapter 6. These are four groups characterized by two factors each. These subjects are sick and diagnosed psychiatrically and in treatment in an institution. Yet the syndromes are not static in that through therapy or favorable life experiences they may return to the phase of borderline personality.

The qualities in general of a healthy personality consist in degrees of realistic self-esteem, good affectional relations with consistency, continued accretion of a reservoir of internalized roles, a sense of identity and a capacity to organize behavior relative to the situational requirements. These are facilitated or handicapped by inner disturbances at critical periods of environmental strains and crises acting on a susceptible system.

Probably as important or more so than capacity for a variety of social roles or plasticity within a number of rapidly changing situations is the ability to develop and maintain affectional relations with one or more other persons. For example, the sample of borderline patients we have been investigating has the ability to adapt and conform to a protective environment. Yet their capacity to form or maintain affectional relations had been damaged so that they greatly feared and avoided personal closeness.

SUMMARY

After this brief résumé we can summarize the discussion of the etiology of the borderline from the point of view of general systems theory as one of viewing the development of a syndrome. Unfortunately because of the dearth of empirical data etiological theory has little content appropriate to the problem. In the future this gap may be closed.

The undifferentiated anlage is molded by hereditary and environmental influences into a specific phenotype. Whether this anlage carries the readiness under appropriate later circumstances to become borderline, we do not know. Nor do we know this about most diseases.

The establishment of a borderline system is prepared for future trouble by the quality, quantity and relationship of its parts—the developmental variants. We have mentioned a few of these. All of dynamic psychiatry considers the mother-infant transactions as the most significant variable. We up to now have no concrete assurance for this. Nor have we been able as yet to differentiate the type of this relation for various subsequent syndromes. The same holds true for specific types of communication patterns in the family although there is growing evidence that the schizophrenic family can be identified.

The borderline personality becomes crystallized as a style of life from its system variants. What aspects of experiences with what kinds of people, or in what situations, are pure conjectures. The borderline personality may shift into the overt syndrome and become irreversible but we do not know the precipitating causes for this shift. Favorable life-situations or treatment may result in a remission back into a borderline personality status, even on a permanent basis.

The influence of genic or constitutional qualities as well as the effect of society and culture in general continue throughout life. To an otherwise open system with reverberating transactions penetrating the individual's boundaries in both directions, constitution and society act as restraining walls. In behavior (action or reaction) or in defensive maneuvers, the human person is limited by his genic physical constitution, the speed and quality of his neurological functions, his intelligence and special talents. What he is born with imposes limitations on his behavior. Likewise the *general* culture of his social environment imposes limitations on his deviancy from the general order. Should he transgress these restrictions he moves from being different or eccentric to becoming criminally or psychotically aberrant and consigned to prison or hospital.

Within the parts of the borderline system and even clearer in the borderline personality, are the components of his life-style. This encompasses not only his usual ways of behavior but his stress-responses to stimuli that strain his integrative capacities. Initial defenses may take the form of internal shifts in functional organization such as compensation of one function for another, acceleration or slowing of communication. In reaction to stimuli which cannot be handled internally the response then becomes generalized to the whole and manifested in overt behavior. It is then that the characteristic withdrawal and denial or obversely the angry attack on others occur. Finally, anxiety may mount and when the individual suffers under the impact of outer stimuli and flooded with rage from within becomes temporarily confused and is labeled psychotic.

It matters little whether we call the borderline syndrome a disease, an arrest of development, an emotional disturbance or a type of behavioral deviance. Likewise it is restrictive to view the borderline from a single frame of reference such as the biological, medical, psychological or social. The borderline like health and illness is a system in process occurring in time: developing, progressing and regressing as a focus of a large biopsychosocial field.

CHAPTER 11 Society, Culture
and the
Borderline

In Chapter 10 we approached the many factors possibly related to the
etiology of the borderline through the use of systems theory. This enabled
us to place the large number of variables concerned with healthy or
faulty development in perspective. We realize that for physiological,
psychological and social systems individual theories are relevant but
something in addition is necessary for multiple systems. As Panzetta
(1967) and many before him have stated, the linkages between cultural-
social and psychological systems are still lacking.

We have considered among the etiological factors two sets of dimensions—invariable and variable. The former include genic or hereditary
from which so-called constitution is derived, although every step in maturation and development is affected by environmental influences. We also
included those general aspects of culture and society extending beyond
the family and its ethnicentricities and subsumed under the disciplines
sometimes called social psychology or social psychiatry.

Panzetta points out that for the constellations of society, culture and personality there is little causal understanding, limited models and only exploratory research. The social context should not be limited to health or disease but include the overt problems of poverty, civil rights and education; the cultural should be focussed on identifiable specific cultures of different kinds, not only Negro or low-economic groups in general; and the psychiatric interest should be on current realities rather than historical relations or reductionistic concepts.

Our unified concept of human behavior considers personality, society and culture as interlocking processes constituting a living system that should not be fractured into causes and effects. Each represents a frame of reference from which to view a specified field. For our present consideration we focus on the borderline syndrome.

It is probable that the borderline always existed. Certainly the published literature indicates that the condition was recognized long ago. Perhaps our diagnostic acumen has improved and our experience with such patients has increased or it is even possible that in this era of neglect of diagnosis the term is a most convenient wastebasket in our uncertain classification. Nevertheless we think that the borderline diagnosis is made more frequently because the neurotic and psychotic syndromes are more clearly understood in patients seeking help in private offices, clinics and hospitals, leaving a middle area unclear.

Not only the cases published under this diagnostic heading, but actual experiences of private psychiatrists and clinic mental health workers clearly show that borderline syndromes appear in the rich and poor, the low and upper social classes, the intellectually dull and the well endowed, in fact in college students including those in Harvard College (Arnstein, 1958).

As we have indicated in Chapter 10, there has been little evidence that infant-mother relations in these patients had been obviously or at least overtly unique and only a bare suggestion that characteristics of their family processes can be identified. Finally, the salient features of the syndrome are only quantitatively greater in patients than in those who function without help but think or talk about their difficulties in maintaining affectional consistency and search for an identity ("Who am I?") with various degrees of existential anxiety. These seem to constitute a borderline character or personality.

We therefore ask: Are there some factors in our rapidly changing western society and/or culture which spawn or facilitate the development of the borderline? Do these act directly on the developing personality at various critical periods such as adolescence or young adulthood or indirectly by influencing the maternal child-rearing practices or both?

With the knowledge that the borderline case is distributed among all socioeconomic classes, in all ethnic groups and in all nations (Vargas, 1966) we are hard pressed in determining what general factors facilitate this abnormal state. If we attempt to find those influences in our society which act directly on the developing individual or indirectly through the family or the mother on the child during its formative years, we can develop a large list of possibilities. These may be divided into categories termed general, family, maternal and paternal. By this maneuver there is no intent to fracture the field since each focus is in intimate transaction with the others. Nor is there an intent to attribute to any or several social or cultural changes the role of final or single cause of the borderline syndrome. The list is obviously incomplete and in places redundant. In fact in itself it portrays our own value judgment of the negative attributes of our current society.

Can we make some general statements concerning these characteristics other than the cliché "an increase in existential anxiety?" Although this is very difficult to do and the causal significance of these abstractions in relation to a specific syndrome is vague we shall make the attempt.

A. *General*
 1. Marked increase in local, national and international violence.
 2. Greater urban unrest and stimulation of hate.
 3. Fewer sanctuaries for relief of anxiety.
 4. Greater latent anxiety requiring a variety of defenses.
 5. Increased expectations of generalized conformity.

B. *Family*
 1. Cramped, restricted, mechanized living conditions.
 2. Nuclear family with loss of "assistant" parents (except among Negroes).
 3. Paucity of verbal communications.
 4. Dissociation of adolescent from adult culture (emphasis on youth).

C. *Maternal*
 1. Fewer full-time mothers.
 2. Decreased orientation toward maternal roles.
 3. Greater insecurity and immaturity (earlier marriages).

D. *Paternal*
 1. Less authoritative.
 2. Concerned with job security.
 3. Decrease in future orientation.

Lichtenstein (1963) brilliantly reviews several recent books concerned with human identity (Riesman, Wheelis, Erikson, Lynd, Strauss). He criticizes the concept that social pressures with the threat of shame create character or personality as if these were static as contrasted with the more enlightened concept of "sense of identity" used by Erikson. The idea that man is born a slave or alienated and becomes freer only through experience and experiment, according to Lichtenstein, is incompatible with what we know about developmental psychology. Wheelis believes that changes in neurotic patterns with fewer hysterical neuroses and more character disorders, which include the borderline, are related to changes in social structures. In his review Lichtenstein performs a valuable service in indicating the restricted view of the social scientist as well as the psychologist each of whom seems blind to the complementarity of the "ground plan" of maturational forces and the learning processes steered by culture and personal life-crises. The development or lack of an evolving identity has to do, not with a state, but with a *sense of* identity. This is not necessarily destined to become organized although its directional plan may be immutable. Nevertheless, the sense of identity may undergo transformation and metamorphosis within the context of adequate experiencing in life. Unfortunately the borderline has not developed or acquired the "ground plan" for self-objectivication. How and why he does not cannot be explained by single causes.

Meerloo (1954) has made three interesting generalizations about the family in the modern technological age. (1) He considers that there has been a technological invasion of the family, "technicizing" it based on the increase in television-viewing and automatic machine deliveries of goods among others. There is little pride in service occupations. These have dehumanized man and increased his dependency on the magic of machines. Life now is not man in relation to man but man in relation to machines. (2) The psychological invasion or the "psychologizing" of the family has intellectualized the emotions into a series of clichés. (3) The confusing semantics of love has "glamorized" the family so that instead of mutual adjustments the ideal is the "external romantic."

In a review of the literature on the "as if" concept, Ross (1967) although he never mentions that this condition belongs to the borderline syndrome writes about retardation of ego maturation with respect to object-relations. The resultant narcissism, weak superego and fragile, magical and grandiose ego-ideal are a result of our culture with its emphasis on material values and the affectlessness in the upbringing of children.

Langer (1964) places the responsibility on science rather than on technology. She states that science has out-run imagination, in fact has overwhelmed us. As a result our traditional institutions seem inadequate so that we tend to abandon them. Members of the younger generation sweep them away but also sweep away their own social symbols leaving their personal lives empty. Culture, she states, which is "the expression of characteristic patterns of feeling leading to patterns of action and their things involved," needs to catch up with the runaway technological civilization.

Langer writes:

> The seeds of civilization are in every culture but it is city life that brings them to fruition. Like every process of fruition, civilization strains and drains the life which engenders and supports it—the culture which reaches its height in the development. Civilized life establishes a new balance between conservative and progressive elements and tips the scales of feeling toward the venturesome personalistic pole and away from piety and decorum. Such a shift of balance does not take place, of course, without flagrant exhibits of complete imbalance—lives culturally lost, degenerated, the familiar 'criminal elements' and irresponsible drifters of every big city in the world.

Many of these drifters are borderline according to our experience with several patients. These are the "beatniks." In a recent editorial article Masserman (1967) attributes the term "beatnik" to the adolescents' assumption that they have been beaten into martyrdom. The movement is not limited to Western civilization since it is now rampant in the Soviet Union, Red China and Japan as well. "Are there special circumstances in our *own* time, place and culture that especially influence some of our youth toward the extremes that we then berate as beatnik?" His answer is again a generalization: that the adolescents' search for identity is an increasingly difficult task in our current incredibly intricate culture. As types of partial or complete failure in adaptation he includes regressions (facilitated by reluctance of families to give up control), stereotypes of peer-group behavior, sexual promiscuity, identity diffusion, premature marriage and various forms of beatnik existence. The "off" withdraw, the "down" rebel and the "up" push for progressive change.

It is frequently pointed out that society and culture are in a period of transition so that the young are being reared with ambiguity between two worlds. Mazlish (1961) points out the current denial of faith, abandonment of tradition, repudiation of values and absence of fixed views. As a result the existing models for identification are weak and defenses against affective commitment are increasing. Attempts are made to utilize cults to replace religion and existentialism as a philosophy to attain a sense of identity. Unfortunately the borderline is unable to use these techniques.

Keniston (1960) has studied a series of uncommitted and alienated youths among Harvard College students who are obviously overprivileged and overwhelmed. His case reports and generalizations indicate that many of his subjects were borderline cases so that his work has direct applicability to our problem. These students developed noncommitment as a way of life related to their "identity diffusion" (ala Erikson) or fragmentation of identity.

They searched for sentience without commitment. This means a refusal to assume the adult role and a rejection of their culture. They are not involved with their parents, particularly in their social problems. They distrust the adult roles which do not inspire enthusiasm or commitment.

Keniston attempts to articulate the psychological and social factors in the development of alienation. Is the syndrome a reaction to the subject's personal past or a social problem? He attempts to use the outmoded either/or approach such as indicated in the statement often repeated by others: "Crime is not a product of psychological disorder but rather a sign of social disorder."

In the early development of Keniston's subjects there was no unusual treatment during the first years of life and no gross deprivation. Yet their mothers were ambivalent about motherhood and developed with their sons a special alliance which the mothers had difficulty in severing. As a result the youths had great difficulty in tearing away from their dependencies. There was little opportunity for masculine identity to be achieved with their fathers. They repeatedly blame their present condition on their past experiences.

On the other hand, Keniston writes about our rapid social changes resulting in the shattering of intimate communications. The ascendency of technological values has been accompanied by work for a living without satisfactions. Keniston states: "Alienation is a response *of* individuals especially sensitized to reject American culture by their early development, a development which in part reflects their families' efforts to solve dilemmas built into American life; and it is in part a response *to* social stress, historical losses and collective estrangement in our shared experiences."

Is it society or culture which prevents development of healthy personality and self-realization or do they create conditions under which development is hindered or blocked? Sanford (1966) states the question: "We must ask concerning any proposed social action or any intervention in social systems how it might affect the individual." Since culture consists of "transmitted and created content and patterns, of values, ideas and other symbolic systems how do they contribute to or are affected by changing sex roles, housing, jobs, position of women?" Sanford also reveals the effect on later personality of college experiences with their crises for which interventions are possible and learning may ensue. But there has been no evaluation of activities directed toward primary prevention of any mental or emotional disturbance. Social psychologists write bravely about the articulation of culture-social personality but seem to be driven back to genetic personality explanations. So, for example, the withdrawn narcissistic character (our borderline) develops out of broken homes from rejecting mothers who maltreat and neglect their children according to Sanford.

If as Keniston states this is an age of alienation and if the problems of identity diffusion and deficient affectional relationships in the individual are general characteristics of the borderline, then all aspects of our culture should demonstrate this condition to some degree. Our own limited expertise prevents us from exploring the cultural areas termed "the arts." It has been said that modern music which is becoming more dissonant is an example, that social dancing with partners not touching is another, and that expressionistic painting with its examples of nothingness (white on white), concern with color and not form or content, the satire of junk and pop art, all express the same trend. In addition the irrational, the violent and the extreme in some art forms seem to be an attempt to achieve otherwise tenuous and weak relationships.

This trend is becoming more obvious in current literature. For example Lionel Abel (1966) states:

> As for the ultra-modern novelists of this time, instead of making writers their heroes or protagonists, they seem to have made writing itself their hero and their only heroism. Their novels tell the stories of no persons, but only of objects and things, of voids, and of absences. Their inspiration comes, I believe, from nothingness and I suspect it was the work of writers such as these that made Gilman think the literary critic should be a 'metaphysician.'

John Barth (1966) in *Giles Goat-Boy* writes:

> Its about *love*, as you say; but a very special kind. People talk about two sorts of *love*, you know, the kind that tries to escape the self and the kind

that affirms the self. But it seems to me there's a third kind of love, that doesn't seek either union or communion with its object, but merely admires it from a position of utter detachment—what I call the Innocent Imagination. . . . He would deal with reality like a book, a novel that he didn't write and wasn't a character in, but only an appreciative reader of . . . But in truth, of course, he *wasn't* finally a spectator at all; he couldn't stay 'out of it'; and the fiascos of his involvements with men and women—in particular the revelation of his single mortal fate—these things would make him at the end, if not an authentic person, at least an expert amateur, so to speak, who might aspire to a kind of honorary membership in the human fraternity.

Stimulated by their patients and by our investigations on the borderline case, Drs. Litowitz and Newman (1967), two of our residents at Michael Reese, have written about the borderline and the theatre of the absurd:

We believe that the characteristics of the borderline as a cultural and clinical descendant of the classical neurosis are manifested in the structure and context of these plays, just as the classical theatre (Sophocles, Shakespeare, Ibsen) reflects the structure and content of the classical neurosis. It is fairly well accepted that the artist, in this case the playwright or poet, is often an avant-garde chronicler of changes in society, be they social, political, philosophical or psychological. We think that the modern playwrights, through their own perceptive intuitions, have picked up certain themes which they philosophically consider to be dilemmas of the human condition and which they have dramatized in a rather unique modern style.

Our intent is to impose a psychiatric interpretation on the manifest themes that the dramatists have presented and hence to reveal that the structure and organization of their plays parallel the dynamic conflicts and personality organization of a group of patients called borderline.

Bearing in mind the characteristics of borderline patients, we were struck by similar themes and relationships in the group of plays referred to as theatre of the absurd. The themes of many of these plays deal with loneliness, isolation, meaninglessness, reality and illusion, uncertainty, and difficulty in communicating with another person. The actual relationships within the plays all showed marked defects in object relatedness, they were always dyadic, and the individuals almost always demonstrated evidence of identity confusion, megalomaniacal tendencies, and futility concerning the future. Most impressive, perhaps, is the lack of meaningful communication as we have come to expect it in a relationship or in a drama that mirrors such a relationship.

The playwrights are attempting to convey, through the evocation of poetic images, the sense of perplexity they feel about the human condition. They are describing life stripped of traditional values, and a world without benefit of ultimate concepts and truths. Man, confronted with a world without illusions, is forced to regard life as meaningless and to experience his isolation completely.

The purpose of their paper was to illustrate the relationship between the borderline personality and certain contemporary plays which Esselin (1961) has grouped collectively as the theater of the absurd (Albee, Beckett, Ionesco, Genét, Gelber). The authors indicate that the theater of the absurd seems to mirror the change in the form of neuroses that has been observed and described since World War II by an ever-increasing number of psychiatrists. In their paper they present excerpts from *Waiting for Godot* by Samuel Beckett (1945) and *The Zoo Story* by Edward Albee (1959). We need not repeat these details available in their published report. We are certain that not only the analysis of other modern plays, dance, painting, sculpture and music will reveal the cultural shifts which are part of the prevailing social and cultural conditions in which the "sick" borderline patient is a precipitant.

What does all this mean? The deficiency in our answers rest with the fact that we have not yet been able to articulate society and culture in general with personality (Ruitenbeck, 1963). For infantile and early childhood experience we may tentatively say that the mother in her child-rearing practices transmits somehow to her offspring the influences of her ethnic subculture but also those of the culture at large. She always is affected for better or worse by the influence of society and culture in her effective mothering. In later phases of development including adolescence and adulthood the individual is directly influenced by his culture, its changes and the rate of change. Does his sense of identity enable him to persist as a person despite minor or major crises?

Only the medical historian may one day tell us whether the borderline syndrome existed in previous eras in historical societies or whether the borderline is truly increasing in numbers in our contemporary societies. There is no doubt that whatever factors are concerned in the production of the syndrome artists, dramatists and writers have caught the feeling, tone and hopelessness of the condition, indicating its universality. Perhaps they too have the borderline personality (not syndromes) and are ventilating their problems. It is highly likely that the "sick" borderline like all psychiatric syndromes represents an exaggeration of a contemporary problem in all civilized mankind. With this background, in some way social and cultural conditions plus some other variables contrive together to produce the overt syndrome.

CHAPTER 12 General Summary
and Conclusions

SUMMARY

The original goal of our research was to define the psychiatric entity frequently referred to as borderline. This term in itself has many historical and contemporary meanings. Although attempts have been made by a number of individual therapists to allocate this diagnosis to a specific syndrome, in general it has been used as a depository for clinical uncertainty. Even this usage is not specific because the same uncertainty existing in many clinics is hidden by the use of at least a dozen terms, ranging from chronic undifferentiated schizophrenia to anhedonism and character neuroses. These special terms seem to designate commonalities of visible symptoms rather than patterns of functions or dysfunctions.

The diagnosis of borderline has been in use for several decades, or even longer, without clear definition. The term has both technical and general implications which are difficult to separate. Our attempt to define what it denotes as a clinical psychiatric syndrome is confusing to those who literally expect the definition to include what borders on what. We have given much consideration to developing a new diagnostic appellation, which is difficult after the long usage of the old even though it is semantically unclear. We wanted to use a new word for the syndrome and other terms for the subcategories, but we have not succeeded in our efforts. This may be accomplished by others in the future.

Our primary goal, then, was to determine whether a borderline syndrome exists and if so what are its attributes (Chapter 1). Secondarily we hoped to ascertain if subcategories could be delineated and to define them if possible. Thus the goal at the onset of the research was to answer the question, *"What is the borderline?"*

We began our investigations in an era when clinical diagnoses and classifications are derogated, diagnostic skills atrophying and the life-history of psychiatric entities of no great concern. These tendencies are self-perpetuating because students are being taught to focus, sometimes to exclusion, on the internal dynamics of individual patients.

Our overview of an extensive professional literature (Chapter 2), although selective, disclosed that no systematic study of the borderline has ever been made. The same deficiency applies to other diagnostic terms, serving the purpose of labeling vague syndromes. The bulk of published reports are based on one or a few patients for whom treatment represents the only method of observation. Conclusions are couched in the form of psychoanalytic interpretations. The raw data are skimpy, "metapsychological" theory is directly applied and conclusions are inferences as to meanings rather than definitions of processes. These reports are carried through the literature as "findings" monotonously confirmed in continuity.

Despite these criticisms which are more general than specific and applicable to a whole specialty, "dynamic" studies disclose patterns that can be translated into hypotheses. The positive contributions suggest that the borderline is a specific syndrome with considerable degree of internal consistency and stability, and not a regression as a response to internal or external conditions of stress. It represents a syndrome characteristic of arrested development of ego-functions. Clinicians recognized that the borderline syndrome is a confusing combination of psychotic, neurotic and character disturbances with many normal or healthy elements. Although these symptoms are unstable, the syndrome itself as a process is recognizably stable, giving rise to the peculiar term "stable instability."

We concluded that despite the value of studies of the internal dynamics of borderline patients and the usefulness of our previous research which classified depressions into syndromes or categories on the basis of symptoms, neither was useful for the study of the borderline. Instead we decided to study the ego-functions of borderline patients in so far as they are exposed by ongoing behaviors thereby revealing what were normal healthy or adaptive functions, and what were unhealthy non-adaptive functions. Utilizing a framework of ego-psychology based on psychoanalytic theory promised a better understanding of the syndrome and its subcategories (Chapter 3).

Our research design was derived, therefore, from a different approach: instead of using the data of dyadic introspection from interviews, or various forms of psychotherapy or tapping historical or anamnestic data, we described observable behaviors (Chapter 4). In essence we observed and described behaviors and *then* rated traits extracted from an ego-psychology framework. This extraction required the redefinition of ego-functions into behavioral variables as exactly as possible and the development of a quantitative coding system sufficiently clear and practiced so that rater-reliability could be achieved.

Our assumptions can be summarized as follows:

1. Behavior can be observed, described and quantified.
2. Behavior assessed in terms of ego-functions is an index of mentation that the psychotherapist does not typically observe; hence the study of such behavior adds to the therapist's store of knowledge of the patient's assets and liabilities and capacities for adaptation.
3. Behavioral evidences have validity in terms of estimating the quality and quantity of internal psychological functions.
4. A large enough time-sample of the behavior of an individual patient is an adequate index of his ego-functions.
5. A finer analysis of ego-functions in a large enough sample of patients designated by a specified diagnostic term can result in a sharper definition of that specific syndrome.

Patients were selected on the basis of the known positive and negative attributes of the borderline described in the extensive literature and corresponding to our clinical experiences (Chapter 4). They were young adults from upper lower or lower middle socio-economic classes. An older age group from a previous study was also available for study. Actually we had anticipated that our selection would include a sufficient number of non-borderline patients, but most of these dropped out (Chapter 9) so that comparison groups of schizophrenics and neuroses were utilized on the basis of information derived from the literature and our own clinical experiences.

In our design we could not include all hypothesized ego-functions since many are not expressed in behavior; others which were included had to be dropped because of insufficient evidence. Some qualities of the borderline could not be evoked and in fact may have been inhibited because of the non-stressful characteristics of the nursing unit. In fact, the behaviors that we observed must be linked to the specificity of the environment within which they occurred—far less stressful than the real world. Even the decision for discharge which we planned for our second period of "observation-description-rating" was not stressful probably because the borderline does not become committed to the institution. Their reluctance to leave was based on a distaste for living away from their families (as advised) or taking a job amidst people.

At least two independent professionals rated the protocols in juxtaposition with the observational evidence for their ratings. The descriptions suitable for each rating were developed by the investigators, the raters were trained by one of us and another reviewed the ratings and reconciled them (in the relatively few cases when they were discrepant) on the basis of the recorded evidence and his clinical judgment. We believe that we achieved reliability which is always the result of well-defined scale points, common language, adequate training of raters and clinical judgments reconciling differences.

The next step was difficult because of the nature of our ratings, the large number of variables remaining viable (93) and the limited sample of patients. Factoring did not appear to be the primary method of choice for our statistical analyses. We were indeed fortunate in our search for a method to join forces with Friedman and Rubin, who utilized our data for their own investigations on clustering (Chapter 5).

They utilized a clustering procedure, the results of which were subjected to a multiple discriminant-function analysis. Ten components accurately identified membership in one of four groups for 49 of 51 patients. In addition 20 variables accurately predicted group membership for all patients. Each of these four groups was separately factor analyzed to develop internal descriptions of each group and make possible between-group comparisons.

The four groups elicited from the statistical analysis when translated into clinical syndromes coincide with clinical experience (Chapter 6). However, using our data which are fully documented, other clinicians may make other interpretations. In general Group I is closest to the psychotic border, Group IV is closest to the neurotic border, Group II represents the core process of the borderline and Group III is the most adaptive, compliant and lacking in identity ("as if").

In defining the overall characteristics of the borderline syndrome we include *anger* as the main or only affect, defect in *affectional* relationships, absence of indications of *self-identity* and *depressive loneliness*.

Within this gestalt the various groups represent different positions. Members of Group I give up attempts at relationship but at the same time overtly, in behavior and affect, react negatively and angrily toward other people and to their environments. Persons in Group II are inconsistent, moving toward others for relations which is then followed by acted-out repulsion, moving away into isolation where they are lonely and depressed. This back-and-forth movement is characteristic and corresponds with the fact that these people are both angry and depressed but at different times. Patients in Group III seem to have given up their search for identity and defend against their reactions to an empty world. They do not have the angry reactions characteristic of Group I. Instead they passively await cues from others and behave in complementarity—"as if." In no other group were the defenses observable as clearly or as consistently as in Group III. Subjects in Group IV search for a lost symbiotic relation with a mother figure which they do not achieve, and then reveal what may be called an anaclitic depression.

In the cluster analysis Groups I and III were shown to be relatively close together and Groups II and IV were likewise close. This makes clinical sense because patients in both Groups I and III have given up hope of meaningful relationships and those in Groups II and IV are still searching. Patients in Group I are angry at the world and their ego integrations are endangered by this strong affect; we hypothesize that they often become temporarily psychotic as a result. Those in Group III have given up even their reactions to frustration and are compliant, passive and relate as others wish, or it may be that they successfully defend themselves against angry behavior and eruptions.

Group II includes patients who are buffeted by virtue of their own ego-dysfunctions as they attempt to relate to others, become stimulated to anger, and then withdraw and suffer loneliness. Group IV, on the other hand, is characterized by abandonment of any but dependent clinging relationships, and when this is not gratified, develop the characteristics of an anaclitic depression, weeping and feeling neglected and sorry for themselves.

The next step after the characteristic behavioral traits of the borderline category, its subgroups and factors had been put together was to check them against total case reports of individual patients. We could utilize published case histories, the protocols of our 51 patients, an in-depth study of 16 additional patients, an experimental group previously studied and one patient in treatment. This was the final pay-off because, by utilizing the behavioral characteristics designating each of the four groups isolated by statistical methods, we were able to place all of the patients in appropriate groups. Thus the statistical differentiation of the whole syndrome and of the four groups made logical clinical sense. This was not true of the finer subdivisions of each group into two factors each because too much overlapping was apparent in them to discriminate clinical entities. The within-group variance was not sharp enough. We demonstrated the way individual patients fall into one of the four groups (Chapter 7).

Interest has shifted from specific mother-child relations as primary causations in the development of neuroses and psychoses to the family of origin. Viewed as a system in its own right and not simply as a collection of individuals, investigators have searched for the families' methods of interaction, problem-solving and especially their methods of communication. The literature contains significant references to disturbed communication systems in families of schizophrenics, but none for the borderline.

Since the study of the family was an after-thought and not included in our original design, we were forced to use routine social service data rated according to specific criteria by an independent rater. Although the families of the borderline showed the usual range of concern about the illness, no specific type of family was correlated with any of the borderline groups. Nevertheless a by-product of this study was a technique for family analysis which discriminated family types. As for the borderline patient in his nuclear family, he marries infrequently and is an inadequate spouse and a poor parent (Chapter 8).

To obtain a perspective on the borderline over time we did a follow-up study (Chapter 9). We were highly successful in interviewing the majority of our residual patient sample (86 per cent) and about 40 per cent of the dropouts. Essentially we found that the borderline in the time-span of 1 to 3.5 years (we designed no set time for the follow-up) after hospitalization did not become schizophrenic except for two patients in Group I. Despite therapy in the hospital oriented toward improving the social aptitudes of the patients, they remained for the most part socially isolated. Yet most of them with some psychiatric contacts returned to school or employment and maintained their instrumental roles successfully. Thirteen patients had to be rehospitalized five of whom had been hospitalized before entering ISPI. Of the dropouts only one turned out to be a borderline.

In an attempt to answer the question—*"How does a human become a borderline?"*—in other words to determine the etiology of the syndrome we realized that we and others had little information. It has been easy, but of little value, for many writers to discuss deficiencies in early child-mother relations, or neglectful mothering or even infantile traumata. Like these genetic factors, genic, familial, and general environmental aspects of etiology are not specific. Only mother- and peer-deprived experimental monkeys suggest an analogy. In brief, no specific etiological agents or conditions are known to produce the borderline syndrome.

To emphasize that search for a single etiological agent or that emphasis on a specific psychodynamic formulation is futile, we have sketched out the value of approaching the borderline or, for that matter, any disease process, within the framework of general systems theory. Within this large field there are appropriate places for many processes, from genic to culture, all of which transact to create the borderline system. The etiology of this syndrome as for any, will come about from knowing the many parts of the system transacting, in its ontogenesis and in its life-cycle (Chapter 10). The questions what, how and why applied to the borderline require different subtheories and hypotheses leading to different techniques of investigation all of which are important. Basic to further research on the borderline is the question, "What is the borderline?" This has been the essential goal of our research which we have reported in detail.

Next we attempted to view society and culture at large in our rapidly changing Western civilization (Chapter 11). We could observe and infer the vast changes occurring but could not articulate these with genetic processes involved in etiology. The question *"Why is the borderline?"* remains unanswered except by vague philosophical approaches to the relationships between modern urban civilization and culture. The "why" becomes a humanistic rather than a scientific question. The essence of the borderline is determined by scientific data that deal with verbal and nonverbal behaviors as processes. The existential aspect is teleological, ideational and abstract, and unrelated to the content of behaviors.

CONCLUSIONS

We should like to make explicit what has been accomplished by our investigations through some generalizations over and above the summary of each chapter. In essence we have taken a psychological theory, that of psychoanalytic ego-psychology, and made of it an operational theory which served as our strategy. As tactics we developed a research design applying methods of observing, describing and rating behaviors in a specific setting.

Essentially our conclusions consist of several *hypotheses* which are now available for replication and retesting. The first hypothesis encompasses the delineation of the dimensions of the class of ego-dysfunctions by which we characterize the borderline syndrome as differentiated from all other psychiatric entities. Second, we hypothesize four groups, divisions or subcategories of the borderline.

At this time the results of our statistical analysis developed four groups which have the best fit with contemporary clinical experience. The dimensions of the syndrome are logical and clinically consistent, as are the divisions into four groups. As clinicians we can easily recognize the general characteristics of the borderline syndrome as well as the sub-syndromes, matching them with cases reported in the literature, with our own clinical experiences and with the clinical study of our current sample of patients.

Our statistical analyses constituted in themselves a research program carried out by independent investigators using our data (Friedman and Rubin). They were able to develop several sets of groupings and probably could have furnished more. Indeed, in the future newer and/or better mathematical and statistical methods may produce other groupings. As clinicians we have the responsibility of choosing which are logically compatible with clinical experience and which have the optimum degree of discrimination for clinical practice.

The latter is exemplified by the fact that our statisticians at first found groupings which were too coarse in that they discriminated only between activity and passivity in overall behavior. The last attempt was too fine in that it resulted in groupings that in essence were fine divisions of what is our final Group II excluding all the others. The results which we accepted resonated immediately with clinical experience.

This last statement requires some explanation because it involves the use of our human internal computers, a process which sometimes is called intuition. Before we began the research and continually during its process we become familiar with the literature on the borderline, diffuse and unsystematic as it is. Yet undoubtedly clinical patterns were taking shape within our mental processes. Second, as we read the descriptions of behavior in our protocols the dimensions of the borderline and its several varieties vaguely developed shape as input of information became programmed. Yet we could not have defined the borderline and its groups in a conscious, logical statement. Then the statistical analysis produced results that clustered items or traits which when retranslated into ego-dysfunctions elicited in us: "That's it—certainly that is what we have been observing." A fit had been accomplished which could not have been possible by clinical scanning or statistical analysis alone.

The clinician should now be able to diagnose the borderline syndrome in general with considerable accuracy and each of the four groups in detail. The investigator can use these for correlations with causes, course, natural history of the disturbance and the effectiveness of various therapies. Eventually such impersonal causal factors as the genic and socio-cultural may be discovered, but as of now our best expectations rest with elucidating what personal experiences contribute most to the development of the borderline in general and its subcategories in particular.

Within the large class or syndrome of the borderline its subcategories must show some commonalities in their manifestations in order to be members of the larger class. Therefore we would expect some overlapping in the deficits of their ego-functions. We cannot as yet apply the factors of each group for clinical discriminations, which is in keeping with the fact that although fine differences among small groups and factors may be statistically feasible, the use of the finer elements of the factors is not yet clinically practical.

We believe that psychonalytic theory of ego-functions has been useful in deriving meanings from psychoanalytic data. We can now add that from our experience we believe that translating this theory into operational strategy is useful in discriminating ego-functions and their disturbances in behavior. From a study of the psychoanalytic literature as well as from our own research there appears to be a good fit between the results of the two techniques. The theory of ego-psychology, furthermore, when translated into operational terms, can serve as the basis of tactics applicable to a wide range of other unclear behavioral deviances or clinical syndromes.

It is far from our intention to separate artificially internal dynamics from external behavior. We have not fractured the field of "mentation–behavior." In our research we have viewed behavior as the final common pathway of a wide variety of internal processes. We have clearly defined our position as observers and our corresponding operational techniques. We could have also taken other positions, but not simultaneously. At any rate it is reassuring that data derived from introspection and that derived from overt behavior are congruent since they deal with the same processes and both reveal in the "adaptation-maladaptation" or "function-dysfunction" axes similar characteristics.

It must be clear, however, that the operational theory applied to ego-functions requires great pains in its translation into an effective research design. If the design is carefully worked out, the resulting observations and descriptions can be utilized for adequate ratings, properly scaled and tested. Raters must be trained and checked, the traits or items to be rated must be specifically defined and the quantities explicated in a useful code. The ratings cannot represent the skill of only one person and results must be fed back to insure refinement of definitions of scale-points.

The many ratings derived from multiple observers are all used for each variable and a summary rating made for each. We utilized the numerical ratings of our 93 variables for clustering and factor analysis. The results then had to be translated back into traits of behaviors which were then checked against the data of clinical experience. In simple terms the essence of this type of research is a double translation. Theory-dependent traits are used for ratings. The resulting numbers are then subjected to statistical analysis. These are then reconverted into behavioral language in clusters or groups. Traits which were fed into the statistical analysis via numbers are recovered in combinations that must make sense and reverberate with clinical experience.

In sum, the question *"What is the borderline?"* as the primary and essential reason for the research was answered by a tentative structure. In addition three by-products accrued representing theoretical, methodological and statistical advances. We utilized a *theory* of functions for classification, a *method* of behavioral observations, descriptions and ratings as our tactics, and a *statistical method* based on a clustering technique.

Questions such as *how* people become borderline characters, or even worse, become ill with the borderline syndrome, and *why* in our current culture both have been appearing in our experience more frequently have not been answered. However, there are many more current questions, and even more will arise to attract investigators' interest in the subject. We hope that our researches have at least established some hypotheses for such future work, that our methods may prove useful for investigations on other unclear clinical syndromes and that we have made a beginning in operational research on ego-functions.

REFERENCES

Abel, L.: In Defense of Edmund Wilson, *Chicago Sun-Times Book Week*, Sept. 4, 1966.

Ackerman, N.: *The Psychodynamics of Family Life*, New York: Basic Books, 1958.

Adler, L. M.: Patients of a State Mental Hospital: The Outcome of Their Hospitalization. In Rose, A. (ed.): *Mental Health and Mental Disorder*, New York: W. W. Norton & Co., pp. 501–523, 1955.

Albee, E.: *The Zoo Story*, New York: Coward-McCann, 1959.

Alexander, F. G., and Selesnick, S. T.: *The History of Psychiatry*, New York: Harper & Row, 1966.

Arnstein, R. L.: The Borderline Patient in the College Setting. In Wedge, B. M. (ed.): *Psychosocial Problems of College Men*, New Haven: Yale University Press, 1958.

Artiss, K. L.: Language and the Schizophrenic Quandary, *Contemporary Psychoanal.*, 3:39–54, 1966.

Barnett, J.: A Structural Analysis of Theories in Psychoanalysis, *Psychoanal. Review*, 53:85–98, 1966.

Barnett, J.: Cognitive Thought and Affect in the Organization of Experience, (in press, 1967).

Bartlett, M. S.: Multivariate Statistics. In Moravitz and Waterman (eds.): *Theoretical and Mathematical Biology*, New York: Blaisdell Publishing Co., 1965, Chap. 8, pp. 199–223.

Barth, J.: *Giles Goat-Boy*, New York: Doubleday, 1966.

Beck, S. J.: Schizophrenia Without Psychosis, *Arch. Neurol. Psychiat.*, 81:85–96, 1959.

Beck, S. J.: Symptom and Trait in Schizophrenia, *Amer. J. Orthopsychiat.*, 34:517–526, 1964.

Beckett, S.: *Waiting for Godot*, New York: Grove Press, 1945.

Benedek, T.: Adaptation to Reality in Early Infancy, *Psychoanal. Quart.*, 7:200–209, 1938.

Benedek, T.: Toward the Biology of a Depressive Constellation, *J. Amer. Psychoanal. Assoc.*, 4:389–402, 1956.

Bentley, A. F.: Kennetic Inquiry, *Science*, 112:775–777, 1950.

Beres, D.: Structure and Function in Psychoanalysis, *Int. J. Psychoanal.*, 46: 53–63, 1965.

Bernstein, H.: Identity and Sense of Identity, *Bull. Philadelphia Assoc. Psychoanal.*, 14:158–159, 1964.

Bertalanffy, Von L.: *Problems of Life,* New York: John Wiley & Sons, 1952.

Birdwhistell, R. L.: The American Family, *Psychiatry,* 29:204–212, 1966.

Bleuler, E.: *Dementia Praecox or the Group of Schizophrenics* (Zinkin, J., translator), Monograph Series in Schizophrenia, No. 1, New York: Int. University Press, 1950.

Bleuler, E.: *Lehrbuch der Psychiatrie,* 9th ed., edited by M. Bleuler, Berlin: Springer, 1955.

Bowlby, J.: *Maternal Care and Infant Health,* Geneva: World Health Organization, 1952.

Bowlby, J.: The Nature of the Child's Tie to His Mother, *Int. J. Psychoanal.,* 39:350–373, 1958.

Brown, J. S., and Kosterlitz, H.: The Social Adjustment of Psychiatric Patients Following Treatment in a Therapeutic Milieu (publication pending).

Bychowski, G.: Psychic Structure and Therapy of Latent Schizophrenia. In Rifkin, A. (ed.): *Schizophrenia in Psychoanalytic Office Practice,* New York: Grune and Stratton, 1957.

Cattell, R. B., Coulter, M. A., and Tsujioka, B.: The Taxonomic Recognition of Types, Functional Emergents. In Cattell, R. (ed.): *Handbook of Multivariate Experimental Psychology,* Chicago: Rand McNally, 1966.

Clark, L. P.: Some Practical Remarks upon the Use of Modified Psychoanalysis in the Treatment of Borderline (Borderland) Neuroses and Psychoses, *Psychoanal. Review,* 6:306–315, 1919.

Cummings, J., and Cummings, E.: *Ego and Milieu,* New York: Atherton Press, 1962.

Deutsch, H.: Some Forms of Emotional Disturbances and Their Relationship to Schizophrenia, *Psychoanal. Quart.,* 11:301–321, 1942.

Eckstein, R., and Wallerstein, J.: Observations on the Psychology of Borderline and Psychotic Children, *The Psychoanalytic Study of the Child,* New York: Int. University Press, 9:344–369, 1954.

Eisenstein, W. W.: Differential Psychotherapy of Borderline States. In Bychowski, G. and Despert, J. L. (eds.): *Specialized Techniques in Psychotherapy,* New York: Basic Books, 1952.

Elkes, J.: Subjective and Objective Observation in Psychiatry, *The Harvey Lecture Series,* 57:63–92, 1963. New York: Academic Press.

Erikson, E. H.: *Childhood and Society,* 2nd ed., New York: W. W. Norton & Co., 1963.

Escalona, S., and Heider, G. M.: *Prediction and Outcome,* New York: Basic Books, 1959.

Esselin, M.: *The Theatre of the Absurd,* New York: Anchor Books, 1961.

Eysenck, H. J.: Psychiatric Diagnosis as a Psychological and Statistical Problem, *Psychological Reports,* 1:3–17, 1955.

Federn, P.: *Ego Psychology and the Psychoses,* New York: Basic Books, 1952.

THE BORDERLINE SYNDROME

Fenichel, O.: *The Psychoanalytic Theory of the Neuroses,* New York: W. W. Norton & Co., 1945.

Fleck, S.: An Approach to Family Pathology, *Comprehensive Psychiatry,* 7:307–320, 1966.

Freeman, H. E., and Simmons, O. G.: *The Mental Patient Comes Home,* New York and London: John Wiley & Sons, 1963.

Freud, A.: *Normality and Pathology in Childhood,* New York: Int. University Press, 1966a.

Freud, A.: Links between Hartmann's Ego Psychology and the Child Analyst's Thinking. In Lowenstein, R. M., Newman, L. M., Schur, M., and Solnit, A. J. (eds.), *Psychoanalysis—A General Psychology,* New York: Int. Universities Press, 1966b.

Fried, E.: Ego Strengthening Aspects of Hostility, *Amer. J. Orthopsychiat.,* 26:179–187, 1956.

Friedman, H. P., and Rubin, J.: On Some Invariant Criteria for Grouping Data, *J. of the Amer. Statistical Assoc.,* Dec., 1967.

Fries, M.: Factors in Character Development: Neuroses, Psychoses and Delinquency, *Amer. J. Orthopsychiat.,* 7:142–147, 1937.

Fromm-Reichmann, F.: Loneliness, *Psychiatry,* 22:1–15, 1959.

Frosch, J.: The Psychotic Character, Clinical Psychiatric Consideration, *Psychiat. Quart.,* 38:81–96, 1964.

Gesell, A., and Armatruda, C. S.: *Developmental Diagnosis,* New York: Hoeber, 1941.

Gitelson, M.: On Ego Distortion, *Int. J. Psychoanal.,* 39:245–257, 1958.

Gitelson, M.: On the Problem of Character Neurosis, *J. Hillside Hospital,* 2:3–18, 1963.

Glover, E.: Psychoanalytic Approach to the Classification of Mental Disorders, *J. Mental Sci.,* 78:819–842, 1932.

Glover, E.: *On the Early Development of the Mind,* London: Harcourt Brace & Co., 1933.

Glover, E.: Metapsychology or Metaphysics, *Psychoanal. Quart.,* 35:173–190, 1966.

Goffman, E.: *Behavior in Public Places,* New York: Free Press, 1966.

Goldfarb, W.: Emotional and Intellectual Consequences of Psychological Deprivation in Infancy. In Hoch, P. H., and Zubin, J. (eds.): *Psychopathology of Childhood,* New York: Grune and Stratton, 1955.

Greenberg, N. H.: Psychosomatic Differentiation in Infancy, *Psychosom. Med.,* 19:293–302, 1957.

Greenson, R.: In Hoch, P., and Zubin, J. (eds.): *Psychopathology of Childhood,* New York: Grune and Stratton, 1955.

Grinker, R. R., Sr.: *Psychosomatic Research,* New York: W. W. Norton & Co., 1953.

Grinker, R. R., Sr. (ed.): *Toward a Unified Theory of Human Behavior,* New York: Basic Books, 1956, Second edition 1967.

Grinker, R. R., Sr.: On Identification, *Int. J. Psychoanal.,* 38:379–391, 1957.

Grinker, R. R., Sr.: Psychiatry Rides Madly in All Directions, *Arch. Gen. Psychiat.,* 10:228–237, 1964.

Grinker, R. R., Sr.: Normality Viewed as a System, *Arch. Gen. Psychiat.,* 17: 320–325, 1967.

Grinker, R. R., Sr., Miller, J., Sabshin, M., Nunn, R., and Nunnally, J. C.: *The Phenomena of Depressions,* New York: Hoeber, 1961.

Hamburg, D. A., et. al.: Classification and Rating of Emotional Experiences, *A.M.A. Arch. Neurol. Psychiat.,* 79:415–420, 1958.

Harlow, H. F.: Development of the Second and Third Affectional Systems in Macaque Monkeys. In Tourlentes, T. T., Pollack, S. L., and Himvich, H. E. (eds.): *Research Approaches to Psychiatric Problems,* New York: Grune and Stratton, 1962, pp. 209–230.

Harlow, H., and Harlow, M. K.: Learning to Love, *Amer. Scientist,* 54:244– 272, 1966.

Harman, H. H.: *Modern Factor Analysis,* Chicago: University of Chicago Press, 1960.

Hartmann, H.: *Ego Psychology and Problems of Adaptation,* New York: Int. Universities Press, 1958.

Hartmann, H.: *Essays on Ego Psychology,* New York: Int. Universities Press, 1964.

Hoch, P. H., and Cattell, J.: The Diagnosis of Pseudoneurotic Schizophrenia, *Psychiat. Quart.,* 33:17–43, 1959.

Hoch, P. H., and Polatin, P.: Pseudoneurotic Forms of Schizophrenia, *Psychiat. Quart.,* 23:248–276, 1949.

Hoch, P. H., and Zubin, J. (ed.): *Psychopathology of Childhood,* New York: Grune and Stratton, 1955.

Home, H. J.: The Concept of Mind, *Int. J. Psychoanal.,* 47:42–49, 1966.

Hughes, C.: Borderline Psychiatric Records—Pro-Dromal Symptoms of Physical Impairments, *Alienist and Neurologist,* 5:85–90, 1884.

Hunt, J. McV., and Kogan, L.S.: *Measuring Results in Social Casework,* New York: Family Service Association of America, 1950.

Jenkins, R. L., and Cole, J. O. (eds.): Diagnostic Classification in Child Psychiatry, *Amer. Psych. Assoc. Psych. Research Reports,* 18:1964.

Jones, W. A.: Borderland Cases, Mental and Nervous, *J. Lancet* (new series) 38:561–567, 1918.

Kanfer, F. H., and Saslow, G.: Behavioral Analyses, *Arch. Gen. Psychiat.,* 12:529–538, 1966.

Kantor, J. R.: Behaviorism: Whose Image? *Psychol. Record,* 13:499–512, 1963.

Kaplan, A.: *The Conduct of Inquiry,* San Francisco: Chandler Publishing Co., 1964.

Keniston, K.: *The Uncommitted: Alienated Youth in American Society,* New York: Harcourt, Brace and World, Inc., 1960.

Kernberg, O.: Borderline Personality Organization, *Journ. Amer. Psychoanal. Assoc.,* 15:641–685, 1967.

Knight, R. P.: Borderline States. In Lowenstein, R. (ed.): *Drives, Affects, Behavior,* New York: Int. Universities Press, 1953, pp. 203–215.

Knight, R. P. (ed.): Borderline States. In *Psychoanalytic Psychiatry and Psychology,* New York: Int. Universities Press, 1954.

Knowlton, P., and Burg, M.: Treatment of a Borderline Psychotic Five-Year-Old Girl. In Caplan, G. (ed.): *Emotional Problems of Early Childhood,* New York: Basic Books, 1955, pp. 451–488.

Kraepelin, E.: *Clinical Psychiatry,* New York: Macmillan, 1912 (translation of 7th ed. by Diefendort, A. R.).

Langer, S. K.: *Philosophical Sketches,* New York: Mentor Books, 1964.

Levine, S.: A Further Study of Infantile Handling and Adult Avoidance Learning, *J. Personality,* 25:70–75, 1956.

Levine, S.: Infantile Experience and Maturation of the Pituitary Adrenal Axis, *Science,* 126:1347–1349, 1957.

Lichtenstein, H.: The Dilemma of Human Identity: Notes on Self-Transformation, Self-Objectivation and Metamorphosis, *J. Amer. Psychoanal. Assoc.,* 11:173–223, 1963.

Lidz, T., Fleck, S., and Cornelison, A. R.: *Schizophrenia and the Family,* New York: Int. Universities Press, 1965.

Litowitz, N. S., and Newman, K. M.: The Borderline Personality and the Theatre of the Absurd, *Arch. Gen. Psychiat.,* 16:268–281, 1967.

Little, M.: Transference in Borderline States, *Int. J. Psychoanal.,* 47:476–485, 1966.

Lorenz, K.: *On Aggression,* New York: Harcourt, Brace and World, Inc., 1963.

Lyerly, S. B., and Abbott, P. S. (eds.): *Handbook of Psychiatric Rating Scales,* Public Health Service Publication No. 1495. Washington, D.C.: U.S. Department of Health, Education, and Welfare, 1966.

Maccoby, Eleanor E., and Maccoby, Nathan: The Interview: A Tool of Social Science. In Lindzey, G. (ed.): *Handbook of Social Psychology,* Cambridge: Addison-Wesley Publishing Co., Inc., 1954.

Masserman, J. H.: The Beatnik: Up—, Down—, and Off—. *Arch. Gen. Psychiat.,* 16:262–268, 1967.

Mazlish, B.: Our Heraclitean Period, *The Nation,* 192:336–338, 1961.

Mead, M.: The Concept of Culture and the Psychosomatic Approach, *Psychiatry,* 10:57–65, 1947.

Meehl, P. E.: Some Ruminations on the Validation of Clinical Procedures, *Canadian J. Psychol.,* 13:102–128, 1959.

Meerloo, J. A. M.: The Development of the Family in the Technological Age. In Lubman, S. (ed.): *Emotional Forces in the Family,* Philadelphia: J. B. Lippincott, 1954.

Meissner, W. W.: The Operational Principles and Meaning in Psychoanalysis, *Psychoanal. Quart.,* 35:233–255, 1966.

Menninger, K.: *The Vital Balance,* New York: The Viking Press, 1963.

Mischler, E., and Waxler, N.: Family Interaction Processes and Schizophrenia. *Int. J. Psychiat.,* 2:375–428, 1966.

Modell, A. H.: Primitive Object Relationship and the Predisposition to Schizophrenia, *Int. J. Psychoanal.,* 44:282–292, 1963.

Nagel, E.: *The Structure of Science,* New York: Harcourt, Brace and World, Inc., 1961.

Offer, D., and Sabshin, M.: *Normality,* New York: Basic Books, 1961.

Oken, D., Grinker, R. R., Sr., Heath, H. A., Sabshin, M., and Schwartz, N.: Stress Response in a Group of Chronic Psychiatric Patients, *Arch. Gen. Psychiat.*, 3:45–46, 1960.

Panzetta, A. F.: Causal and Action Models in Social Psychiatry, *Arch. Gen. Psychiat.*, 16:290–297, 1967.

Parkin, A.: Neuroses and Psychoses: I. Historical Review, *Psychiat. Quart.*, 40:203–216, 1966. II. Modern Perspective, *ibid.*, 216–227, 1966.

Pavenstedt, E.: Environments That Fail to Support Certain Areas of Early Ego Development. In *Ego Development and Differentiation*, Des Plaines, Ill.: Forest Hospital Publications, 1964.

Piaget, J.: *Origins of Intelligence in Children*, New York: Int. Universities Press, 1951.

Rapaport, D.: The Structure of Psychoanalytic Theory. In Koch, S. (ed.): *Psychology: A Study of a Science*, 3:55–183, New York: McGraw-Hill, 1959.

Rangell, L. (Reporter): Panel Report on the Borderline Case, *J. Amer. Psychoanal. Assoc.*, 3:285–298, 1955.

Rao, C. R.: The Utilization of Multiple Measurements in Problems of Biological Classification, *J. Royal Statistical Soc.*, Ser. B, 10:159–203, 1948.

Rao, C. R.: The Use and Interpretation of Principal Component Analysis in Applied Research, *Sankhya Ser. A*, 26:329–358, 1964.

Robbins, L. L. (Reporter): Panel Report on the Borderline Case, *J. Amer. Psychoanal. Assoc.*, 4:550–562, 1956.

Rosenfeld, S. K., and Sprince, M. P.: Some Thoughts on the Technical Handling of Borderline Children, *The Psychoanalytic Study of the Child*, 20:495–517, 1963.

Ross, N.: The "As If" Concept, *J. Amer. Psychoanal. Assoc.*, 15:59–83, 1967.

Rosse, J. C.: Clinical Evidence of Borderline Insanity, *J. Nerv. Ment. Dis.*, 17:669–674, 1890.

Royce, J. R.: *Psychology and the Symbol*, New York: Random House, 1965.

Rubin, J.: *Optimal Taxonomy Program* (7090-IBM-0026), Int. Business Machines, Corp., Program Information Dept., Hawthorne, New York, 1965.

Rubin, J.: Optimal Classification into Groups: An Approach for Solving the Taxonomy Problem, *J. Theoret. Biol.*, 15:103–144, 1967.

Ruesch, J.: Hospitalization and Social Disability, *J. Nerv. & Ment. Dis.*, 142:203–214, 1966.

Ruitenbeck, A. M. (ed.): *Varieties of Modern Social Theory*, New York: E. P. Dutton & Co., 1963.

Sanford, N.: *Self and Society: Social Change and Individual Development*, New York: Atherton Press, 1966.

Sargent, H. D.: Intrapsychic Change. Methodological Problems in Psychotherapy Research, *Psychiatry*, 24:93–109, 1961.

Schmideberg, M.: The Borderline Patient. In Arieti, S. (ed.): *American Handbook of Psychiatry*, 1:398–418, New York: Basic Books, 1959.

Searles, H. F.: Concerning the Development of an Identity, *Psychoanal. Review*, 53:7–30, 1966.

Shapiro, D.: *Neurotic Styles*, New York: Basic Books, 1965.

Singer, M. T., and Wynne, L. C.: Communication Styles in Parents of Normals, Neurotics and Schizophrenics, *Amer. Psychiat. Research Rept.*, 20:25–38, 1966.

Skinner, B. F.: *Verbal Behavior*, New York: Appleton-Century-Crofts, Inc., 1957.

Spiegel, J.: Paradigms Must Be Coordinated. *International Journal of Psychiatry*, 2:422–431, 1966.

Spitz, R. A.: Relevancy of Direct Infant Observations, *The Psychoanalytic Study of the Child*, 5:66–75, 1950.

Stengel, E.: Classification of Mental Disorders, *Bull. World Health Organization*, 21:601–663, 1959.

Stern, A.: Psychoanalytic Investigation of and Therapy in the Borderline Group of Neuroses, *Psychoanal. Quart.*, 7:467–489, 1938.

Strauss, A. L.: A Sociological Perspective on Abnormality, *Arch. Gen. Psychiat.*, 17:265–271, 1967.

Strauss, A. L., Schatzman, L., Bucher, R., Ehrlich, D., and Sabshin, M.: *Psychiatric Ideologies and Institutions*, New York: Free Press, 1964.

Suslick, A.: Pathology of Identity as Related to the Borderline Ego, *Arch. Gen. Psychiat.*, 8:252–262, 1963.

Tinberger, N.: *The Study of Instinct*, London: Oxford University Press, 1951.

Vargas, E.: *Changes in the Symptomatology of Psychotic Patterns*, Budapest, Hungary: Academiai Kradó, 1966.

Waelder, R.: *Basic Theories of Psychoanalyses*, New York: Int. Universities Press, 1960.

Werner, S., and Dunn, O. S.: Elimination of Variates in Linear Discrimination Problems, *Biometrics*, 22:268–275, 1966.

Weingarten, L. L., and Korn, S.: Psychological Test Findings on Pseudoneurotic Schizophrenic, *Arch. Gen. Psychiat.*, 17:448–454, 1967.

Weiss, J. (Reporter): Clinical and Theoretical Aspects of the "As If" Characters (Participants: Atkin, Tartakoff, Ross, Greenson, Katan, Deutsch, Chase, Bychowski, Kaywin), *J. Amer. Psychoanal. Assoc.*, 14:569–591, 1966.

Wilks, S.: *Mathematical Statistics*, New York: John Wiley & Sons, 1962.

Wolberg, A.: The "Borderline Patient," *Amer. J. Psychotherapy*, 6:694–701, 1952.

Wynne, L. C., and Singer, M. T.: Thought Disorder and Family Relations of Schizophrenics, *Arch. Gen. Psychiat.*, 9:199–206, 1963.

Wynne, L. C., and Singer, M. T.: Thought Disorders and Family Relations of Schizophrenics. I. A Research Strategy, *Arch. Gen. Psychiat.*, 9:191–198, 1963.

Zuk, G. H. and Boszormenyi-Nagy, I.: *Family Therapy and Disturbed Families*, Palo Alto, California, Science and Behavior Books, Inc., 1967.

APPENDIX I

Patient_____

Number_____

Caseworker_____

SOCIAL DATA SCHEDULE

1. Birthdate_____   Admitted to ISPI_____

Circle (0) the appropriate code number for each of the following items:

2. Sex:
   0 Male
   1 Female
3. Race:
   0 White
   1 Negro
   2 Other (specify)
4. Religion:
   0 Protestant
   1 Catholic
   2 Jewish
   3 Other (specify)
5. Marital status:
   0 Single (never married)
   1 Married (living with spouse)
   2 Married (separated)
   3 Divorced (remarried)
   4 Divorced (not remarried)
   5 Other (specify)

6. If ever married, how many children does patient have:
   0 None
   1 One
   2 Two
   3 Three
   4 Four or more
7. Education:
   00 Grammar school: completed
   01 Entered but not completed
   10 High School: Completed
   11 Entered but not completed
   20 College: Completed
   21 Entered but not completed
   30 Additional formal education
       Specify

8. Occupation:
   0 Professional, technical or similar
   1 Manager, official, proprietor, except farm
   2 Clerical, kindred
   3 Sales worker
   4 Craftsman, foreman, kindred
   5 Operative, kindred
   6 Private household
   7 Service worker (except private household)
   8 Laborer
   9 Other (specify)
9. Living arrangements—degree of stability in recent years:
   8 Highly stable
   5 Moderately stable
   2 Little stability
   X Unknown
10. Financial support—at the time of admission patient was responsible for:
    0 No one
    1 Self, partially
    2 Self, fully
    3 Self and others—no. of people (   )
    4 Other (specify)
11. Type of admission to hospital:
    0 Voluntary entry
    1 Commitment
12. Comments

APPENDIX II

GUIDE FOR INTERVIEWING REPORTERS

Period Covered
Reporter:_____Date:_____by Report:_____

A series of four frames of reference is suggested to guide the interviews with reporters. These are offered to insure coverage and not to suggest the order of an interview. Points should be used only when relevant and as needed.

   I. Description of Reporter's Contact with Patient
      A. Amount of contact for the period
      B. Kinds of contact
         1. Observation and interaction
         2. Observation only
         3. Hearsay
         4. None
      C. Places of contact
  II. Description of What, When, Where, Who
      A. What was going on (or might go on)—present, past, future
         1. As perceived by reporter
         2. As perceived by patient
         3. As perceived by others (specify)
         4. Combinations of 1, 2, 3
      B. When did the "What" take place; as perceived by
      C. Where did the "What" take place; as perceived by
      D. Who was involved in the "What"; as perceived by
 III. Description of Patient's Behavior
      (In the context of II; *What, When, Where, Who*)
      A. What did the patient say
         1. In time and space

2. As heard by; as reported by

B. How did the patient sound
1. In time and space
2. As heard by; as reported by

C. What did the patient do—how did he act
1. In time and space
2. As observed by; as reported by

D. How did the patient look
1. In time and space
2. As observed by; as reported by

E. How did the patient feel
1. In time and space
2. As elicited by; as reported by

IV. Description of Behavior of Others
(In the context of II; *What, When, Where, Who;* and III; *Patient's Behavior*)

A. What did others, including the reporter, say (specify others)
1. In time and space
2. As heard by; as reported by

B. How did others sound
1. In time and space
2. As heard by; as reported by

C. What did others do—how did they act
1. In time and space
2. As observed by; as reported by

D. How did others look
1. In time and space
2. As observed by; as reported by

E. How did others feel
1. In time and space
2. As elicited by; as reported by

APPENDIX III

PROTOCOL SAMPLES

From these three samples of behavioral reports—(1) male aide, (2) female occupational therapist, (3) female nurse—it is possible to see the repetitive behavior of the patient, her modes and manner, something of her strengths and weaknesses.

The samples illustrate the transactional quality of the reporting elicited by the interview guide that was used (Appendix II). The four sections are spaces provided for coding the behavioral evidences to the variables to which they relate. Sections are: I. Outward Behavior, II. Perception, III. Messages, IV. Affects and Defenses. The codes shown are the original numbers used on the schedule for individual ratings of ego-functions. The first code shown, male aide report, A2aM, was on the original schedule, the variable "Negative Behavior to Male Staff."

Date: Friday, October 26, 1962
Reporter: Male Aide—Mr. C.

	I	II	III	IV
The first night I met Rose she called me stupid. I walked up to her and told her my name and that I was an aide on the floor. "Anything you want, any time you feel that you'd like to talk to me, feel free to do so." "Oh, stupid, get away from me." I didn't know how to take this at that time, so I just walked away. The next evening, I found out that she was calling everybody on the floor stupid.	A2aM A3aM	A2a&b B1a3	Alb	A2a1M B1a1 B2

	I	II	III	IV
I was reading in the chart that she gets in this mood and curses and uses all kinds of profane language. She told me that she expresses her compulsions with this. I sat and talked to her. She said that she didn't mean to call people names, but she gets on these compulsions and this is the only way she can express herself. She said that the nurses and doctors told her that the best thing for her to do when she gets like this is to go to her room and lie down and go to sleep.	A1aM A3aM	A1b A1b A1a	A1b A2b A3b	C1-3
Yesterday I took Rose down for some shots. When I first walked in the door, she started calling me all kinds of profane names. All I'd said was, "Rose, it's time for your shots." When she does this, I just stand right there and look at her. After she gets finished, she'll get up and come with me.	A2aM A3aM			A2a1M B1a1 B2
She went down for her shots. After that, there was a meeting. After she came from the meeting, she was very pleasant. I presumed that the meeting was good for her. At first she told me that she didn't think she could stay through the meeting. Dr. L. and Miss H. suggested that she stay, but if she couldn't understand what they were talking about she could leave. I was very surprised and happy to know that she did stay for all of the meeting.	A1e A3e B1b-B3 A1a A3a B1c1- B3D1	A4 A3a&b		A7e2
Today she was crying. I sat by her. She used some profane names and hit me with a book. She had been read-	A2aM A3aM			B4a&b B1a2

ing a magazine. She asked me, "Are you teasing me, Mr. C.?" "No, I'm not teasing you. I just sat down. You hit me with the book." "I didn't mean to hit you with the book. All I was doing was flipping the book back."

She called me some profane names and then got to her problem. She said that she has a great big crush on Mr. L., but he didn't notice her last night. When he didn't, she got angry at him and threw a milk carton and hit him. She told me that she thought this was very funny. Nobody cares about her feelings and how they hurt her feelings. I asked her how did she feel about his feelings, hitting him with the milk carton. She said that she'd done it just playing.

She said that the things Mr. L. said to her made her throw the milk carton. I asked her what did he say. She said that he came over to her and kissed her on her leg. I guess he was just playing, and she had one of her spells on and thought that he meant something else.

"When are your parents coming to visit you?" She said that her doctor had taken all of her privileges away from her.

She also said that she doesn't mean to say or do the things that she does, but she feels that everybody she talks to and is with is trying to harass her or get on her back.

She feels that someone should be with her and talk to her at all times.

I	II	III	IV
	B1a3 A2a&b		B2
	A5 B1a6	A1b A2b	C1-5
A1aM A3aM	A1c1 A1a	A1b	B1a1 B2 A1b1M A7a2M
A2bM A3bM	A5 A1b C2 A2a&b	A2b A3b	B1a2 B2 A2b2M C1-15
	A2a&b B1ab		C1-15 A3b1
	A3a&b		
	A1a A1B C2		
			A9a

If they aren't she gets very angry. When the patients do get with her, she calls them stupid and other names.

One night her parents visited. I was here but I didn't get a chance to go in the room. We were all sitting in the music room—Rose, G., E., Miss B. and myself. G. told Rose that she would like to see how her visitors looked. Rose got very upset. This is one reason I think she got upset and cursed in front of her parents. She left the dayroom and went to her room with her parents.

The only one on the floor who talks to her is Mr. L. Whenever anyone else talks to her, she figures they are teasing her and she gets upset. She curses and calls them names. When she starts this, she goes to her room and cries.

The other day we were sitting at the piano and she was playing. I told her that her playing was very nice. She said, "That's not all the nice things about me when you get to know me." "I think you are a wonderful person and that you have a lot of nice qualities about you that will come out in time to come." "Yes, they will. All I want to do is get well." She didn't curse.

There are times when I can sit down and talk to her and she won't curse at all. She said, "I will change." She looked at me and said "stupid." She smiled when she said this.

I	II	III	IV
			A2b1
			B1a1
A1c			
A3c	A4		B1a1
			B2
A2a&b	A2a&b	B4b1	B1a1
A3a&b			B2
			A2b1
B1c2	A5		
B3d2	A1d	A1b	A9a
A1aM	C1	A2b	
A3aM		A3b	
	A2a&b		
	C1		

She looks very unhappy to me. She looks like an unhappy child. The only way she'll smile is for someone to go and talk to her. Other than that, she'll walk around with a gloom on her face.

She participated pretty well in activities. She loves to dance. When she goes down to the dances, she dances almost every record. That's one of her favorite hobbies, she says. She's a very good dancer. She'll dance with anyone who asks her. They do ask her.

One night at a dance, she and Mrs. F. had an argument. Both of them wanted to leave the table at the same time. Rose wanted to come upstairs and she walked out. J. walked out too. J. had a grounds pass and didn't need supervision, and went to the canteen. Rose wanted to go to the canteen too and asked me, but I told her that I was the only aide there and she couldn't go. She asked me if I was being smart. "If I want to go, will you stop me?" I told her that I'd have to, at least I'd try. "I wouldn't want to have to do that."

She told me that I was trying to boss her. I told her that I wasn't, that I had a job to do and that was part of my job—to look after her. She said, "Come on. Let's dance." We danced, and she told me what had happened was that she and J. had an argument. Some fellow had sat down at the table. She told him to move and he

I	II	III	IV
			B4a&b
B1b-			
B3b			
B1c1&2	A4		
B3d-	A1c2		
1&2			
			A7b2
	A4		
B1b-			
B3b			
A2aM			B1a1
A3aM	A2a&b		B2
B2b			
B3c	A2a&b		
		A1b	
A1aM	B1a3	A2b	
A3aM		A3b	A7a2M
	A2a&b		A2b1
	B1b3		A7b2
A2bF			

I	II	III	IV
A3bF			
	B1b3		B1a1
	A1c2		B2
A2b			
A3b			
			A7b2M
	C2	A1b	A1b1M
	C1	A2b	A9b1M
		A3b	
	A1c1		
A2b	A2a&b		B1a1
A3b			B2
B1a2	A4		
B3a2			
B2a3			C1-18

didn't want to. She and J. got into some kind of argument. I don't know what the argument was about. After we danced, they sat at the same table and stayed there through the rest of the dance. This was last Wednesday.

She calls the guys who ask her to dance names, too. I see some of them look at her and their eyes stretch. One night she was dancing with some fellow and they stopped in the middle of the floor. She just snatched away from him and came and sat down.

One fellow, in particular, that she would like to dance with at all times is Mr. L. She'll tell you, "I'm just throwing myself at him. He doesn't want me." I don't know too much about Mr. L. I think he's trying to be nice. He'll talk or dance with her like he will with anyone else. She takes it for granted that he should fall in love with her. At least, that's the idea she gives me. Mr. L. doesn't really seem interested in anybody.

When Rose first came to the hospital, she had a crush on Mr. D. Mr. D. got tired of hearing her calling him names. He couldn't take it. I guess Mr. L. just laughs it off. She calls him names too. He'll just smile and laugh it off. He doesn't get upset about them. They said that he kind of got upset last night when she hit him with the milk carton.

She comes out for meals. She doesn't get up in the mornings. I asked her this morning why did she sleep so late. She said that there was nothing to do.

She went to the gym this morning and participated in volleyball. She plays real well. That's the only time I don't hear her calling names. She'll holler over at me sometimes when I'm smiling or laughing, and ask me if I'm laughing at her. I'll tell her that I'm laughing at the game or something.

She'll tell me, "You're my friend. In spite of everything you do, you're my friend." I tell her, "Look, if you are going to call me names, I'm leaving." "Sit down. Don't leave." I didn't leave.

She smiles when she's dancing. The thing she enjoys most is when I show her how to do the Mash Potatoes—that's a dance. I showed her how to do the Bird too—another dance. She's like a little child when he gets a toy. She jumps up and starts clapping her hands. She does this too when she wins when we're playing ping-pong. She's as happy as if she was given a prize for something.

I	II	III	IV
B3a3			
B1c1- B3d1	A4		
B1b- B3b	A1c2		
	A2a&b		
	C2		A1a1M
A1aM A3aM			A8a1M
	A1c2		
B1c2 B3d2			B1b2 B2

Date: Wednesday, October 31, 1962
Reporter: Occupational Therapist—
Miss B.

The first time Rose came into O. T., she bustled in like she's been there before. She walked down the aisle and commented, not talking to anybody in particular, "I don't plan to do any woodworking," in a loud voice.

Then she decided that she would do some woodworking. She sat down on a stool by the window in a secluded area of the room. She spoke to no one, and made no approach to anyone except me when she had difficulty or wanted to go to the next step.

She drew a picture inside the serving bowl. It was a very typical stereotype of an American kid, bouffant hairdo.

Throughout she was using these off-colored words. It was like, "Oh hell." It sounded like a period or punctuation mark. It was just there.

I finally got her out. She didn't want to go. She came back later asking to do more work. I tried to explain to her that we had two groups coming in and just didn't have enough room.

The second time she came in, she felt angry. She was hammering away steadily, hitting very hard and swearing to herself under her breath. She threw down the hammer, got up. There was another patient with whom she was having some difficulty standing off to one side of her. She got up, turned to this patient, called her a few names, and stalked out.

I	II	III	IV
B1c1			
B3d1			A9a
B1b-	A4	A1a	
B3b			
		A4a	
A2b			C1-18
A3b			
	A2a&b		
C1	A5		
C3a			
C3b1			
		B4a1	B1a1
			B2
C1	A4		
	B1a6		
B1c1	A1a		
B3d1	A1a		B1c2
			B2
A2b			B1a1

A couple of minutes later, she came back. She was holding her arms over her stomach. She was really feeling sick. She walked back in and told me that she wanted to apologize. She said, "I'm sorry." She was looking, at this point, for the patient to say, "It's OK. Forget about it." The patient looked at her, turned around and walked out, leaving Rose standing there.

It had been hard enough for her to come back and apologize, because she didn't really mean the apology as such. It made her so angry that this girl didn't understand and she said, "Oh, you're still a bitch."

The next I saw her was at the patient meeting where she got up and talked at length. I think she was successful to the point that she got across that she wanted to be liked and she didn't really know how she wanted to behave, but she did know that she wanted to be accepted. I think she got this across very well.

I also saw an incident where she was accepted by the patients. She

was at a dance last Wednesday night. She was following this patient around. She asked him to dance with her and he did.

She says that she feels D. is one of the patients who is able to express her anger as much as she wants to and gets away with it. She says that people favor her. They treat her like she's dynamite about to go off. I don't

I	II	III	IV
A3b	A2a&b		B2 A2b1
A1b A3b	A2a&b A1b B1b6	A1a	C1-6 C1-14
A2b A3b	A2a&b		B1a1- B2 A2b1F
A1e A3e	A4	A1a A2a A3a	
	A1a A1b A1d C1		
B1c1 B3d1 A1bM	A1c1		
A3bM			A7b2M
	A3a&b		

know how it is on the ward, but I don't think it's so in this situation. Of course, D. denied this, as did other patients. Rose said that she was sorry, but this was the way she felt.

I've seen her a couple of times in the last week or so, and I think she is able to handle her anger much better. She is much more controlled. She doesn't get angry and jump up and run out. She's trying to be more direct. She's swearing less.

Yesterday she said that she felt like hammering. She also said that she was self-conscious because she was making so much noise and disturbing other people. I told her that I would get her some more material so that she could put it between the copper and canvas, pound as much as she wanted to and no one could hear it. She thought this was pretty good idea. I gave her the material.

Yesterday when she was hammering, for the first time since she's been working on this thing, it started to take something of a shape. Before she was just mangling the metal. Now she is directing her blows. She took this piece of metal that was completely messed up, straightened it back out and went to work on it.

At the end of the period she just wanted to hit it one more time. I told her to go ahead and she hit it real hard. "Oh shit, I want to call you a bitch so bad. I haven't done it all day. Just let me say it once." She smiled and said, "You know, I feel much

I	II	III	IV
		A1a	
		A2a	
		A3a	
	A1a		
A1a	A1a		
A3a		A1a	
		A2a	
		A3a	C1-11
	A2a&b		
	B1a6		
	A5		
C1			
C3b1,2			
A2a			
A3a	A2a&b	A1a	B1a1
			B2
			A2a1

	I	II	III	IV

better now," and she was able to go without coming back.

She hasn't been coming regularly, but she's been in four out of the last six or seven sessions. This is good for her. Before she would come in maybe once a week. — B1c1, B3d1 | A4

She seems to relate to me very well. She talks to me. She regards me, pretty much, as a peer. She kids with me and I kid her back. — A1a, A3a | A2a&b | | A7a2

The first day she wanted a lot of help. She looked kind of depressed that day. I was going out of my way to do things for other people, but also getting things for her. I made the comment that I had never worked so hard for a patient since I'd been here. She said, "You're a snot." "Why am I a snot?" "That was a very snotty thing to say." "I'm sorry," but I hadn't intended to be snotty. She told me to go away. I said all right, "Call me when you need me." — A2a, A3a | | | B4a&b, B1a1, B2, A2a1

She does ask for a lot of help. It's not so much a lot of help as it is that she kind of likes to have somebody there. She's pounding on this thing and feels silly pounding, and she wants to tell somebody that she feels silly. She wants to tell somebody that it's not working, or it is working. I try to stay as close to her as I can. — A1a, A3a | A2a&b, A5, A1a, A1b, C2 | | A7a2

A lot of times she'll say something to me like, "You mean you have a degree for this?" I usually joke back with her from time to time. She takes it well usually. Sometimes she says, "You're being snotty." What she's asking for is for people to take this sarcasm because this is the only way she can relate to people. If she makes me feel like I've stepped on her toes, then I'll say I'm sorry, but then I also tell her to let me know what she means. If she means what she says, then everything will be fine.

There have been times when someone like Dr. R. will come in. He asked how she was doing. She was swinging this hammer and said, "This is really doing me a lot of good." He was pleased and said, "I'm very glad to hear it." She retorted, "But I didn't mean it." He told her to say what she means. If it's not doing any good, then say so.

After he left, she told me that he was really a snot too, and didn't have to say that. I repeated to her again, to please say just what she means, because people don't know.

Sometimes she looks depressed. Generally, if she is depressed, she'll show it. She's slower in her movements and speaking. I don't know if anyone else has noticed it or if it's valid. To me, she seems to move slower. Otherwise, she's very energetic and kind of the athletic type.

I	II	III	IV
A2a A3a	A2a&b		A2a1
		A1a A2a A3a	
A1aM A3aM	A2a&b		C1-14
			A2a1M
	A1c2		B4a&b

Date: Friday, November 2, 1962
Reporter: Female Nurse—Miss H.

Several patients went to the Ice Capades last Wednesday. Rose came up to me, "Miss H., I'm just so upset. I want to go." "Why didn't you sign up?" "Well, can't you make an exception for me?" "You had time." "But they made exceptions for other people. Take me." "No." "Well, the patients can vote that I can go. It's OK with them." "That's fine and good, but this is your own fault. You should have signed up for it."

She went to her room. When we came back, they said that she had been in her room crying. She kept saying, "I just have to get out of this place." Everybody kept telling her that it was her own fault. From what I heard, she was like a little kid, "I wanted to do something. I didn't do it, but it's my fault; yet, I don't want to be mad at myself." I think she really wanted to go. She was afraid of being angry at herself and kept blaming it on us. "Please take me. Make an exception." She looked so frustrated.

While she was upset, there were tears, her face was red. There wasn't as much of the language that she usually uses. I felt that she was frustrated and didn't know exactly what to do. She knew that she should be mad at something. When she was telling me about how much she wanted to go and how much she wanted to get out, there was this real, "I want to go. I can't go." Then she'd turn around and say something. "Oh, are you dumb." When she switched

I	II	III	IV
	A3a&b		
			A9a
B1b-B3b	A1a	A1b	
A1aF	A2a&b	A2b	
A3aF	C2	A3b	
	A1b		B4a&b
	A4	A1b	
		A2b	
		A3b	
	A1a		
			B4a&b

back to this, I didn't think there was
the emotion that was in the other
part when she wasn't using these
words.

She was sitting on her bed knitting.
She only made about five rows. She
was ripping it out, putting it back in.
She's been pretty well controlled.

Thursday, I came in at 2:00. I go
to these discussion groups that they
have downstairs. We have a group
going with Miss H. and Dr. L. Six
patients are involved and Rose is one
of them. Yesterday only 3 patients
showed up—Rose, Judy and Dave M.

I can kid with her and yet she
knows that I'm making a point. She'll
sit down there and say, "I really got
upset. If I'm upset with somebody,
that's OK; but if someone else is
upset with the same person, I get
upset with this same person and with
the person who's upset with the
person I'm upset with. I don't know.
I don't think it's controlling my emotions. I don't think that's my problem.
I think my problem is finding emotions."

She has this thing with Judy. She
says, I like you, but I have to call you
names. "I have to call you bastard."
This eased up while I was gone, they
said. Yesterday, she was saying, "You
know I haven't had to say this to you,
but right now, I feel like calling you
a bastard." There was no emotion in
the whole thing.

Judy got angry yesterday, but it
wasn't because of Rose. Rose kept

I	II	III	IV
A2a A3a	A2a&b		B1a1 B2 A2a1
	A5		
A1e A3e1e			A7b2
	A1a A1b		A9a C1-3
A1e A3e		A1a A2a A3a	
	C1		
	A1a A1b A2a&b		C1-14

coming back to herself. She wasn't as upset as they were about what was going on on the ward. She was concerned about herself. They'd be talking about something, and she'd go, "Well, I feel I just have to do this."

When we got back on the ward, she came up to me and said, "You know I've been sitting out in that dayroom. I've been waiting for something to happen. Yes, I just know something is going to happen. R. came up and asked me to go downstairs with him. You know how upset I get with him. Should I go down?" "No. If you're going to get upset, stay here." "Oh are you dumb." "Listen, why don't you go down. You're been waiting for something. Maybe you'll be satisfied." "Oh, be quiet."

She finally went down. She didn't get upset. I went down about 8:45. They were supposed to be back on the ward at 8:30. I went down for coffee and there she was with L. I told her that they were supposed to be upstairs. She was very pleasant.

I guess what they were talking about was how everybody's upset with what's happening on the ward now. S. is real manicky. T's. in bed and falls out on the floor. The new patient is yelling. We have another male patient who is very upset. It's just a bunch of things all together, occurring at once.

Rose wanted to know if he was talking about her when she said he was upset. When we got upstairs,

I	II	III	IV
			A9a
A1a A3a		A1b A2b A3b	
	A1a		
			B1a1 B2
	A2a&b		A2a1
A2a A3a			
B1b- B3b			
A1b- A3b	A4		
			A7b2
B2b			
B3c	A2a&b		
	A1a	A1b	A9a
A1a	A1b	A2b	C1-3

she comes up to me. "Everybody's upset on this floor. I'm not. I see people like that. I'm not upset about it. I'm upset that I'm not upset."

I went and sat down with her and tried to explain, "Rose, when you came in, you acted out so much. You have sympathy because you know these patients are acting out." "Oh, shut up. Gee, are you dumb."

About 5 after 12, she decided that she wanted to talk to me again. I told her no, I was going home.

This morning she was playing pool. S. was acting out. Again, Rose was upset because she wasn't upset about S.

I was in her room Wednesday. She was crying because she wanted to go, and I wasn't giving her any sympathy at all. She was getting a little perturbed. She wanted me to sympathize with her because it was our fault. I wouldn't do it. She said, "I feel like saying something." "What?" "Stick it up your vagina." "Don't." She looked at me, started laughing.

She told me before I left that she feels she's taking so much more in. She says, "You people think I'm really giving a lot out. You can't imagine how much more I'm taking in. It's like getting out the bad stuff when you vomit. I just have to get this stuff out of me. That's the way I do it."

She gets a tickle. The tickle usually is down at the bottom of the sternum.

I	II	III	IV
A3a	C1	A3b	
A2a A3a	A2a&b		B1a1 B2 A2a1
	A2a&b		
B1c2- B3d2			C1-3
A2a A3a	A2a&b A1a A1b	A1b A2b A3b B4b1	B1a1 B2 A2a1
A1a A3a	A1a A1b C1	A1b A2b A3b	C1-3 A9a
	B2		C1-6 A9a

As it rises, she gets upset. If she degrades somebody by using these words, this relieves the tickle.

She said two things. She said that she appreciates a person who doesn't take this personally. She can get along better with this type of person. She can reach some type of understanding with this type of person and feels comfortable with them. But she gets a lot of relief out of a person who will react to this. She is able to react too. If a person does react, which she doesn't really like them to do, she does get relief from it.

She is really a cute kid. She's got a personality. When you get to know her, and she becomes comfortable with you, she'll joke with you, laugh and talk. She's got a pixie haircut and has very bad acne, but she's cute.

I consider her age level about 4 or 5—the way she reacts. I watched her with her mother one time and it was, "Mommy, Mommy." She sat there all rolled up in a fetal position.

One day I worked a double shift. At the end of the 4 to 12 shift, I went out there to watch television. I sat in a chair and put my feet up. I was tired. I sat there leaning back, and she was sitting next to me. She put her feet up too. The two of us were slouched down in the chair watching television. We were joking around. In between episodes we were talking like two people our age.

She had been talking about L. She has affection for L. She switched over

I	II	III	IV
	A1a	A1b	C1-3
	A1b	A2b	
		A3b	
A1a			
	A1d		
A1cMo			C1-13
A3cMo			
		A1b	A7a2
A1a		A2b	
A3a	A2a&b	A3b	

	I	II	III	IV
to this girl conversation, and said, "How would you like to kiss that guy?" She does have a sense of humor. This is when you get the impression that she's so cute. If you can get comfortable enough with her, and have her feel the same way, she comes out with this.	A1a A3a	A1c1		A9a
Once I woke her up in the morning. She went, "Oh get out of here." I went around to her, "Get out of that bed." She looked at me and just laughed.				
Afterwards we were talking again, about how other patients react to what she says. I said "Rose, remember when I woke you up this morning? Your reaction to what I said? I thought you were kidding. I didn't think you were angry at me." "I wasn't."				
She was a management problem in the beginning when we had to keep asking her to go down to her room, and one of us would stay with her. Possibly Monday of last week, she started controlling herself, going to her room when she felt upset. Now, she is staying out in the dayroom all the time. She'll watch all these other interactions that are going on, and come up and tell us about them. "Why don't I get upset?"	B1b- B3b	A4 A3a&b		
In the patient meeting, they were trying to tell her that she was pushing away and pulling at the same time. She actually got around to saying this, but yet she wouldn't admit that she'd said it. She still won't.	A1e A3e	B1e3		C1-3

APPENDIX IV

LIST OF 93 EGO-FUNCTION VARIABLES
THAT ENTERED INTO DATA ANALYSIS
(SCHEDULE FOR INDIVIDUAL RATINGS OF EGO-FUNCTIONS)

PATIENT_____No._____

OBS. PERIOD: 1st_____ UNIT: 1st_____

            2nd____   2nd _____

RATER(s)_____

I OUTWARD BEHAVIOR

  A. To People

	1*	2	3	18
1 Positive Behavior to Male Staff				
2 Positive Behavior to Female Staff				
3 Positive Behavior to Male Patients				
4 Positive Behavior to Female Patients				
5 Negative Behavior to Male Staff				
6 Negative Behavior to Female Staff				
7 Negative Behavior to Male Patients				
8 Negative Behavior to Female Patients				
9 Appropriateness of Behavior to Male Staff				
10 Appropriateness of Behavior to Female Staff				
11 Appropriateness of Behavior to Male Patients				
12 Appropriateness of Behavior to Female Patients				
13 Appropriateness of Behavior in Groups				
B. To the Environment				
14 Positive Behavior to Grooming				

* Each column provides separate space for entering the ratings based on the behavioral evidence for a given report; that is, in column 1 the ratings based on the evidence in report 1 were entered.

	1	2	3	18

15 Positive Behavior to the Routine of Eating
16 Positive Behavior to the Routine of Sleeping
17 Positive Behavior to Freedom
18 Positive Behavior to Organized Programs
19 Positive Behavior to Informal Programs
20 Negative Behavior to Grooming
21 Negative Behavior to the Routine of Eating
22 Negative Behavior to the Routine of Sleeping
23 Negative Behavior to Limits
24 Negative Behavior to Organized Programs
25 Negative Behavior to Informal Programs
26 Appropriateness of Behavior to Grooming
27 Appropriateness of Behavior to Eating
28 Appropriateness of Behavior to Sleeping
29 Appropriateness of Behavior to Freedom
30 Appropriateness of Behavior to Organized
   Programs
31 Appropriateness of Behavior to Informal Programs

C. To Tasks

32 Positive Behavior to Tasks
33 Negative Behavior to Tasks

II PERCEPTION

A. Patient's Awareness

34 Perception of Self—Inner
35 Perception of Self—Outer
36 Awareness of Body Qualities
37 Self-Identity
38 Awareness of Others—Speed of Identification
39 Awareness of Others—Spontaneity of Identification
40 Awareness of Situations and Events—Speed of
   Identification
41 Awareness of Situations and Events—Spontaneity
42 Awareness of Time/Place—Speed/Spontaneity
43 Awareness of Things—Speed/Spontaneity

	1	2	3	18

B. Patient's Differentiation of Roles

44 Self from Staff*

C. Patient's Assessment

45 Self (Self-Esteem)
46 Others in Relation to Self (Trust)
47 Situations, Events and Institutions (Confidence)

III MESSAGES

48 Quantity of Verbal Messages in the Organized Situation
49 Quantity of Verbal Messages in the Informal Situation
50 Degree of Logical Talk in the Organized Situation
51 Degree of Logical Talk in the Informal Situation
52 Degree of Personal Talk in the Informal Situation
53 Congruence of Behavior with Verbal Messages

IV AFFECTS AND DEFENSES
A. Relations with People

54 Positive Affect to Male Staff Stated Verbally
55 Positive Affect to Female Staff Stated Verbally
56 Positive Affect to Male Patients Stated Verbally
57 Positive Affect to Female Patients Stated Verbally
58 Negative Affect to Male Staff Stated Verbally
59 Negative Affect to Female Staff Stated Verbally
60 Negative Affect to Male Staff Stated Nonverbally
61 Negative Affect to Female Staff Stated Nonverbally
62 Negative Affect to Male Patients Stated Verbally
63 Negative Affect to Female Patients Stated Verbally
64 Negative Affect to Male Patients Stated Nonverbally
65 Negative Affect to Female Patients Stated Nonverbally
66 Tolerance for Physical Closeness to Male Staff
67 Tolerance for Physical Closeness to Female Staff

* This variable was originally based on checks of the occurrence of three categories of role behavior: "Complementarity," "Imitation," "Individualism." For data analysis the categories and their combinations were placed on a hierarchical scale. Frequency of occurrence of the role pattern was the basis for coding the patient on the scale.

	1	2	3	18

68 Tolerance for Physical Closeness to Male Patients

69 Tolerance for Physical Closeness to Female
   Patients

70 Relationship Constancy for Male Staff

71 Relationship Constancy for Female Staff

72 Relationship Constancy for Male Patients

73 Relationship Constancy for Female Patients

74 Investment in Self

75 Investment in One Male

76 Investment in One Female

77 Investment in More Than One Male

78 Investment in More Than One Female

B. Control of Affect and Behavior

79 Quantity of Impulse Discharge to People Stated
   Verbally

80 Quantity of Impulse Discharge to People Stated
   Nonverbally

81 Quantity of Impulse Discharge to Situations Stated
   Verbally

82 Quantity of Impulse Discharge to Situations Stated
   Nonverbally

83 Quantity of Impulse Discharge to Things Stated
   Verbally

84 Quantity of Impulse Discharge to Things Stated
   Nonverbally

85 Quantity of Physiological Process Stated Verbally

86 Quantity of Physiological Process Stated
   Nonverbally

87 Capacity to Delay Impulse Discharge

88 Free Anxiety—Intensity

89 Free Anxiety—Duration

90 Depression—Intensity

91 Depression—Duration

C. Defenses*

92 Defense Checked with Highest Frequency

* Since these variables were based originally on checks of occurrence of the defenses observed in behavior, for data analysis the defenses were placed on a hierarchical scale ranging from 1–9; for example, regression was 1 on the scale.

	1	2	3	18
93 Defense Checked with Second Frequency				
List of Defenses				
Intellectualization				
Humor				
Rationalization				
Compulsivity				
Somatization				
Projection				
Displacement				
Withdrawal				
Denial				
Dissociation				
Regression				

Frequency of occurrence of the defense was the basis for coding the patient on the scale.

APPENDIX V

GENERAL DEFINITIONS AND SCALE POINT CUES

I OUTWARD BEHAVIOR

Outward behavior means the publicly observable or visible actions of the individual. Excluded from the meaning are introspective data, consciousness or references to mind. To make quantitative and qualitative assessments of outward behavior usually requires transactional evidence. The evidence should express the mutual, reciprocal effects of processes experienced by several people in a given field. Although such processes involve implicit and explicit social roles, outward behavior by definition deals with the explicit. A role is defined as a goal-directed pattern or sequence of acts tailored by the cultural process for the transactions a person may carry out in a social group or situation. Social roles involve complementary or reciprocal expectations of behavior, and the criteria for a number of ratings in this section are stated as expectations inhering in social roles.

A. Outward Behavior to People

The categories *Staff* and *Patients* are defined by name. The category *In Groups* is described by a series of transactions that culminates in the development of leadership roles with the consequent ordering of behavior and establishing of controls. First, there must be interaction, then functional interdependence—commonality of purpose, problem, and feeling about something significant—and finally, a flow of communication resulting in the development of leadership roles. Leadership roles may be implicit or explicit and there may be more than one in a group. Some roles relate to tasks and some to feelings. The group must accord leadership to an individual, and the individual must have the capacity to assume the role. Thus the identification of leadership is the necessary condition for specifying the *Group* as the field in which the patient's behavior occurred.

1–4 *Positive Behavior to People* can be characterized as action that moves one toward others in the interest of furthering relationships.

	Rating	Scale Point Cues
1–2 Staff	8	Patient seeks out staff and uses their assistance.
	5	Patient accepts the presence of staff in their routine contacts on the ward; accepts assistance when offered.
	2	Patient only accepts the presence of staff when staff makes a positive effort.
3–4 Patients	8	Patient seeks out other patients; makes a special effort to include them in his ward behavior.
	5	Patient accepts the presence of other patients in spontaneous contacts.
	2	Patient only accepts other patients if they make a special effort to include the patient in their behavior.

5–8 *Negative Behavior to People* can be characterized as action that diminishes relationship.

	Rating	Scale Point Cues
5–6 Staff	8	Patient activity avoids contact with the staff, asking them to go away.
	5	Patient passively rejects staff by missing appointments, avoiding opportunities for meeting.
	2	Patient will allow staff to remain but expresses preference that the contact be brief.
7–8 Patients	8	Patient actively drives other patients away.
	5	Patient avoids other patients.
	2	Patient will accept other patients, but reluctantly.

9-13 *Appropriateness of Behavior:* Behavior is considered appropriate when actions meet socially acceptable expectations of behavior for the setting generally and for the situation specifically. Behavior may sometimes realistically reflect an existing affective relationship, but if socially unacceptable, the behavior should be rated at the low end of the appropriateness scale. For example, conflictual, unhappy marital relations acted-out during visits on the unit would, under the terms designated, be considered inappropriate behavior.

9-10 To Staff. Appropriateness of behavior to staff covers the expectations that: (1) patients will communicate with staff, (2) patients will act toward staff in accordance with their known functions.

Rating	Scale Point Cues
8	Patient actively engages staff in discussion of personal problems and current problems on the unit.
5	Patient accepts suggestions of staff and cooperates with them.
4	Patient follows suggestions of staff only if offered; patient does not use or misuse staff.
2	Patient tends to avoid or disregard staff.

11-12 To Patients. Appropriateness of behavior to patients covers the expectations that: (1) patient will understand that he is part of a formal group which requires living together reasonably comfortably, (2) patient will work toward resolution of a conflict in a group.

8	Patient actively uses other patients for emotional support, recreational activities, and discussion of problems. (Discussion of detailed personal problems, particularly in groups, would be inappropriate.)
5	Patient accepts presence of other patients on the unit as people with problems with whom it may or may not be useful to work.

Rating	*Scale Point Cues*
2	Patient treats other patients on the unit as mentally ill people with whom he could not possibly have anything in common and who can be of no help to him.

13 In Groups. Appropriateness of behavior in groups covers the expectations that the patient will be present and participate in group activities.

8	Patient, during patient meetings and other group activities, actively engages in discussion of common problems.
5	Patient accepts group situations but does not seek them out.
2	Patient does not bring up group problems in groups, or else discusses personal problems in detail.

B. Outward Behavior to the Environment

Environment means the aggregate of the external conditions and forces affecting the life of the patient (excluding the people in the environment accounted for in the ratings under IA). Our observations will refer primarily to the hospital, its facilities, and to the unit on which the patient lives. However, the patient's life space is as inclusive as the observations that are reported.

Routines refers to current customs and observances. The concept includes specified rules but the notion of routines is more general covering customs, order, observances.

Freedom refers to the advantages that the hospital has to offer.

Limits refers to the specified rules and regulations of the hospital.

Programs or Situations: (1) Organized, (2) Informal. Everything that occurs against the relatively steady background of the hospital should be considered informal. When the situation is specifically formalized within the total, then the situation should be considered organized. Organized implies structure and expectations. Thus, occupational therapy, the dance, the ward meeting are organized. Card games, ping-pong, pool are informal when they do not reach tournament proportions.

14–19 *Positive Behavior to the Environment* can be characterized as affirmative management of oneself in relation to the demands of the environment. (Rate "passive resistance" at the lower end of the continuum.)

	Rating	*Scale Point Cues*
14 Grooming	8	Patient is almost always well groomed.
	5	Patient is well groomed when required.
	2	Patient is well groomed only with encouragement from staff.
15 Eating	8	Patient actively approaches mealtimes and snacks; requests trips to canteen.
	5	Patient accepts meals and snacks.
	2	Patient accepts meals and snacks with support from staff.
16 Sleeping	8	Patient goes to bed early (between 10 and 12); sleeps through night.
	5	Patient stays up occasionally.
	2	Patient goes to bed when reminded by staff.
17 Freedom	8	Patient makes a special effort to obtain privileges (passes, access to telephone, to hospital activities) as soon as possible.
	5	Patient asks for privileges in the usual course of events.
	2	Patient takes or uses privileges when offered.

Programs/Situations—(See general definition distinguishing organized from informal.)

18 Organized	8	Patient looks for organized activities and requests additional activities at patient meetings.
	5	Patient attends organized activities consistently.
	2	Patient attends organized activities when reminded by staff.
19 Informal	8	Patient organizes informal activities; shows leadership on the unit in this respect.
	5	Patient participates in informal activities such as card games, etc.

2   Patient occasionally participates in informal activities; usually when reminded by staff or patients.

20–25 *Negative Behavior to the Environment* can be characterized as active protest or overt noncompliance with the demands of the environment.

	Rating	*Scale Point Cues*
20 Grooming	8	Patient remains in pajamas with no attention to appearance.
	5	Patient prefers to dress sloppily even when reminded by staff.
	2	Patient will dress or groom himself under protest when encouraged by staff.
21 Eating	8	Patient will not eat by himself.
	5	Patient eats irregularly with encouragement.
	2	Patient eats meals on wards irregularly; depends on snacks.
22 Sleeping	8	Patient sleeps during the day and is up at night and insists on this.
	5	Patient stays up at night unless heavily sedated or sent to bed by staff.
	2	Patient complains about sleeping and arising hours, but conforms.
23 Limits/ Regulations	8	Patient disregards ward and hospital rules.
	5	Patient disregards rules unless constantly directed by staff.
	2	Patient tests limits, but complainingly conforms.
Programs/ Situations		
24 Organized 25 Informal	8	Patient refuses to attend any of the organized or informal programs.
	5	Patient avoids organized or informal programs.
	2	Patient avoids programs unless reminded by staff.

26-31 *Appropriateness of Behavior to the Environment* is behavior that conforms to or accommodates to the social demands defined by the environment. Scale point cues will vary with the environment.

26 Grooming
27 Eating
28 Sleeping
29 Freedom
30 Organized Programs
31 Informal Programs

C. Outward Behavior to Tasks

Tasks mean any work that the patient undertakes for himself or any that might be assigned to him. Exclude casual, incidental offers of help such as, "I can show you how to play hearts."

32 *Positive Behavior to Tasks* suggests moving constructively toward making or doing something.

Rating	Scale Point Cues
8	Patient looks for jobs on the ward or in activities (occupational therapy).
5	Patient accepts assigned tasks.
2	Patient will perform tasks or participate in activities only with strong support.

33 *Negative Behavior to Tasks* suggests moving toward making or doing something destructively or else moving away from the task.

Rating	Scale Point Cues
8	Patient refuses to do anything on the ward or in activities.
5	Patient can occasionally be encouraged to accept a job assignment on the ward.
2	Patient occasionally participates in an activity or accepts a ward assignment, but protests.

II PERCEPTION

Perception refers to what the patient discerns, knows, apprehends, about himself, about others, and about what transpires in his life space. Perception as used here involves cognitive processes such as thinking, judgment and memory.

A. *Patient's Awareness of*

34–37 *Self* means that the patient recognizes impulses, affects, thoughts, attitudes and actions intrinsically arising in himself as belonging to himself. At the pathological extreme are delusional systems and hallucinatory experiences.

34 *Inner* covers internal phenomena such as impulses, fantasies, feelings reported by the patient or assessed from clear, concrete observations of affective behavior.

Rating	Scale Point Cues
8	Patient describes a strong impulse in a vivid way; for example, "I should be out working, but I feel very depressed about my chances of getting a job."
5	Patient describes some fantasies or impulses but in a vaguer way; for example, "Sometimes I wonder what I'm doing here. Maybe I'm trying to get out of responsibility."
2	Patient denies feelings such as anger when looking angry, or says, "I don't know how I feel today," or, "I'm never sure what I'm going to do."

35 *Outer* covers external phenomena expressed in nonverbal as well as verbal behavior.

8	Patient is highly aware of his behavior; e.g., "I've sure been grouchy today."
5	Patient is moderately aware; e.g., "Did I say something wrong?"
2	Patient is scarcely aware: "I can't understand why you people won't listen to my problems," or "What did I do?"

36 His Body Qualities

8	Highly aware: Patient's body movements indicate an easy awareness of himself and the physical body; for instance, dancing and athletics.
5	Is confused: Patient is somewhat awkward in gross physical activities: Questions staff; for instance, "Am I putting on weight?"

2   Misidentifies: Patient is physically
awkward and needs cues from staff to
manage the simple physical tasks.

37 *Self-Identity.* We have defined self-identity as the integrated
perception of oneself moving through life. Stated another way,
self-identity is the organized and enduring conception of oneself
and his place in the social scheme of things. Patients may talk
about themselves and their lives in such a way that the evidence
for the rating is specified and can be coded directly to the item.
However, self-identity is a global concept and a global rating.
Once ratings based on sufficient and substantial evidence have
been made for "inner," for "outer," and for "body image" then
the global rating for self-identity may emerge from the previous
parts. A high rating on self-identity involves some awareness of
both inner and outer.

8   High consistency.
5   Moderate.
2   Low consistency.

38–39 *Others* means that the patient recognizes (and implies that the
patient knows): (1) the culturally defined behavioral expectations tacitly held for the variety of people of differing age, sex,
race, social, cultural group, occupational class, etc.; and (2) their
invitations and demands on him.

38 *Speed of Identification* is the rapidity or swiftness with which
the patient identifies explicit and implicit messages.

Rating	*Scale Point Cues*
8	Patient behaves entirely realistically at the time, in relation to the other individual's personal and occupational characteristics.
5	Patient has to wait for a minute or two to respond to another person; for example, patient needs a few sentences from the other person before he is sure who they are.
2	Patient needs repeated explanations of who people are.

39 *Spontaneity of Identification* means that the patient can

proceed in the absence of explicit messages; the patient can take cues.

8	Patient can judge who people are and what they want without explanations and understands immediately.
5	Patient understands who people are and what they want, when told.
2	Patient can only respond to repeated definite statements about who people are and what they want, nor does patient inquire about people and their wants.

40–41 *Situations and Events* refers to transactions which the patient observes, without involvement (for example, the behavior of others), and events such as games in which the patient may be a participator without interpersonal involvement.

	Rating	*Scale Point Cues*
40 Speed of Identification	8	Patient identified the events at the time.
	5	It took a few minutes before patient could identify what was going on.
	2	Patient did not identify or delayed responses for a considerable time.
41 Spontaneity of Identification	8	Patient behaved entirely realistically in relation to the event.
	5	Patient behaved as though he were trying to understand what was going on; e.g., is Mrs. M. drunk?
	2	Patient behaved as though he scarcely understood; e.g., it is a shame the way these nurses treat Mrs. M.

42 *Time and Place* refers to awareness of "when" and "where."

	Rating	*Scale Point Cues*
42 Speed and Spontaneity	8	Since admission patient has been aware of where he is and what time it is.
	5	Patient needs some explanation of the hospital.

Rating	Scale Point Cues
2	Patient needs repeated cues each day to maintain his orientation, or even has difficulty maintaining his orientation with repeated cues.

43 *Things* refers to inanimate objects.

	Rating	Scale Point Cues
43 Speed and Spontaneity	8	Patient is aware of furnishings and facilities of the unit and the general hospital areas, and has no difficulty with their use. Patient is able to distinguish public from personal property.
	5	Patient is aware of the nature and purpose of equipment and property, but needs reminders of what belongs to whom and how to care for and use property.
	2	Patient is unable to distinguish objects, for instance, "This chair is a spaceship," or else patient has gross distortions as to whom what belongs and how objects should be used; e.g., patient takes food off other patients' trays.

B. *Patient's Differentiation of Roles*

44 *Role Identity* refers to the awareness of one's role in transactions with others. In a single transaction three discrete categories of behavior are possible:

Complementarity is defined as acting in accord with the expectations of others.

Imitation is defined as taking on the role of the other.

Individuality is defined as acting independently of the other.

C. *Patient's Assessment of*

45–47 *Assessment* refers to judgment or appraisal.

	Rating	Scale Point Cues
45 *Self* Assessment of	8	Though unable to handle his problems in some areas, patient feels that he is

Rating	Scale Point Cues
self may be equated with *Self-esteem*	basically worthwhile and that his troubles are temporary.
5	Patient feels uncertain of his own worth, looks down on himself for his weakness and illness.
2	Patient feels worthless, no good, unlovable.

46 *Trust* 8 Optimistic about help, feels people
Assessment of are basically well intentioned and good.
others in re- Questioning: "Can I be helped?"
lation to self 5 "Can one trust others?"
may be equated
with *trust*. 2 Suspicious and mistrustful; won't or
can't be helped.

47 *Con-*
fidence 8 "Everything can't always go wrong."
Assessment 5 Uncertain of future, patient vacillates
of situations, between hope and despair. "Sometimes
events, and in- I feel that nothing good can happen to
stitutions may me, but then I think that everything
be equated can't always go wrong."
with *confidence*.
2 "Nothing good can happen to me."

III MESSAGES

Messages are verbal and nonverbal communications which report fact, impart thought, idea, meaning, and feeling.

Patient's Verbal Messages means all that the patient communicates verbally.

48–49 *Quantity of Verbal Messages*

Rating	Scale Point Cues
8	Patient talks practically all of the time.
5	Patient talks back and forth conversationally.
2	Patient rarely talks; usually only when spoken to.

50–51 *Degree of Logical Talk:* Logical talk has precise meaning, is clear and coherent.

Rating	Scale Point Cues
8	When patient talks, what he says has precise meaning.
5	Patient gives a general drift, but I have to ask him to be sure I understand.
2	I don't understand what the patient is talking about.

52 *Degree of Personal Talk:* Personal talk may be characterized as relating to the individual—his behavior, his motives, his private affairs.

Rating	Scale Point Cues
8	Patient talks mostly about himself.
5	Patient talks about himself some, but also about other people on the ward.
2	Patient rarely mentions himself.

53 *Congruences of Behavior with Verbal Messages:* Congruence means that the total behavior including the nonverbal coincides with and is in harmony with the verbal messages.

Rating	Scale Point Cues
8	Patient does what he says.
5	If patient says something, he usually does it.
2	What the patient says doesn't have much to do with what he does.

IV AFFECTS AND DEFENSES

Affect means the feelings and emotions associated with various forms of action, and various modes and means of communication. Love, tenderness, longing, jealousy, shame, guilt, anger and rage are examples of affects that may be manifest in behavior and communicated in any of several forms, currently or retrospectively. Affects may be rated on:

(1) A reportable feeling of which the patient is conscious and of which he may have a fairly good quantitative metric;

(2) Observations supported by behavioral evidence that the patient looked "as if" he were angry;

(3) A diagnostic inference based on interpretation of extensive behavioral evidence, in which event the patient's feelings may be
below his awareness.

A. *Relations with People* deals with the feelings associated with transactions with others and with the quality of observable response and
behavior.

54–57 *Positive Affect Toward Others* can be characterized as feelings
and emotions that tend in the direction of establishing and maintaining amicable relations, liking, affection, and tenderness for
others.

	Rating	*Scale Point Cues*
54–55 Staff	8	Enthusiasm, adoration, love: "Mr. Jones, you are the best aide in the hospital."
	5	Active liking: "Mr. Jones, I would like to go to the patio with you."
	2	Weak approval: "Mr. Jones is OK, as aides go."

56–57 *Patients:* The scale point cues illustrated for Staff may be
applied to patients.

58–65 *Negative Affect Toward Others* can be characterized as feelings
and emotions that tend in the direction of pushing others away
and of decreasing rapport.

	Rating	*Scale Point Cues*
58–59 Staff Verbal	8	Strongly repelling, hate, anger: "I don't want to talk to you now, or in the future." "You are the most repulsive person I have seen; who tells you you are a psychiatrist?"
	5	Moderately repelling, active dislike: "If I have to go down to the patio with you instead of Mr. Jones, all right; but he isn't available."
	2	Critical, complaining: "Mr. Jones isn't much good as an aide, but what can you expect at these salaries?"
60–61 Staff Non-verbal	8	Strongly repelling, e.g., overt angry avoidance, or physical attack.

Rating	Scale Point Cues
5	Moderately repelling, active dislike, e.g., in behavior overtly pushing others aside.
2	Weakly repelling, e.g., in behavior tending to ignore the invitations and demands of others.

62–65 Patients   The scale point cues illustrated for staff may be applied to patients.

66–69 *Tolerance for Physical Closeness* means to be able to endure or to bear the presence of other people within the hospital unit, physically close, or in actual bodily contact.

	Rating	Scale Point Cues
66–67 Staff	8	Seeking, clinging: Mr. So-and-so likes me to stay very close with him particularly when he's anxious.
	5	Acceptance: Mr. So-and-so joins in the ward activities but seems uncomfortable if somebody sits with him for any length of time.
	2	Avoidance: When Mr. So-and-so sees me coming, he heads off the ward.

68–69 Patients   The scale point cues illustrated for staff may be applied to patients.

70–73 *Capacity for Relationship Constancy* means to be able to continue relationships over time. Continuance does not imply a positive relationship. The relationships of patients that will be rated "low" on constancy will be marked by frequent exchange of people or by gross investment in self.

	Rating	Scale Point Cues
70–71 Staff	8	Highly consistent over time: Mr. So-and-so always asks me to take him to the patio; if I'm not around, he waits on the ward.
	5	Moderately consistent: Mr. So-and-so usually asks me, but can go with somebody else.
	2	Little consistency over time: It doesn't seem to make any difference to Mr. So-and-so which nurses or aides he does things with.

72–73 Patients   The scale point cues illustrated for staff may be applied to patients.

74–78 *Quality of Object Relations:* Degree of interest and/or investment in:

74 Self represents all facets of one's ego.

Rating	Scale Point Cues
8	Patient is only interested in what he wants
5	Patient puts himself first, but can listen to the requests and opinions of others.
2	Patient considers his own wishes or preferences realistically in relation to those of others.

Others. In this category the individual invests in others.

75–76 One Individual

8	Patient seems to be able to talk about pretty much anything with me.
5	Patient seems to get fairly close to Mr. So-and-so. They do a lot of different things together.
2	Patient keeps all people at a distance.

77–78 More Than One

8	Patient has some very complicated relationships with other people. He can relate in a number of ways.
5	Patient seems to be able to talk to a lot of different people. He gets along, depending on what he wants, with a variety of people.
2	Patient keeps all people at a distance.

B. *Control of Affect and Behavior:* Control implies the maintenance of ordinary rational processes.

Impulse Eruption or Discharge: Impulse refers to impelling wishes or urges to action. Underlying ratings of high discharge is the assumption that uncontrollable feelings and emotions were associated with the impulse. High discharge implies low control, but low discharge does not necessarily imply high control. Impulse eruption is rated in terms of the object of the response, since the stimuli are not always known.

	Rating	*Scale Point Cues*
79–80 People	8	Patient stated, "Get the hell out of here
79 Verbal		and don't come back!" in a loud voice.
	5	Patient said, "Why do you keep coming around, and bothering me?"
	2	Patient said, "I wish he wouldn't come around," in a low voice.
80 Nonverbal	8	Patient threw Mr. Jones right out of the room.
	5	Patient got up and walked out as soon as Mr. Jones started to visit.
	2	Patient acted extremely bored and sleepy but didn't ask Mr. Jones to leave.

81–82 Situations, Events

	Rating	*Scale Point Cues*
	8	When the fire drill started, the
81 Verbal		patient shouted to the nurses, "You're going the wrong way."
	5	Patient kept talking about how he hoped this was only a drill.
	2	The patient waited patiently for the fire drill—didn't say much to the staff.
82 Nonverbal	8	When the fire drill started, the patient ran to the end of the hall and began banging on the fire door.
	5	The patient went to the head of the line as we approached the stairs.
	2	The patient plugged along at the tail end, not seeming very excited.

	Rating	*Scale Point Cues*
83–84 Things	8	Patient yelled so loudly when the lights
83 Verbal		went on that he woke everybody up.
	5	Patient said to the man next door, "Get in here and fix that."
	2	Patient stayed in bed muttering.
84 Nonverbal	8	Patient pulled the lights all on when the man next door disturbed him.
	5	Patient unscrewed his lightbulb and went back to bed.
	2	Patient turned over and faced the wall.

85–86 Physiological Processes

	Rating	Scale Point Cues
85 Verbal	8	Patient sits in the dayroom yelling, "Do something, I'm getting weaker all the time!"
	5	This patient frequently complains he is hungry and is not getting enough to eat.
	2	Patient occasionally comments on his appetite.
86 Nonverbal	8	Patient takes stuff right off other people's trays without asking and glares at them if they interfere.
	5	Patient is always taking off for the canteen.
	2	Patient is usually late for meals.

87 *Capacity to Delay Impulse Discharge* refers to an estimate of the time span between the stimulus and the response. Discharge may be immediate in response to a stimulus or may occur only after efforts at control or for other reasons.

Rating	Scale Point Cues
8	We got to talking today and the patient was complaining about what I said to him yesterday.
5	After I walked back to the dayroom, the patient came in and said, "What the hell do you mean by talking to me that way when you got me up?"
2	As soon as I asked the patient to get out of bed, he began yelling and throwing pillows.

Free Anxiety is equivalent to felt anxiety. It is an anticipatory feeling of dread, doom, a feeling that something horrible is going to happen. Symptomatically, free anxiety is marked by sweating, dilation of the pupils, tremors.

	Rating	Scale Point Cues
88 Intensity	8	Intense.
	5	Impressive.
	2	Distinct, but not impressive.

	Rating	Scale Point Cues
89 Duration	8	Approximately an hour or more.
	5	Approximately less than an hour.
	2	Approximately less than a quarter of an hour.

Depression is characterized by hopelessness, helplessness, failure, sadness, gloom.

	Rating	Scale Point Cues
90 Intensity	8	Intense.
	5	Impressive.
	2	Distinct, but not impressive.

	Rating	Scale Point Cues
91 Duration	8	Lasting.
	5	Temporary.
	2	Transient.

C. *Defense Mechanisms*

Defense mechanisms or characterological defenses are the repetitive, automatic techniques which a person uses to protect himself against the arousal, the awareness, and the intensity of affects.

	General Definition	Behavioral Cues
Intellectualization	Reasoning or thinking about impulses, affects and actions as a precaution against danger.	"Do patients here get psychoanalysis or psychoanalytically-oriented psychotherapy?" (From patient—first day on floor.)
Humor	Substituting the ludicrous or the comic for painful, disturbing affects, thus gaining pleasure despite the pain.	Reporter states: He tries to make a joke out of everything.
Rationalization	Selecting the most acceptable and apparently reasonable from a complex of motives to explain behavior originally unacceptable.	"Of course I'm worried about the H-bomb, isn't everybody."

Compulsivity	Routinized concentration of behavior, task, or game.	
Somatization	Reacting organically to unacceptable impulses or affects.	Reporter states: Patient always has aches and pains instead of worries; or patient states: You must think this is all in my head?
Projection	Divesting oneself of and blaming others for an unacceptable impulse or action.	"Tell this man to keep his hands off of me!"
Displacement	Expressing a repressed impulse in some other category of functioning.	Reporter: When she's angry at her roommate, she picks a fight with me.
Withdrawal	Moving away from reality.	"I don't choose to talk about that any more."
Denial	Negation of conscious awareness of inner or outer stimuli —literally seeing but refusing to acknowledge what one sees, or hearing and negating what is heard. Denial should be distinguished from avoidance manifested; for example, by the actual closing of the eyes or the refusal to look.	"What disturbance? Nobody is crazy here."
Dissociation	Separating from consciousness some part of mental activity which then	Reporter: Patient acts like she doesn't know what she's doing.

	functions as an independent unit of mental life.	
Regression	Currently using ego-functions which were once adequate even though now less effective.	"I feel too bad to get out of bed. I want my meals in my room."

APPENDIX VI

Patient_____No._____
Observational Period:
1st_____2nd_____
Rater_____

SYNTHESIS SCHEDULE

1. *Capacity for Problem-Solving.* Rate the patient using the following scale:
   8—High; 5—Moderate; 2—Low; 0—None; IE—Insufficient Evidence; NE—No Evidence.

   Rate Each Part
   (a) Delays actions appropriately in pursuit of solutions to problems   _____
   (b) Weighs and selects among the demands of social pressures and influences   _____
   (c) Applies his thoughts to a problem   _____
   (d) Foresees consequences of decisions and actions*   _____
   (e) Chooses realistically among alternative courses of action   _____
2. *Capacity to Carry on Usual Life Processes.* Rate the patient using the following scale: 8—High; 5—Moderate; 2—Low; 0—None; IE—Insufficient Evidence; NE—No Evidence.

   To what degree is the patient able to carry on his usual life processes   _____

---

* This question implies using ordinary experience leading to adjustment to the social environment.

APPENDIX VII

SYNTHESIS DEFINITIONS

Synthesis is the ego-function that unites, binds, and creates concepts, percepts and actions.

1. *Capacity for Problem Solving.** The problem-solving item and its parts (a—e) are bound up with the internal logic and thought processes of raters. Inferences may be colored by their culturally determined value systems.

   (a) *Delays Actions Appropriately in Pursuit of Solutions to Problems* implies resistance to acting before obtaining sufficient and adequate information.

   (b) *Weighs and Selects Among the Demands of Social Pressures and Influences* implies the ability to choose among the demands, claims, and suggestions made by other people.

   (c) *Applies His Thoughts to a Problem* suggests that the patient reports consideration of a problem, trial and error thinking, and tentative decisions are not expressed in action.

   (d) *Foresees Consequences of Decisions and Actions* implies using experience generally.

   (e) *Chooses Realistically Among Alternative Courses of Action* suggests that the patient apparently chooses realistically among alternatives for the problem presented.

2. *Capacity to Carry on Usual Life Processes.* This is the rater's impressionistic assessment of the patient at rest.

---

* To make realistic cause-effect connections is part of the problem-solving process. The capacity to connect causally is being omitted from this scheme because psychiatric patients have, by the nature of their illness, inevitably failed in this task.

APPENDIX VIII

AGREEMENT ON 90 VARIABLES

Detailed data on the amount and nature of agreement for 90 variables are presented in the table in this Appendix. For all of these variables the number of effective categories is ten (0 through 9), since no scales were reduced for analysis. Using "no evidence" (NE) and "insufficient evidence" (IE) as effective categories is excluded. Since raters were required to code evidence prior to making ratings, the occasions when one rater used NE or IE and the other made a rating, 10 per cent of all possible ratings (453 out of 4,590 total sets) are treated as an assessment of the raters' use of evidence rather than of scale points. Thus for 90 per cent of all possible ratings both raters located the evidences for their ratings. The NE-rating occurrences were resolved by a third rater who reviewed the evidence coded by the person who had used a scale point. The decision of the third rater went to one or the other of the pair 409 out of the total of 453. The base for computing the proportions of agreement in the following table excludes the NE-rating occurences. For variables 1 through 8, 13, 20 through 25, 33, 54 through 73, 75 through 86, 88 through 91, NE-NE was equated with zero, since if the behavior did not appear in the observational period, it was assumed the sample of behavior was adequate for a determination of not present.

PROPORTION OF INSTANCES OF
INDEPENDENT AGREEMENT BETWEEN TWO RATERS

Variable* Number	Base	Exact Agreement	One-Step Difference	Exact and One-Step Cumulated	Two-Step Difference	Cumulated
1	49	.49	.39	.88	.12	1.00
2	51	.43	.39	.82	.18	1.00
3	50	.44	.48	.92	.08	1.00
4	50	.40	.50	.90	.10	1.00
5	46	.46	.32	.78	.20	.98
6	48	.35	.44	.79	.19	.98
7	45	.40	.42	.82	.09	.91
8	50	.44	.34	.78	.12	.90
9	49	.31	.61	.92	.06	.98
10	51	.31	.57	.88	.10	.98
11	51	.34	.50	.84	.12	.96
12	51	.37	.47	.84	.14	.98
13	49	.33	.51	.84	.14	.98
14	49	.45	.47	.92	.08	1.00
15	46	.35	.41	.76	.20	.96
16	46	.36	.42	.78	.18	.96
17	51	.24	.40	.64	.30	.94
18	51	.49	.41	.90	.10	1.00
19	51	.45	.43	.88	.12	1.00
20	45	.71	.16	.87	.11	.98
21	41	.76	.12	.88	.10	.98
22	43	.65	.26	.91	.09	1.00
23	40	.50	.23	.73	.17	.90
24	41	.27	.49	.76	.22	.98
25	36	.69	.22	.91	.06	.97
26	51	.46	.42	.88	.12	1.00
27	47	.32	.47	.79	.17	.96
28	49	.25	.51	.76	.14	.90
29	51	.28	.32	.60	.26	.86
30	51	.40	.54	.94	.06	1.00
31	51	.51	.41	.92	.06	.98
32	47	.36	.34	.70	.21	.91
33	35	.77	.09	.86	.06	.92
34	51	.29	.31	.60	.29	.89
35	51	.33	.43	.76	.18	.94
36	49	.25	.55	.80	.18	.98
37	49	.25	.51	.76	.14	.90
38	51	.29	.33	.62	.24	.86
39	51	.28	.45	.73	.25	.98
40	51	.20	.49	.69	.12	.81
41	51	.29	.43	.72	.22	.94

Variable* Number	Base	Exact Agreement	One-Step Difference	Exact and One-Step Cumulated	Two-Step Difference	Cumulated
42	51	.39	.39	.78	.12	.90
43	51	.41	.33	.74	.20	.94
45	49	.22	.41	.63	.27	.90
46	49	.35	.47	.82	.16	.98
47	47	.45	.40	.85	.13	.98
48	49	.41	.39	.80	.16	.96
49	51	.39	.53	.92	.04	.96
50	41	.27	.46	.73	.24	.97
51	51	.32	.50	.82	.14	.96
52	51	.26	.29	.55	.29	.84
53	41	.22	.32	.54	.19	.73
54	40	.73	.10	.83	.10	.93
55	36	.44	.36	.80	.17	.97
56	41	.90	.05	.95	.05	1.00
57	45	.93	.05	.98	.02	1.00
58	42	.62	.21	.83	.12	.95
59	45	.53	.25	.78	.18	.96
60	34	.50	.32	.82	.09	.91
61	38	.50	.37	.87	.05	.92
62	40	.53	.25	.78	.12	.90
63	42	.52	.26	.78	.12	.90
64	39	.54	.33	.87	.10	.97
65	39	.54	.36	.90	.10	1.00
66	32	.34	.34	.68	.22	.90
67	33	.36	.30	.66	.21	.87
68	45	.38	.26	.64	.29	.93
69	44	.39	.27	.66	.27	.93
70	29	.58	.21	.79	.10	.89
71	29	.48	.35	.83	.10	.93
72	44	.41	.32	.73	.16	.89
73	40	.43	.32	.75	.20	.95
74	51	.35	.55	.90	.09	.99
75	38	.42	.24	.66	.21	.87
76	45	.42	.22	.64	.16	.80
77	37	.38	.30	.68	.13	.81
78	34	.44	.29	.73	.15	.88
79	41	.41	.39	.80	.10	.90
80	47	.43	.32	.75	.19	.94
81	27	.52	.37	.89	.11	1.00
82	33	.55	.18	.73	.21	.94
83	37	.87	.05	.92	.05	.97
84	34	.56	.23	.79	.09	.88
85	35	.51	.37	.88	.09	.97
86	33	.67	.09	.76	.06	.82

Variable* Number	Base	Exact Agreement	One-Step Difference	Exact and One-Step Cumulated	Two-Step Difference	Cumulated
87	46	.35	.41	.76	.13	.89
88	35	.40	.28	.68	.26	.94
89	38	.52	.24	.76	.08	.84
90	47	.53	.19	.72	.15	.87
91	42	.55	.31	.86	.04	.90

* Variables 44, 92, and 93 were originally based on checks of occurence of categories. For data analysis the categories were placed on hierarchical scales, 1 through 9. The most frequent category for the patient was the basis for coding the patient on the scale. Only the checks in exact agreement were used for coding the patient on the scale.

APPENDIX IX

TEN COMPONENTS THAT PREDICT
GROUP MEMBERSHIP FOR 49 OF 51 PATIENTS

COMPONENT I

VARIABLES

OUTWARD BEHAVIOR	FACTOR LOADINGS*
2 Positive Behavior to Female Staff	.45
3 Positive Behavior to Male Patients	.52
4 Positive Behavior to Female Patients	.41
5 Negative Behavior to Male Staff	−.63
6 Negative Behavior to Female Staff	−.66
10 Appropriateness of Behavior to Female Staff	.63
11 Appropriateness of Behavior to Male Patients	.49
12 Appropriateness of Behavior to Female Patients	.48
13 Appropriateness of Behavior in Groups	.45
14 Positive Behavior to Grooming	.48
15 Positive Behavior to the Routine of Eating	.53
17 Positive Behavior to Freedom	.43
18 Positive Behavior to Organized Programs	.48
19 Positive Behavior to Informal Programs	.43
20 Negative Behavior to Grooming	−.57
21 Negative Behavior to the Routine of Eating	−.30
22 Negative Behavior to Sleeping	−.32
23 Negative Behavior to Limits	−.42
24 Negative Behavior to Organized Programs	−.36
25 Negative Behavior to Informal Programs	−.31
26 Appropriateness of Behavior to Grooming	.54
27 Appropriateness of Behavior to Eating	.46
28 Appropriateness of Behavior to Sleeping	.43

Only factor loadings of .30 or more are presented.

OUTWARD BEHAVIOR	FACTOR LOADINGS
29 Appropriateness of Behavior to Freedom	.62
30 Appropriateness of Behavior to Organized Programs	.70
31 Appropriateness of Behavior to Informal Programs	.64
32 Positive Behavior to Tasks	.36
33 Negative Behavior to Tasks	−.34

PERCEPTION

34 Perception of Self—Inner	.38
35 Perception of Self—Outer	.42
36 Awareness of Body Qualities	.51
37 Self Identity	.38
38 Awareness of Others—Speed of Identification	.38
39 Awareness of Others—Spontaneity of Identification	.53
40 Awareness of Situations and Events—Speed Identification	.37
41 Awareness of Situations and Events—Spontaneity	.44
42 Awareness of Time/Place—Speed/Spontaneity	.54
43 Awareness of Things—Speed/Spontaneity	.56
44 Differentiation of Self from Staff	.33
45 Patient's Assessment of Self (Self-Esteem)	.54
46 Patient's Assessment of Others in Relation to Self (Trust)	.65
47 Patient's Assessment of Situations, Events and Institutions (Confidence)	.57

MESSAGES

50 Degree of Logical Talk in the Organized Situation	.36
51 Degree of Logical Talk in the Informal Situation	.49

AFFECTS AND DEFENSES

58 Negative Affect to Male Staff Stated Verbally	−.54
59 Negative Affect to Female Staff Stated Verbally	−.57
60 Negative Affect to Male Staff Stated Nonverbally	−.57
61 Negative Affect to Female Staff Stated Nonverbally	−.53
64 Negative Affect to Male Patients Stated Nonverbally	−.51
65 Negative Affect to Female Patients Stated Nonverbally	−.38
73 Relationship Constancy for Female Patients	.38
74 Investment in Self	−.55
76 Investment in One Female	.39
77 Investment in More Than One Male	.60
78 Investment in More Than One Female	.62
79 Quantity of Impulse Discharge to People Stated Verbally	−.42

COMPONENT II

OUTWARD BEHAVIOR	FACTOR LOADINGS
1 Positive Behavior to Male Staff	.47
2 Positive Behavior to Female Staff	.45
3 Positive Behavior to Male Patients	.36
4 Positive Behavior to Female Patients	.36
5 Negative Behavior to Male Staff	.39
6 Negative Behavior to Female Staff	.53
7 Negative Behavior to Male Patients	.49
8 Negative Behavior to Female Patients	.72
13 Appropriateness of Behavior in Groups	.45
17 Positive Behavior to Freedom	.37
18 Positive Behavior to Organized Programs	.35
19 Positive Behavior to Informal Programs	.37
23 Negative Behavior to Limits	.38
29 Appropriateness to Freedom	.36
31 Appropriateness to Informal Programs	.40

PERCEPTION

34 Perception of Self—Inner	.39
38 Awareness of Others—Speed of Identification	.32
44 Differentiation of Self from Staff	.35

MESSAGES

48 Quantity of Verbal Messages in the Organized Situation	.60
49 Quantity of Verbal Messages in the Informal Situation	.54

AFFECTS AND DEFENSES

58 Negative Affect to Male Staff Stated Verbally	.39
59 Negative Affect to Female Staff Stated Verbally	.63
60 Negative Affect to Male Staff Stated Nonverbally	.59
61 Negative Affect to Female Staff Stated Nonverbally	.69
62 Negative Affect to Male Patients Stated Verbally	.60
63 Negative Affect to Female Patients Stated Verbally	.54
64 Negative Affect to Male Patients Stated Nonverbally	.46
65 Negative Affect to Female Patients Stated Nonverbally	.56
67 Tolerance for Physical Closeness to Female Staff	.46
72 Relationship Constancy for Male Patients	.34
79 Quantity of Impulse Discharge to People Stated Verbally	.66
80 Quantity of Impulse Discharge to People Stated Nonverbally	.62
81 Quantity of Impulse Discharge to Situations Stated Verbally	.41

OUTWARD BEHAVIOR	FACTOR LOADINGS
82 Quantity of Impulse Discharge to Situations Stated Nonverbally	.40
85 Quantity of Physiological Process Stated Verbally	.36
92 Defense checked with highest frequency	.48
93 Defense checked with second frequency	−.45

COMPONENT III

OUTWARD BEHAVIOR

1 Positive Behavior to Male Staff	.35
2 Positive Behavior to Female Staff	.46
3 Positive Behavior to Male Patients	.34
9 Appropriateness of Behavior to Male Staff	.41
10 Appropriateness of Behavior to Female Staff	.37
11 Appropriateness of Behavior to Male Patients	.42
20 Negative Behavior to Grooming	.30

MESSAGES

49 Quantity of Verbal Messages in the Informal Situation	.34
52 Degree of Personal Talk in the Informal Situation	.51

AFFECTS AND DEFENSES

67 Tolerance for Physical Closeness to Female Staff	.32
68 Tolerance for Physical Closeness to Male Patients	.35
69 Tolerance for Physical Closeness to Female Patients	.44
70 Relationship Constancy for Male Staff	.34
72 Relationship Constancy for Male Patients	.48
73 Relationship Constancy for Female Patients	−.56
75 Investment in One Male	.45
76 Investment in One Female	−.49
84 Quantity of Impulse Discharge to Things Stated Nonverbally	−.45
87 Capacity to Delay Impulse Discharge	.33
92 Defense Checked with Highest Frequency	.37

COMPONENT IV

OUTWARD BEHAVIOR

15 Positive Behavior to the Routine of Eating	.33
16 Positive Behavior to the Routine of Sleeping	.49
22 Negative Behavior to the Routine of Sleeping	−.53
24 Negative Behavior to Organized Programs	−.37
27 Appropriateness of Behavior to Eating	.36

OUTWARD BEHAVIOR · FACTOR LOADINGS

28 Appropriateness of Behavior to Sleeping · .51

PERCEPTION

38 Awareness of Others—Speed of Identification · −.71
39 Awareness of Others—Spontaneity of Identification · −.55
40 Awareness of Situations and Events—Speed of
  Identification · −.66
41 Awareness of Situations and Events—Spontaneity · −.61
63 Negative Affect to Female Patients Stated Verbally · .38
66 Tolerance for Physical Closeness to Male Staff · .34
68 Tolerance for Physical Closeness to Male Patients · .33
71 Relationship Constancy for Female Staff · −.33

COMPONENT V

OUTWARD BEHAVIOR

11 Appropriateness of Behavior to Male Patients · −.31
18 Positive Behavior to Organized Programs · −.54
19 Positive Behavior to Informal Programs · −.46

PERCEPTION

41 Awareness of Situations and Events—Spontaneity · −.36

AFFECTS AND DEFENSES

55 Positive Affect to Female Staff Stated Verbally · .46
57 Positive Affect to Female Patients Stated Verbally · .31
65 Negative Affect to Female Patients Stated Nonverbally · .35
67 Tolerance for Physical Closeness to Female Staff · .36
68 Tolerance for Physical Closeness to Male Patients · −.32
69 Tolerance for Physical Closeness to Female Patients · .33
71 Relationship Constancy for Female Staff · .36
74 Investment in Self · −.36
76 Investment in One Female · .33
81 Quantity of Impulse Discharge to Situations Stated
  Verbally · .41
82 Quantity of Impulse Discharge to Situations Stated
  Nonverbally · .51

COMPONENT VI

OUTWARD BEHAVIOR

14 Positive Behavior to Grooming · −.32
17 Positive Behavior to Freedom · .38
24 Negative Behavior to Organized Programs · −.31

OUTWARD BEHAVIOR	FACTOR LOADINGS
26 Appropriateness of Behavior to Grooming	−.35
33 Negative Behavior to Tasks	−.33

PERCEPTION

34 Perception of Self—Inner	−.31
47 Patient's Assessment of Situations, Events and Institutions (Confidence)	.45

MESSAGES

49 Quantity of Verbal Messages in the Informal Situation	.32
53 Congruence of Behavior with Verbal Messages	−.38

AFFECTS AND DEFENSES

86 Quantity of Physiological Process Stated Nonverbally	−.37
88 Free Anxiety—Intensity	−.71
91 Depression—Duration	−.62

COMPONENT VIII

OUTWARD BEHAVIOR

11 Appropriateness of Behavior to Male Patients	−.36
12 Appropriateness of Behavior to Female Patients	−.42
21 Negative Behavior to the Routine of Eating	.39
22 Negative Behavior to the Routine of Sleeping	−.31
27 Appropriateness of Behavior to Eating	−.32

AFFECTS AND DEFENSES

64 Negative Affect to Male Patients Stated Nonverbally	−.41
72 Relationship Constancy for Male Patients	−.37
75 Investment in One Male	−.50
85 Quantity of Physiological Process Stated Verbally	.37
86 Quantity of Physiological Process Stated Nonverbally	.33
92 Defense Checked with Highest Frequency	.36

COMPONENT X

OUTWARD BEHAVIOR

1 Positive Behavior to Male Staff	−.30
9 Appropriateness of Behavior to Male Staff	−.30
12 Appropriateness of Behavior to Female Patients	.41
16 Positive Behavior to the Routine of Sleeping	.39
20 Negative Behavior to Grooming	.31
25 Negative Behavior to Informal Programs	−.34

PERCEPTION

44 Differentiation of Self from Staff	−.32

AFFECTS AND DEFENSES	FACTOR LOADINGS
55 Positive Affect to Female Staff Stated Verbally	.31
56 Positive Affect to Male Patients Stated Verbally	−.35
78 Investment in More Than One Female	.33

COMPONENT XII

OUTWARD BEHAVIOR

14 Positive Behavior to Grooming	−.33

PERCEPTION

44 Differentiation of Self from Staff	−.35

MESSAGES

53 Congruence of Behavior with Verbal Messages	.30
70 Relationship Constancy for Male Staff	.39
71 Relationship Constancy for Female Staff	−.37
81 Quantity of Impulse Discharge to Situations Stated Verbally	−.33
93 Defense Checked with Second Frequency	−.41

COMPONENT XIII

PERCEPTION

34 Perception of Self—Inner	.33
35 Perception of Self—Outer	.35

AFFECTS AND DEFENSES

68 Tolerance for Physical Closeness to Male Patients	−.35
87 Capacity to Delay Impulse Discharge	−.33

APPENDIX X

SCHEDULE FOR STUDY OF FAMILIES
OF BORDERLINE PATIENTS

Patient's Name:_____

Address: _____

1. Type of family group from which patient came into the hospital:
   a. Nuclear family_____
      Patient's position in nuclear group is:
      _____husband and father
      _____wife and mother
      If there are children, specify age and sex of each child and specify age of patient's spouse:_____

      Also specify age and sex of any other member of the family living in the home and relationship to patient:_____

   b. Family of Origin_____
      Specify the age and sex composition of the members of the family and relationship to patient:_____

   c. Broken family home: Nuclear_____; Origin_____.
      _____husband and father not present; Specify why:_____

      _____wife and mother not present; Specify why:_____
      Specify the age and sex composition of the members of the family and relationship to patient:_____

   d. Patient did not live in a family group, (lived independently) but has a family_____.

e. Patient lived independently, has no family because: _____

2. If condition a, or b, or c above was checked, what is the occupation of the head of the family. Specify head and occupation: _____

*

I. *How does the family function in relation to the patient's illness and hospitalization?*
   a. Describe the social worker's evaluation of the family's involvement on behalf of the patient, that is, keeping appointments, providing patient with needed articles such as clothes, planning for discharge.
   b. Describe the family's attitude toward the patient's hospitalization:
   c. Does the family see the relevance of the patient's illness to them? Explain:

Patient's Name _____ Family: Origin _____
                                Nuclear Family _____

CHECK LIST OF TRAITS

Check as many as apply:

II. *How does the family function to maintain its integration?*
   A. The Marriage
      1 Marriage is highly discordant.
      2 Partners engage in mutual devaluation and criticism.
      3 Partners unable to achieve a mutuality of purpose in major areas of living, conflicting demands remain unresolved.
      4 Spouses fail to form a nuclear family since one or both retain primary loyalties to their families of origin.
      5 Parents and/or spouses are deficient in achieving reciprocal role relationships.
      *6 Specify any other signs of pathology in the marriage not listed above:
   B. Family Life
      7 Family relationships marked by chronic overt conflict or competition.

---

* Traits marked with an asterisk were deleted from the data analysis, because of infrequency of occurrence, five or fewer.

8 Family life marked by denial of problems; conflict does not reach the surface; familial friction is avoided.

9 Family is not a mutually protective unit.

10 Family is excessively protective.

*11 Shared interests are minimal or lacking.

12 Shared interests are centered on inanimate objects.

*13 Specify any other signs of pathology in family life not listed above.

C. Functional Activities

14 Delineation of family role functions of male and female is unclear.

15 Outright rejection of parenthood or excessive conflict over parenthood; family does not provide adequate nurturant care for children.

*16 Maintenance of a discrete household is not possible or has been abandoned.

*17 Discrete household maintained, but household conditions and practices are substandard.

*18 Health conditions and practices are substandard.

*19 The task of financial independence cannot be sustained.

20 Parents do not maintain leadership over children, that is, no evidence of parental authority or discipline.

21 Authority is confused and diffused; evidence of parental uncertainty.

22 Authority is strongly centralized in father.

23 Authority is strongly centralized in mother.

24 Parents fail to give guidance to children in the development of self-reliance.

25 Mother-child relationships are problematic.

26 Father-child relationships are problematic.

*27 According to patient—mother discriminates against him.

*28 According to patient—father discriminates against him.

*29 According to patient—others: Specify_____ discriminate against him.

30 Parents are impervious to the feelings and communications of the children.

31 Parents impede and destroy the initiative of children.

*32 Specify any other signs of pathology not listed above in functional activities of the family.

D. Affects and Communication

The quality of the affect and emotionality in this family may be characterized as:

33 Absent or neutral for wife or mother.

34 Absent or neutral for husband or father.

35 Mixed for wife or mother.

36 Mixed for husband or father.

37 Predominantly negative for wife or mother.

38 Predominantly negative for husband or father.

39 Overdevotion for wife or mother.

40 Overdevotion for husband or father.

*41 Other, specify_____for wife or mother.

*42 Other, specify_____for husband or father.

*43 Specify affect_____for significant other person, e.g., grandmother.

44 Contact among family members is at a minimum, family members are isolated and detached one from the other, communication is absent.

45 Contact among family members is excessive and intrusive, very involved.

*46 Contact among family members is present but impersonal, members are suspicious of one another.

47 In general, communication may be characterized as confused.

*48 Specify any other signs of pathology not listed above in family affect and communication.

III. *How (by what means) does the family and its component parts resist the natural process of disintegration?*

49 The family is currently in a static state; there is no evidence of change in the state of the component parts of the system relative to each other.

50 The family and its parts has not set eventual separation as a goal; the family does not want the children to pry themselves loose and/or the children do not want to.

51 The family displays no discomfort about its static state and the absence of goals for change; there is no evidence of anticipation of separation from home ties.

In part at least, one or more of the following accounts for the static state of the family:

52 Self interest of one of the parents, specify:_____

53 Dominance of one of the parents, specify:_____

54 Overinvolvement of one of the parents with child(ren), specify:_____

55 Discouragement of independent strivings of child(ren)

*56 Other, specify:_____

57 Self-identity of child(ren) has been submerged by the family; parents do not see child(ren) as having a separate identity.

*58 Specify any other signs of family resistance of redistribution of its parts into new families.

IV. *How does the family function in relation to the other social systems?*

*59 The family is unable to provide either the basic information or attitudes toward work that are essential for performance of tasks in the economy.

*60 The family hampers participation in the economy with excessive pressure for performance.

*61 Family is unable to encourage or facilitate the principal wage earner to participate in the economy.

*62 Family fails in transmitting the basic adaptive techniques of the culture to its child or children.

*63 Family does not support the social value system, or define behavior that is socially legitimate or desirable; family engages in antisocial behavior.

*64 There is no evidence of family identity with the community or adherence to community patterns.

*65 The family is chronically unsure of its standards and values.

*66 The pressures in the family are so great, or lack of knowledge so great there is no capacity for participation in community and wider society.

*67 The family seeks stability in society with a static pattern of conformity, has relapsed into a state of passive resignation.

*68 Family's position in society does not permit children to assimilate behavior patterns and feelings of worth.

*69 Specify any other signs of family pathology not listed above in relation to larger social systems, namely the economy, the culture and value systems, the community and its institutions.

1. Why was the patient hospitalized? Describe from the information in the record why the patient got into the hospital, what precipitated

hospitalization; what behaviors and problems led to the patient's hospitalization:

2. Is there a history of mental illness in the family; that is, have parents or siblings been hospitalized for mental illness? Describe:

3. Comments:

APPENDIX XI

INSTRUCTIONS FOR STUDY OF FAMILIES OF
BORDERLINE PATIENTS

Instructions for completing the schedule.

Fill out one "sheet 1" and one "sheet 2" for each patient. When information is available for both the family of "origin" and the "nuclear family," complete separate check list of traits for each.

Fill out the schedule for the information available in the record for the patient's hospitalization as of our study period, the dates of which will be supplied.

Nuclear family is composed of a man, a woman joined in a socially recognized union and their children.

Family of origin is the family of birth or adoption.

Broken family home may be either a nuclear family or the family of origin. Specify age and sex of children as follows: 2 years (M); 6 months (F).

When *specifying family members* include only those living in the home, with two exceptions: specify siblings out of the home (for example, those married) and specify children out of the home (for example those who may be in institutions). Specify family members under question 1b and 1c in terms of their relationship to the patient, for example, brother, sister, uncle.

Occupation—Write in whatever information is available about occupation. The head of the family will typically be the husband or father, or the wife or mother. There may be any kind of exception, for example, a grandparent.

Unknown—Unk. Write Unk. when information is not available to answer the questions on "sheet 1" and "sheet 2."

Underline applicable words and phrases, for example, husband and father when the relationship to patient is father rather than husband. Also underline the phrase within a check list statement that is applicable when the whole statement does not fit as well as one of the phrases within the statement. For example, "The pressures in the family are so great, or *lack of knowledge so great* there is no capacity for participation in community and wider society." In spaces provided write in statements that will clarify and elaborate the check list checks, and briefly state the basis for the check.

You should check the *check list* for the nuclear family and/or the family of origin using whatever data are available, the source of information should be a family member, for example, source may be a sibling, or a spouse, any family member but not the patient himself.

Check list, Section III, statements 1, 2, 3, and 4 apply to families of origin and do not apply to the nuclear family composed of parents and young children. Statements 1, 2, 3, and 4 apply only to the current situation.

There are two levels at which statements in the check list may be checked:

(1) *No inference* is required when specific concrete data directly applicable to the statement are available to answer a question, for example, you may check "Task of financial independence cannot be sustained" when you have such concrete data as the fact that wife is receiving ADC. When the record states only that the father is a fundamentalist minister, but his parish was always in poor session, and the family was always poor, there is not enough data to check the category "Task of financial independence cannot be sustained." From this evidence alone there is no basis for the inference that the family did not manage to remain financially independent. From this one may infer that the family did not have enough to get along comfortably or without deprivation.

(2) *Inference* may be thought of as coming to a conclusion on the basis of a cluster of evidence which leads logically to the conclusion. You may infer from the following evidence that "parental authority was confused and diffused; evidence of parental uncertainty": Patient was preferred by his father, and handled inconsistently by his family who gave him whatever he wanted. On a couple of occasions, following his marriage, the patient determined to "give himself up to the police" so that he might be freed from charges which were pending, but his mother reportedly urged him not to.

APPENDIX XII

SCHEDULE FOR FOLLOW-UP OF BORDERLINE PATIENTS

Patient's Name_____

Date of discharge from ISPI:_____

1. Data obtained from:
   00 No data obtained
   01 Patient
   02 Family member, Specify: _____
   03 Other, specify:_____
2. Data obtained by means of:
   00 Inapplicable
   01 Interview (personal contact) at ISPI, Date: _____
   02 Interview (personal contact) elsewhere, Specify:_____
   Date:_____

   03 Telephone contact, Date_____
   04 Mail contact
3. Reason for nonresponse of patient and/or family:
   00 Inapplicable
   01 Refused personal contact: 10 Patient;   11 Family member;
      Explain why:
   02 Could not be found at address: 10 Patient;   11 Family
      member;   12 Whereabouts unknown;   13 Whereabouts
      known, Specify:_____
   03 Patient deceased: 10 Suicide;   11 Other, Specify:_____
   04 Patient currently hospitalized
      Name and location of hospital:_____
      Date of admission:_____
   05 Other, Specify:_____

4. Living situation:
   A. HOME ARRANGEMENTS
      (1) Patient currently living
         00 Alone
         01 Family, Specify:_____
         02 Friends, Specify: _____
         03 Other, Specify:_____
      (2) Housing
         00 Room
         01 House
         02 Apartment
         03 Other, Specify:_____
      (3) Does patient have complaints about his current home arrangements:
         10 No;   11 Yes, Specify:
      (4) Since discharge from ISPI, has the patient changed his living situation?
         10 No;   11 Yes;
         Number of changes:_____; Kind of changes:
   B. COMMUNITY AND LEISURE TIME ACTIVITIES
      (1) Patient's assessment
         00 No data
         01 None
         02 Patient asserts that his leisure time activities support his functioning
         03 Patient complains that his leisure time activities impede his functioning
         04 Patient claims that his leisure time activities are not a significant factor in his functioning
         05 Other, Specify:_____
      (2) If 01 or 03, why does patient think that this is so?
      (3) Since discharge from ISPI, has patient experienced any modifications in his use of leisure time?   10 No;   11 Yes; Specify:_____
5. Interpersonal relations
   A. MARITAL
      (1) Current marital status
         00 Single (never married)
         01 Married (living with spouse)
         02 Married (separated)

03 Divorced (remarried)
04 Divorced (not remarried)
05 Other, Specify:_____

(2) Patient's assessment
00 No data
01 Inapplicable
02 Patient asserts that his spouse supports his social functioning
03 Patient complains that his spouse impedes his functioning
04 Patient claims that his spouse is not relevant to his social functioning
05 Other, Specify:_____

(3) If 03, about what does the patient complain?
(4) Since discharge from ISPI, marital status changes:
00 No data
01 Inapplicable
02 Married
03 Remarried
04 Separated
05 Divorced
06 Other, Specify:_____

B. CHILDREN
(1) Number of children for whom patient is responsible
00 None or inapplicable
01 One
02 Two
03 Three
04 Four
05 Five or more, Specify No._____

(2) Ages of children for whom patient is responsible
00 Inapplicable
01 Less than five years, Specify No._____
02 Five less than 10 years, Specify No._____
03 Ten less than 15 years, Specify No._____
04 Fifteen less than 20 years, Specify No._____
05 Twenty years or more, Specify No._____

(3a) Since discharge from ISPI, have changes taken place in patient's responsibilities for children?　10 No;　11 Yes;
Specify:_____

(3b) Are there new children in the family?   10 No;   11 Yes;
Specify:_____

(4) Patient's assessment
    00 No data
    01 Inapplicable
    02 Patient asserts that his children support his functioning
    03 Patient complains that his children impede his functioning
    04 Patient claims that his children are not a significant factor in his functioning
    05 Other, Specify:_____

(5) If 03, about what does the patient complain?

C. PATIENT—PARENT

(1) Parents in the home
    00 No data
    01 Inapplicable
    02 Both parents in home
    03 One parent in home, Specify:_____
    04 Both in-laws in home
    05 One in-law in home, Specify:_____
    06 Other, Specify:_____

(2) Patient's assessment
    00 No data
    01 Inapplicable
    02 Patient asserts that parents/in-laws support functioning
    03 Patient complains that parents/in-laws impede functioning
    04 Patient claims that parents are not relevant to his functioning
    05 Other, Specify:_____

(3) If 03, about what does the patient complain?

D. FRIENDS, CO-WORKERS, EMPLOYERS

(1) Patient's assessment
    00 No data
    01 No friends
    02 Patient asserts that friends support his social functioning
    03 Patient complains that friends impede his social functioning
    04 Patient claims that friends, or co-workers, or employer are not significant factors in his social functioning
    05 Other, Specify: _____

(2) If 01, why?

(3) If 03, about what does the patient complain?

6. Occupation, education and economic circumstances

A. OCCUPATION

(1) Classification

00 No data

01 Inapplicable

02 Unemployed

03 Professional, technical, kindred

04 Manager, official, proprietor, except farm

05 Clerical, kindred

06 Sales worker

07 Craftsman, foreman, kindred

08 Operative, kindred

09 Private householder

10 Service worker (except private householder)

11 Laborer

12 Other, Specify:_____

(2) Stability of employment

00 No data

01 Inapplicable

02 Less 1 month

03 One month less 3

04 Three months less 6

05 Six months less 1 year

06 One year or more

(3) Since discharge from ISPI, have there been changes in occupational classification and in employment?   11 No;
12 Yes; Specify:_____

(4) Patient's assessment

00 No data

01 Inapplicable

02 Patient asserts that employment supports his functioning

03 Patient complains that employment impedes his functioning

04 Patient claims that employment is not a significant factor
in his functioning

05 Other, Specify:_____

(5) If 03, about what does the patient complain?

(6) Housewife
    00 No data
    01 Inapplicable
    02 Able to take full responsibility for care and maintenance of household and family
    03 Able to take partial responsibility
    04 Able to take little responsibility
    05 Able to take no responsibility
    06 Other, Specify:_____

B. EDUCATION
Since discharge from ISPI, has the patient attained a higher level or modified his educational level in any way?   10 No;   11 Yes; Specify:_____

C. ECONOMIC CIRCUMSTANCES
(1) Financial adequacy
    00 No data
    01 Inapplicable
    02 Complete financial self-sufficiency
    03 Supplementary financial assistance required
    04 Occasional financial assistance required
    05 Complete financial assistance required
    06 Other, Specify:_____
(2) Financial assistance obtained from
    00 No data
    01 Inapplicable
    02 Family
    03 Welfare agency
    04 Other, Specify:_____

7. Health
A. PHYSICAL CONDITION
(1) Patient's assessment
    00 No data
    01 No physical illness
    02 Patient asserts that good physical health supports his functioning
    03 Patient complains that poor physical health impedes his functioning
    04 Other, Specify:_____
(2) If 03, about what does patient complain?

(3) Since discharge from ISPI, has patient experienced improvement in physical health, or physical trauma, or setback? 10 No; 11 Yes; Specify:_____

B. PSYCHOLOGICAL CONDITION

   (1) Patient's assessment

      00 No data

      01 Patient asserts that good psychological health supports his functioning

      02 Patient complains that poor psychological health impedes his functioning

      03 Other, Specify:_____

   (2) If 01, what improvement does the patient think he has experienced since discharge from ISPI?

   (3) If 02, does the patient think he has experienced a setback, since discharge from ISPI? Specify:_____

   (4) Since discharge from ISPI, has the patient attempted suicide? 10 No;   11 Yes;   Describe:

   (5) Since discharge from ISPI, type of psychiatric service:

      00 No data

      01 Inapplicable

      02 Public psychiatric hospital, Name:_____ Duration of service:_____

      03 Private psychiatric hospital, Name:_____ Duration of service:_____

      04 Public psychiatric clinic, Name:_____ Duration of service:_____

      05 Private psychiatric clinic, Name:_____ Duration of service:_____

      06 Private psychiatrist:_____ Duration of service:_____

      07 Other, Specify:_____

   (6) Since discharge from ISPI, type of social services:

      00 No data

      01 Inapplicable

      02 Private casework service

      03 Family service

      04 Court or correctional service

      05 Vocational or employment service

      06 Public assistance, Specify:_____

      07 Other, Specify:_____

8. Social conflict (except minor traffic charges)
        00 No data
        01 Inapplicable
        02 None
        03 Violation, Specify:_____
        04 Arrest
        05 Jail sentence
        06 Other, Specify:_____
9. Use of drugs
        00 No data
        01 Inapplicable
        02 No use of drugs
        03 Little
        04 Some
        05 Extensive
        06 Other, Specify:_____
10. Use of alcohol
        00 No data
        01 Inapplicable
        02 No use of alcohol
        03 Little
        04 Some
        05 Extensive
        06 Other, Specify:_____
11. At this time, patient's goals for himself are:
        00 No data
        01 Inapplicable/none
        02 Clearly defined
        03 Ambiguous
        04 Conflictual
        05 Indecisive
        06 Other, Specify:_____
12. What was the patient's affective response to being approached by an ISPI representative and to being questioned?
13. What were the patient's most vivid memories and recollections of ISPI?
14. Does the patient maintain contact and relations with former ISPI patients?
15. Comments:

INDEX

behavior (*cont'd*)
46, 47, 80, 81, 83–89, 95, 211–212,
216–222, 243–249; passive, 85, 109,
110, 176, 179; positive, 80–83, 86–89,
174, 211, 212, 217, 219–222, 243–249;
role, 47, 266
behavioral cues, 234–236
behaviorism, 30–31
behavior-observation-inference model, 31
Benedek, T., 158
Bentley, A. F., 5
Beres, D., 29, 35
Bernstein, H., 16–17
Bertalanffy, L. von, 154–155
Birdwhistell, R. L., 125
Bleuler, E., 10, 19, 92
borderline: in children, 18–19, 145–147;
classifications and, 3–7, 10, 11, 173;
culture and, 156–157, 161, 163–171,
178, 180; diagnosis of, 3–7, 9–11, 164,
172–173, 180; early use of term, 10–
11; etiology of, *see* etiological factors;
general characteristics of, 17, 90–91,
98, 142; genic components of, 145, 154,
156, 161, 163, 178, 189; literature on,
9–22; problem of meaning of, 3–4, 6,
11, 172; psychodynamic formulations
and, 14–18, 178; society and, 156–157,
161, 163–171, 178, 180; subcategories
of, 4, 8, 173, 174, 179, 180
borderline defenses, 96
borderline family, 115–116
borderline personality, 95, 159, 161, 164,
171
Boszormenyi-Nagy, I., 116
Bowlby, J., 157, 158
Bucher, R., 141
Burg, M., 146
Bychowski, G., 19

catatonic states, 19–20
Cattell, J., 20, 61
character, meaning of, 150
character disorders, 10, 12–14, 17, 166,
172, 173; diagnosis of, 95–97
characterological attributes, 159–160
Chicago Psychoanalytic Institute, 13
child analysis, 27
child-mother relations, 11, 16–17, 143,
145–146, 148, 151, 157–158, 164, 165,
171, 177, 178
chronic depression, 109–112
chronic undifferentiated schizophrenia, 91,
95, 172
civil rights, 164
Clark, L. P., 10
classifications, 3–7, 10, 11, 173

clinical descriptions, 11–14, 19, 21–23, 32,
36, 126
clinical interpretations, 23, 24, 27, 28, 34,
36, 82, 173, 175
closeness: fear of, 14, 15, 17, 96, 143, 144,
160; longing for, 14; tolerance for, 87,
213, 214, 230
cluster analysis, 8, 46, 52–59, 62–72, 74,
98–112, 175, 176, 181
coding, 45–49, 174, 193–210
cognition, 28–29, 46, 150
communication systems, schizophrenia
and, 92, 96, 114, 177
compulsions, 10
compulsive character, 95
compulsivity, 215, 235
computers, 57, 58, 72
constitutional factors, 145, 161
conversion symptoms, 102
conversions, 17
core borderline syndrome, 85–87, 103–106
Cornelison, A. R., 114
corrective emotional experience, 148–149
Coulter, M. A., 61
cults, 167–168
culture, borderline and, 156–157, 161,
163–171, 178, 180
Cummings, E., 32
Cummings, J., 32
current behavior, 23, 160

data analysis, *see* statistical analysis
defense(s), 33, 34, 46, 47, 81, 86–90,
214–215; against affective commitment, 167; against anxiety, 11, 96, 165;
borderline, 96; ego–, 93, 142; ego-
syntonic, 96; against loneliness, 22; narcissistic, 14; neurotic, 18, 94; against
primitive unconscious impulses, 15;
pseudoneurotic, 18; psychotic, 18, 94;
schizophrenic, 93
defense mechanisms, 34, 96, 234–236
delusions, 13, 20, 93, 98, 108
dementia praecox, 10, 92
denial, 12, 14, 96, 110, 127, 161, 215, 235
depression, 12, 13, 83–87; anaclitic, 90,
95, 98, 143, 144, 176; anxiety and, 94;
chronic, 109–112; diagnosis of, 94–95;
and guilt, 95, 98; melancholic, 13; neurotic, 89, 90; periodic, 10, 14; schizophrenic, 17
depressive loneliness, 91, 94–95, 98, 105,
142, 144, 176
depressive-masochistic character structure, 18
descriptions, clinical, 11–14, 19, 21–23, 32,
36, 126